**OFFICIAL**
WAYNE ROONEY
ANNUAL

CONTENTS

WANT MORE WAYNE?
visit www.waynerooneyclub.com

THE OFFICIAL WAYNE ROONEY WEBSITE

WAYNE'S

From chilling with 50 Cent and Ronaldinho to meeting up with Prince William, it's been a hectic 12 months in Wayne's world

YEAR!

THE HIGHS AND LOWS OF 2005-06

APRIL 24, 2005

Wayne is snapped for the first time with his new tattoo. The word 'Coleen' sits above a large Celtic cross on his right bicep.

MAY 21, 2005

Wayne plays brilliantly against Arsenal in the FA Cup final at Cardiff's Millennium Stadium but ends up on the losing side. United are held 0-0 after extra-time, despite having most of the possession and the better chances. Wayne scores in the penalty shoot-out but it isn't enough to prevent United going down 5-4.

JUNE 23, 2005

With the new football season still well over a month away, Wayne and Coleen take a well-earned break in the Caribbean. The pair head for the £1,300 a night Sandy Lane resort in Barbados where they meet up with Wayne's then Man United team-mate Phil Neville and his family.

AUGUST 13, 2005

Man United beat Everton 2-0 on the opening day of the new Premiership season. Wayne gets on the scoresheet for the first time against his old club.

MAY 17, 2005

Wayne and fiancée Coleen help lay the foundations for a £2 million wing at Claire House Children's Hospice in Bebington, Merseyside. Coleen's adopted sister – Rosie, aged six – is a patient at the hospice. The pair put on their hardhats to pose for photographs before spending the afternoon talking to the hospice's young patients and carers.

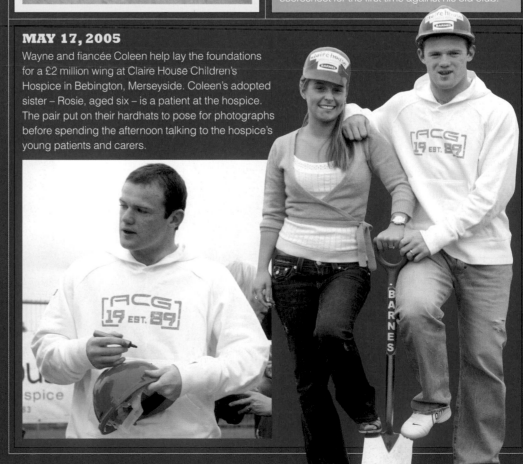

SEPTEMBER, 2005

Wayne teams up with Barcelona and Brazil superstar Ronaldinho to film a TV ad for the latest FIFA 06 football computer game, under the slogan 'You Play They Obey'. Called 'Winner Stays On', the ad sees Rooney and Manchester United dish out a 4-1 beating to Brazil. Ronaldinho trudges off the pitch, only to be told he's got to get back out there immediately because United's next opponents are none other than Barcelona. The ad ends with Wayne looking none too happy about taking Ronaldinho on again. Filmed at the Olympic Stadium in Barcelona, it is the first time that Rooney and Ronaldinho had met. "It was great to meet him," said Wayne. "He seems a great lad, and he is one of my favourite players." As for the game itself, it seems that Wayne is an old pro. "I've played the FIFA games for a number of years but when I play it I only ever choose Man United and England as it would feel weird to be anyone else. At United I usually play with Wes Brown, Darren Fletcher and Alan Smith."

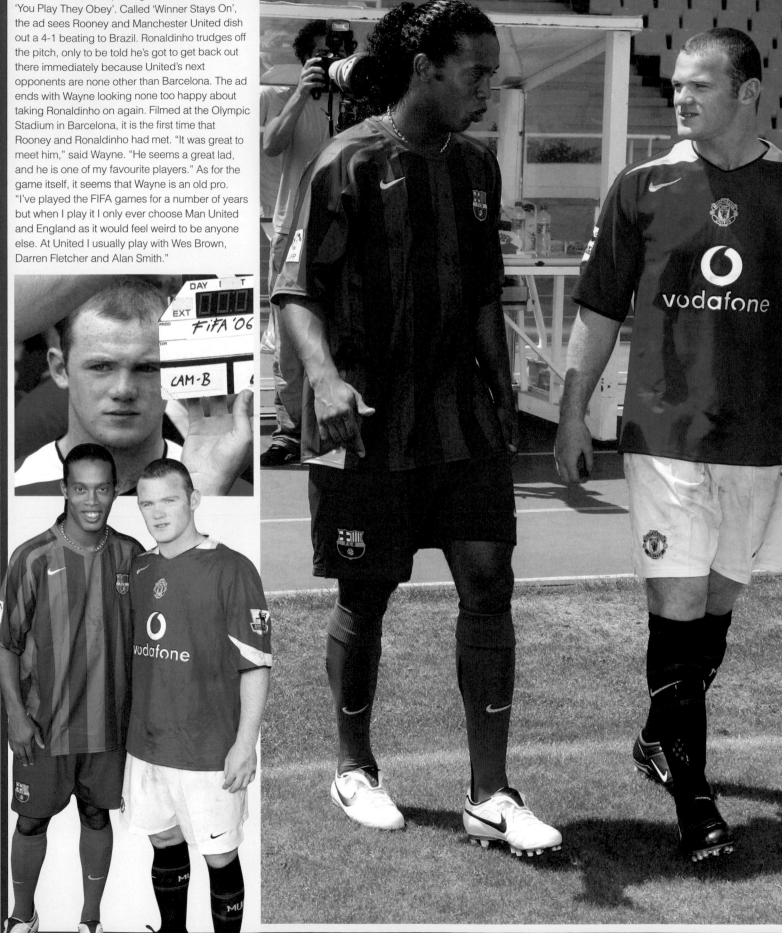

WHO IS BETTER AT 'KEEPY UPPIES', YOU OR RONALDINHO?
Wayne: "Ronaldinho."

WHAT CAN YOU DO WITH A BALL THAT RONALDINHO CAN'T?
Wayne: "Don't know. I've not played against him yet."

WHAT IS YOUR BEST TRICK WITH A FOOTBALL?
Wayne: "I don't do tricks really, but I work hard at striking the ball well from all sorts of angles and deliveries."

DID YOU LEARN ANY NEW TRICKS FROM RONALDINHO DURING THE FILMING OF THIS TV AD?
Wayne: "Yeah. Don't let the make up artists put fake mud on you."

WHAT MAKES RONALDINHO SUCH A GREAT FOOTBALL PLAYER?
Wayne: "There is no one thing, but it's his all round ability, plus his vision and awareness is breathtaking."

WOULD YOU BE ABLE TO BEAT HIM AT FIFA 06?
Wayne: "I think I would give him a good game."

SEPTEMBER 7, 2005
England's World Cup qualification campaign is dealt a blow after they are beaten 1-0 by Northern Ireland in Belfast. It really is a night of frustration for England and for Wayne, who is booked for a foul on Keith Gillespie.

SEPTEMBER 17, 2005
Wayne and Rio Ferdinand share a stage with infamous US rapper 50 Cent. Their brief cameo appearance at the gig at Manchester's MEN Arena is seen by 20,000 people.

SEPTEMBER 19, 2005
Wayne is named Young Player Of The Year at the inaugural MasterCard FIFPro World XI Player awards, as voted for by about 40,000 professional footballers around the world. Wayne and Coleen attend the gala ceremony, which is held at the BBC TV Centre in White City, west London.

SEPTEMBER 23, 2005
Toy company Bandai announce that they're to produce a 30cm high Wayne Rooney action figure as part of their Kick-O-Mania range. The doll is a 'fully bendable' model, it boasts a 'goal shooting action' and comes complete with its own Manchester United strip, shin-pads and a ball.
It retails at £20 and promises hours of endless fun!

OCTOBER 7, 2005
Work on Wayne and Coleen's £4 million mansion in Prestbury, Cheshire nears completion after a year of renovation and improvement. The house boasts splended landscaped gardens, cinema, swimming pool, games room, and an all-purpose sports court. Where better place to relax after a tough Man United or England match?

OCTOBER 11, 2005
Wayne becomes an official ambassador for SOS Children, a charity dedicated to finding homes for the world's poorest orphans. "I was made up when I was asked to get involved," said Wayne. "The work the charity does is for kids who have suffered and have no families to help them. I know how much it means to have a family that supports you, so I am delighted to be giving my support to these kids."

OCTOBER 12, 2005
Wayne has an outstanding game as England qualify for the 2006 World Cup with a 2-1 win against Poland at Old Trafford. The result means Sven-Goran Eriksson's side finish top of their qualification group ahead of the Poles.

OCTOBER 24, 2005
Wayne celebrates his 20th birthday by having a night on the town in Manchester with a group of friends, including his Manchester United team-mate Rio Ferdinand. Coleen is reported to have spent £3,500 on a jukebox from Selfridges as his birthday gift for the new house.

OCTOBER 26, 2005

Wayne is photographed for Coca-Cola by Jason Bell, one of the world's leading celebrity snappers. The idea behind the shoot is to 'Capture Wayne in a way no one ever had before – away from the training ground and the football pitch, and back in his natural environment where he played football as a kid'. The shoot took place at the South Manchester Studios and at a series of outdoor venues in Stockport. A set of ten stunning images were produced and used by Coca-Cola as banners at the World Cup Trophy Tour, which saw the world's most famous sports trophy visit 32 cities in 30 countries over a period of three months.

WAYNE'S YEAR! THE HIGHS AND LOWS OF 2005-06

NOVEMBER 12, 2005

Wayne scores England's opener in a thrilling 3-2 friendly win against Argentina in Geneva. Victory is sealed with two late Michael Owen goals.

DECEMBER 7, 2005

Man United crash out of the Champions League, after losing 2-1 to Benfica. The defeat means United finish bottom of their group and therefore don't even qualify for a place in the latter stages of the season's UEFA Cup competition.

DECEMBER 19, 2005

Wayne is voted the second most famous person in the world after God in a survey of 2,500 under-ten-year-olds. The poll sees Jesus Christ placed third and Wayne's England team-mate David Beckham is voted fourth.

FEBRUARY 6, 2006

Wayne takes a trip to Disneyland Paris with Coleen and Rosie, her seven-year-old adopted sister. Coleen's brothers Joe and Anthony, and her niece Sophie, are also present in the group as they test out the Wild West Goldrush and Space Mountain themed rides.

FEBRUARY 26, 2006

Wayne scores twice as Man United thrash Wigan Athletic 4-0 in the Carling Cup final at Cardiff's Millennium Stadium. It's the first piece of silverware Wayne has lifted as a professional.

FEBRUARY 8, 2006

Wayne helps launch Nike's new 'Joga Bonito' campaign at the Truman Brewery in East London, taking part in a new form of football – called 'Joga 3' – that uses a 'futsal' (a smaller, heavier ball) to encourage skilful play. The three-a-side match sees Wayne team up with Jose Antonio Reyes and Rio Ferdinand to take on Cristiano Ronaldo, Cesc Fabregas and Robbie Keane. Sir Alex Ferguson and Arsene Wenger are also on hand, as is Eric Cantona. "It was brilliant to play alongside Jose, his pace and skill is something else," said Wayne. "It was also great to play with the futsal, it definitely creates a different kind of game."

MARCH 10, 2006

Book publishers Harper Collins sign up Wayne to one of the biggest sports book deals in history. The £5 million, five-book deal will include the first volume of the player's autobiography.

FEBRUARY 15, 2006

Wayne hosts a Coca-Cola-sponsored game of Street Soccer for ten teenage competition winners in the backstreets of central Manchester. As well as the five-a-side match (in which Wayne played for a different team in each half), he also takes part in a street skills session before making himself available for autographs and photos with the winners. "I just love playing football and today's game really reminded me of the days when I used to play football on the streets with my mates," said Wayne. "The games would go on for ever and everyone would get involved – we'd play for hours. I think everyone should get out to the park, or wherever, and have a kick-about whenever they can!"

MARCH 10, 2006

Wayne and Coleen become the new faces of supermarket chain Asda in a two-and-a-half year deal said to be worth £3.5 million. As well as appearing in adverts for the supermarket, the deal will also see Coleen designing clothes for Asda's 'George' clothing label.

MARCH 18, 2006

Wayne meets his boxing hero Mike Tyson at a private dinner held at swanky Manchester restaurant Lounge 10. Welterweight boxing champ Ricky Hatton and Liverpool striker Djibril Cisse are also in attendance.

MARCH 23, 2006

Wayne is guest of honour at the London leg of the FIFA World Cup Trophy Tour organised by Coca-Cola. Wayne helps to unveil the trophy to 500 competition winners, the first time it had been seen in the UK. Wayne also joins ex-England keeper Peter Shilton and Match Of The Day pundit Mark Lawrenson in an exclusive 'Audience With' show for the winners, where England's World Cup hopes and ambitions are discussed.

MARCH 24, 2006

Wayne is featured in a new Nike television advert to publicise the Joga Bonito campaign. The ad sees Wayne going between the posts as a goalkeeper when his team concede a goal. He pulls off a string of brilliant saves before rolling the ball out, taking on a host of opponents and scoring at the other end. "That boy will drive me mad," concludes an exasperated Sir Alex Ferguson as it finishes. The ad, called 'Heart', also features United legend Eric Cantona and is designed to capture Wayne's 'wholehearted approach and enthusiasm' to the game.

APRIL 23, 2006

Wayne is named the PFA Young Player Of The Year for the second year running. "To win it twice on the run is a great honour and I am delighted with the award," said Wayne after picking it up. "I voted for Cesc Fabregas, but it was close between him and Darren Bent."

APRIL 29, 2006

Wayne breaks his foot in Man United's 3-0 defeat at Chelsea. "Wayne Rooney has fractured the base of the fourth metatarsal on the right foot and will be out for six weeks," reads a Man United statement as Wayne leaves Stamford Bridge on crutches. The injury deflates a nation as Wayne's involvement in the World Cup is put into serious doubt.

MAY 4, 2006

Coleen appears on the cover of Marie Claire magazine for the first time. She also finds herself included at number 45 in the 100 Sexiest Women In The World list in FHM magazine.

MAY 15, 2006

Sven-Göran Eriksson names Wayne in his final England squad of 23 players for the World Cup. However, the Manchester United player must prove his fitness by June 9 at the latest or Eriksson will have to call up a replacement.

MAY 26, 2006

A new wax figure of Wayne is unveiled at Madame Tussauds. The Rooney figure took five months to make, with over 450 hours of specialist sculpting. He'll be sporting the new red England World Cup kit, and will be joined on display by likenesses of England team-mates David Beckham, Michael Owen and coach Sven-Goran Eriksson.

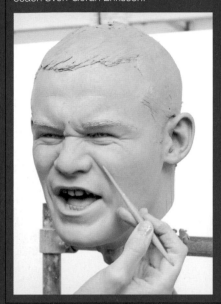

MAY 26, 2006

A scan on Wayne's injured foot reveals the striker will definitely miss England's first three World Cup games. A second scan is scheduled for June 14.

MAY 29, 2006

Wayne's make-or-break foot scan is brought forward to June 7 as the striker hooks up with the England World Cup squad for the first time at Man United's training complex at Carrington.

JUNE 1, 2006

Prince William meets up with the England squad ahead of the World Cup and spends some time chatting to Wayne about his injury and, of course, his chances of playing in Germany.

MAY 21, 2006

Wayne and Coleen attend David and Victoria Beckham's ultra-swanky pre-World Cup party at the England captain's home in Hertfordshire. The massive event takes place in a marquee the size of a football pitch and as well as most members of the England squad being present, also in attendance are Gordon Ramsay, Robbie Williams, Ray Winstone and Kate Moss on the 600-strong guest-list. Wayne and Rio Ferdinand outbid Sharon Osbourne to win a weekend with rapper P Diddy in his £1.5 million New York mansion. Their winning bid? A cool £152,000.

JUNE 15, 2006

Wayne's amazing recovery is complete as he takes to the field as a 58th minute sub for Michael Owen in the second group game against Trinidad and Tobago. The tournament ends in frustration, though, as he is sent off in the quarter-finals against Portugal and England crash out 3-1 on penalties.

MAY 23, 2006

While Wayne's appearance at the World Cup remains in some doubt, hopes are raised when it is revealed in the newspapers that he was seen dancing at the Beckhams' World Cup bash.

11

THE ROONEY CHALLENGE 1

Reckon you know more about Wayne than even he does? Have a go at the ultimate Rooney quiz and if you've done well, there are more challenges lying in wait throughout the book. Answers can be found on page 95

50 out of 50? You've got no chance mate!

SUPER STRIKER

WAYNE SCORED 19 GOALS FOR UNITED IN SEASON 2005-6 BEFORE HIS INJURY AGAINST CHELSEA. BUT HOW MUCH CAN YOU REMEMBER ABOUT THEM?

1

His first goal of the season was in Europe, but who was it against?
A. Debreceni B. Galatasaray
C. Paris Saint-Germain

ANSWER

2

Wayne grabbed two goals in a game four times… twice against the same north-west team. Can you name them?

ANSWER

3

Wayne scored the second goal as United beat Everton 2-0 in August. Which striker scored the other goal?

ANSWER

4

Wayne scored both goals as United beat Newcastle in March. Can you name the Toon keeper that day?

ANSWER

5

Wayne scored as United won 2-1 at West Ham in November. Which former team-mate was in goal for the hosts?

ANSWER

PLAYER SEARCH

Wayne made his last start for Everton versus Man City in May 2004 and his first for Man United that September. Can you spot his former and current team-mates?

F	C	A	R	R	O	L	L	U	Y	T	C	F	I	O	E	S	A	H
S	N	O	S	U	G	R	E	F	S	Q	W	E	T	N	D	F	R	Y
D	E	B	S	I	L	V	E	S	T	R	E	R	D	S	A	H	A	K
J	D	H	G	F	E	T	Y	U	U	I	O	D	P	U	I	O	D	F
E	D	X	Z	R	V	G	Y	O	B	O	M	I	L	L	E	R	Z	H
M	A	W	E	R	B	B	E	F	I	B	F	D	N	H	J	E	K	I	O
B	F	R	K	L	E	B	E	R	S	O	N	A	O	T	R	I	N	K
A	C	A	M	P	B	E	L	L	L	C	P	N	H	T	I	M	S	C
D	M	E	Z	N	E	V	I	L	L	E	D	D	C	U	O	I	K	I
J	S	A	O	S	L	Y	T	O	O	J	I	U	A	S	O	V	I	W
E	O	O	S	O	L	K	S	J	A	E	R	W	R	O	E	D	U	D
M	N	O	X	S	I	V	T	E	T	F	E	E	S	U	I	H	I	A
B	A	M	A	W	O	S	M	D	T	F	G	H	L	S	E	I	U	H
A	D	W	U	O	N	Y	T	W	R	E	W	X	E	W	S	B	I	C
D	V	A	N	N	I	S	T	E	L	R	O	O	Y	F	G	B	I	O
E	B	T	E	D	V	D	F	I	Y	S	H	E	I	N	Z	E	U	I
D	R	S	G	G	I	G	T	R	M	L	U	M	U	Y	L	R	O	L
A	M	O	L	E	A	J	S	P	O	S	M	A	N	W	M	T	H	J
D	M	N	Y	T	R	A	M	I	F	L	E	T	C	H	E	R	M	P
L	Z	A	M	V	L	I	N	D	E	R	O	T	H	G	P	M	R	Y

- Carroll
- Neville
- Heinze
- Ferdinand
- Silvestre
- Djemba Djemba
- Kleberson
- Giggs
- Fletcher
- Miller
- Carsley
- Weir
- Watson
- Martyn
- Yobo
- Osman
- Stubbs
- Hibbert
- Linderoth
- Chadwick
- Jeffers
- Solksjaer
- Van Nistelrooy
- Bellion
- Campbell
- McFadden
- Radzinski
- Ferguson
- Smith
- Saha

ACES HIGH?

Wayne signed for United from Everton in a deal which could eventually cost £30 million. But can you match up his United team-mates with the amount of money they cost to buy?

1	CRISTIANO RONALDO	A	£12.8 MILLION
2	RIO FERDINAND	B	£30 MILLION
3	GABRIEL HEINZE	C	£12.2 MILLION
4	LOUIS SAHA	D	£6.9 MILLION

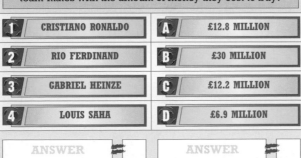

ANSWER ⟍ ANSWER
ANSWER ⟍ ANSWER

GUESS THE STRIKE PARTNER

Can you work out who this strike partner of Wayne is?

ANSWER

WHAT A YEAR!

OKAY, EVERY ROONEY FAN KNOWS HE WAS BORN IN OCTOBER 1985… BUT WHAT ELSE WAS HAPPENING IN FOOTBALL THAT YEAR?

1 Which British team won the 1985 European Cup Winners' Cup, beating Rapid Vienna 3-1 in the final?
ANSWER

2 Everton romped to the League title in season 84/85, but which teams finished second and third?
ANSWER

3 How many points did Everton finish that successful season with?
a. 86; b. 90; c. 79
ANSWER

4 The start of the 85/86 season saw Man United make a flying start to the campaign. But how many games did they win in a row?
a. 8; b. 12; c. 10
ANSWER

5 Who was the Manchester United manager in the 85-86 season?
ANSWER

6 Scotland's football manager died seconds before the end of his team's game against Wales that year. He was a legend at Celtic, but can you name him?
ANSWER

7 Who was appointed Liverpool's player-manager on May 30?
ANSWER

8 Barcelona won the Spanish title for the first time in 11 years, and with four games to spare. Who was their English manager?
ANSWER

9 Manchester United were involved in a tug-of-war with Cologne before the 84-85 season, which they eventually won by signing which Aberdeen player, who is currently a top manager north of the border?
ANSWER

10 Who was manager of Everton in the year Wayne was born?
ANSWER

PAGE TOTAL

OUT OF 50

FA chief Brian Barwick tries his best to keep Wayne firmly under wraps as the squad head off for Germany

Will he? Won't he? A broken foot almost scuppered Wayne's World Cup dream, but he made it only to endure a rollercoaster ride!

WAYNE'S WORLD CUP VERY NEARLY ENDED before it had ever started. An awkward tumble at Chelsea on April 29 saw the Manchester United star break his foot. "Wayne Rooney has fractured the base of the fourth metatarsal on the right foot and he will be out for six weeks," read a statement issued by his club. It didn't take a genius to work out that his injury was six weeks to the day before England's first World Cup game. "All these last ten years," he says recalling how he felt the day he was injured, "all that hard work, all the dreams, playing football in the streets imagining I was Michael Owen. All that effort and sacrifice. It wasn't luck, getting to this stage. I deserved it. Now it looked as if my World Cup would be over before it had begun."

The injury came as a bitter blow to Wayne but he refused to let go of his dream. "I didn't know how bad it was," he said. "I had an x-ray, but nothing showed up, so I had a scan and it was only a small break. Obviously I was gutted. I had one day off and then I went back in and decided to stay fit and keep working hard. The doctors told me it would heal. I kept believing that I'd play in the World Cup. I never let a negative thought come into my mind."

Both Wayne and Sven-Göran Eriksson remained hopeful in the face of some dismal media predictions. His plight dominated every newspaper and led all TV and radio news bulletins, while even his United boss was less than convinced that Wayne would play at the World Cup. "You never know," said Sir Alex Ferguson, "but at the moment I doubt that he'll take part because of the recovery time."

Throwing himself into his rehabilitation at United, Wayne wasn't alone. "It was lucky for me that Alan Smith was doing the same thing," said Wayne. "He was in every day and we were working together and that helped me. If I'd been on my own it would probably have been a lot harder."

After a scan on May 26, Wayne was told that he would not know whether he would be passed fit until a follow-up scan on June 14 – after the World Cup had started. But, with a certain conviction that he would be okay, he joined up with the England team and headed off to Germany. It would still be a few more days before he found out his fate…

Touchdown in Germany

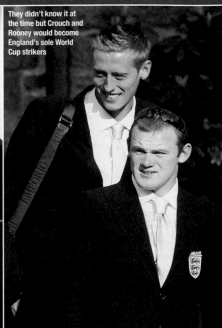
They didn't know it at the time but Crouch and Rooney would become England's sole World Cup strikers

MONDAY JUNE 5

Despite all the media talk about his injury Wayne travels to Germany with the England squad, departing Luton Airport at 3.30pm. The players are dressed in smart Armani suits and their plane, piloted by captain Paul Smiles, is renamed Pride Of The Nation for the occasion. The players receive a rousing send-off, while onboard they are delivered good luck messages, including one from England cricket captain Andrew Flintoff, and they are served a traditional English afternoon tea, including sandwiches and scones, with jam and clotted cream.

The England charter flight BA9200C arrives at Baden-Airpark at 5.40pm. Direct from the runway the players are then taken by coach, decorated with the slogan 'One Nation, One Trophy, Eleven Lions', through large crowds of fans to the luxurious Schlosshotel Buhlerhohe, near the spa town of Baden Baden in the Black Forest region of Germany. On their arrival the squad are serenaded by a traditional German 'oompah' band and child rappers called Sternfanger, which translates as Starcatchers, perform for them.

Tottenham striker Jermain Defoe is also travelling with the 23-man squad, just in case Wayne is ruled out before the final deadline for changes to the squad. Just days earlier Pelé advised England against taking Wayne. "It's dangerous to take a player whose fitness is in question," he said. "It can disturb the way the coach chooses his team. The World Cup lasts only four weeks. You need players who are at the top of their game, which includes their fitness."

WAYNE SAYS: *"Perhaps it's my age or lack of experience, but ahead of the tournament I didn't feel at all nervous, only excited. I love the big stage. The newspapers were full of the story, all about me being irreplaceable, the country's talisman, and how England now wouldn't win the World Cup in Germany without me. It was flattering, I suppose, but rubbish."*

The squad enter the gates of their plush Baden Baden hotel for the first time

TUESDAY JUNE 6

The England team have breakfast between 8am and 9.30am, although Wayne only ever has a piece of toast – it's about as much as he can manage at this time of the morning. They have their first World Cup training session scheduled for 10.30am at the nearby Mittelberg Stadium in Bühlertal, home of local team SV Bühlertal. Training is followed by a press conference with Sven-Göran Eriksson and several players who have been chosen to represent the squad. Wayne joins in with the training as he is determined to be passed fit to play in the World Cup. Walking across the training pitch, a ball comes flying towards him – and he dispatches it in to the far corner of the net with a left-footed volley.

The England players are getting settled into their luxury hotel, which has been hired out exclusively by the FA and adapted especially for the team. The hotel, which has one guarded road leading to its gates, has had thousands of pounds spent on it to install an amusement arcade for the players. There is also a plasma television screen in the ballroom so the players can watch other World Cup games together – and they have English TV channels in their bedrooms if they'd rather enjoy the football alone. They have a communal jukebox and there are rows of computer terminals for them to use. The players also have access to spas, golf courses and swimming pools. Each player has been given an electric toothbrush, as well as golf clubs and tennis and badminton racquets.

WAYNE SAYS: *"These days I'm used to staying in posh hotels, but here the hotel has a mind-boggling list of facilities and all our bedrooms have been fitted with computer games. They've added a games room for table-tennis and darts, and one suite is used as the massage and treatment room."*

WEDNESDAY JUNE 7

England train at 10.30am at Mittelberg Stadium in Bühlertal, while Wayne flies back to England for a second scan on his injured leg at a hospital in Manchester. The scan was originally scheduled for June 14, several days after the World Cup starts, but by moving it forward it means that both England and Manchester United will have a definitive verdict on Wayne's state of health before the start of the tournament. Wayne is so determined that he will be rejoining the England squad immediately that he doesn't pack his bags when he travels home and he returns to Germany on a late-night flight before the outcome of the scan has been made public.

THURSDAY JUNE 8

Wayne is given the all clear to stay with the squad for the World Cup and Sven insists that the last say on the player's fitness "is Rooney's and mine". After his one day away from the squad, Wayne returns to training with the others at 10.15am in Bühlertal. The session is followed by press conference with captain David Beckham. Wayne can now get into the daily routine of the tournament, knowing that he is here for the duration.

Wayne kicks a ball and thrills a nation

The plush hotel gym, where Wayne no doubt completed his rehabilitation

Wayne leaves a Manchester hospital with the all-clear on his broken foot

"So do you think you'll ever start a game this World Cup?"

The hotel's plush marble foyer: now riddled with studmarks

Rooney trains on the Frankfurt pitch prior to the Paraguay game: the closest he'd get to playing

Three Lions, one sunburnt striker!

WAYNE SAYS: *"When I got told my foot had fully healed it was brilliant news. I could now start full training and the only thing they warned me about was that I shouldn't think of playing before the Sweden game. But it was great to be back at the hotel where the lads had already heard the news. In the hotel I was in room 144, with Stevie Gerrard on one side and Frank Lampard on the other. The next morning I was to find my training kit, which has been assigned by the kit manager for that day: that way all the squad will be dressed the same and look and feel like a team, even on the training pitch. We congregate in the lobby of the hotel, most of us carrying our own boots.*

"It's a 15-minute ride to the training pitch at Mittelberg Stadium in Bühlertal and the journey there is beautiful with picture-book perfect German houses and vineyards as far as the eye can see. It's a fantastic training facility and the FA even arranged to have the pitch re-turfed so that we have an international standard pitch similar to the one in Frankfurt. Nothing is being left to chance."

FRIDAY JUNE 9

ON THIS DAY: Germany 4-2 Costa Rica (Munich); Poland 0-2 Ecuador (Gelsenkirchen)

It's the first day of the tournament and this evening Germany kick-off against Costa Rica, but the England players are concentrating on their own first game, tomorrow against Paraguay. They have breakfast at 9.30am before making the 90-minute coach journey from Baden Baden to Frankfurt in the early afternoon. It is hot and the players travel in their shorts and polo shirts, just taking an overnight bag with them for the short stay away from their training base. World Cup rules dictate that teams should stay in the vicinity of their venue on the night preceding a game. To get used to the match pitch there is a training session at the Wald Stadium, followed by a press conference with manager Sven-Göran Eriksson.

SATURDAY JUNE 10

ON THIS DAY: England 1-0 Paraguay (Frankfurt); Trinidad & Tobago 0-0 Sweden (Dortmund); Argentina 2-1 Ivory Coast (Hamburg)

England say goodbye to Jermain Defoe, who leaves the training camp for home following Wayne's recovery. Before their first game against Paraguay, the England team receive a visit in their dressing room from Prince William, delivering a handwritten letter of good luck from his grandmother, the Queen. He hands the correspondence to Sven-Göran Eriksson before the match and asks him to read it out to the team. England win by a single own-goal, deflecting into the net off Carlos Gamarra from a David Beckham cross.

Rooney may be on the bench, but every time his face appears on the giant screen hanging above the centre-circle the England fans chant his name.

After the match, Wayne is among the players warming down on the pitch in front of the handfuls of England fans who have remained in the stadium, impressing them with his ballwork.

WAYNE SAYS: *"I was itching to come on but Sven had made it clear before that I would not be playing. Perhaps just before the end he might change his mind? That's what was in my head. After it was all over I went out on the pitch with the other subs and we did a warm down. I belted a ball into the goal from about 30 yards and all the England fans cheered. When we came off I threw my shirt into the crowd of fans who'd been cheering me. We'd won not very convincingly but it gave us three points and a great start."*

SUNDAY JUNE 11

ON THIS DAY: Serbia & Montenegro 0-1 Holland (Leipzig); Mexico 3-1 Iran (Nuremberg); Angola 0-1 Portugal (Cologne)

The England team train at the Mittelberg Stadium in the morning. There is a press conference afterwards at 11.30am, with Joe Cole and Stewart Downing chosen to face the press this time. Despite the muted performance against Paraguay the team spirit in the camp is still very strong.

WAYNE SAYS: *"On the bus to training we have plenty of music and banter. And we keep playing the DVD of 'Rio Ferdinand's World Cup Wind-Ups', a programme shown on ITV. If you've seen it, you'll know I was well and truly stitched-up on a supposed visit to a dog's home, but the lads love the David James episode when he starts talking about art and shows his paintings on his mobile phone. He's never going to live that down."*

ROONEY'S MATCH DAY ROUTINE

Wayne explains exactly how he approached each match day during the 2006 World Cup,

"We will have travelled to the town where we're playing the day before, mostly by a chartered plane and settled into the team hotel. An advance party will already have arrived and set up the massage and medical suite, put our bags in our rooms, generally making our transition to the new location as painless as possible. In fact everything is geared to making our lives as easy as possible so we can focus entirely on playing.

"Match days begin for me with a chance to sleep-in. My agent says never mind football, I could sleep for England. He's right and I rarely make it down for breakfast. Later, we all attend a pre-match meal and then the final team meeting where Sven emphasises again all the things he wants each of us to do – who will pick up who, how we should approach free-kicks, corners and so on. This is the boss's key meeting and it usually lasts 15 minutes or so.

"Every player has a microchipped ID tag, with your photograph, name and team printed on it. We also have to hand over our passports to a FIFA official before each game, but I'm not sure why. Most of the players spend the next half-hour or so on their mobiles to their wives, girlfriends and families and deal with all the good luck texts and messages that flood in – except Gary Neville who apparently didn't get any!

"Then it's on to the team coach for what is usually a short journey to the stadium. The drive to the stadium is supported by the local police stopping traffic at junctions and traffic lights, and we're accompanied by police outriders. I have to say that I've only recently realised why we have such clear runs to the stadium because, by the time I get on to the coach, I am totally in a world of my own, completely focussed on what's ahead of me. My earphones are clamped to my head and the outside world hardly exists.

"We arrive at the stadium, collect our bags and head for the changing room. By now it's about one-and-a-half hours before kick-off. Our kit is already laid out and some of the lads sit around chatting before getting changed. I always pick up a ball, juggle with it or kick it against a wall.

"The changing room is absolutely off limits to pretty much everyone other than the squad and coaches. A last haven of privacy and bonding, it's our exclusive territory. The lads get changed, the physios strap up some players and the coaching staff have quiet words with individuals. We usually have music in the changing room. We need both to up the tension and to remain calm – a tricky mix.

"I don't get nervous, but sometimes I get a few butterflies. Once I've crossed the white line, however, I'm in the place where I feel the most comfortable in the world.

"As you would expect, a World Cup is the most organised of all football tournaments: we're told when to come out of the dressing room, where and when to line up and take the hands of the mascots. And then we start the walk up the tunnel. I find it hard to make much eye contact with the opposition, even when I know a player well. I just look ahead and keep thinking about what my job is.

"You would think that the crowd noise would be even greater than we get at Old Trafford, but there is quite a lot of ceremony before each game, with the national flags, FIFA Fair Play banner and so on going out ahead of the teams, so some of the raw energy of the crowd gets a bit diffused. What I did notice was how respectful all the crowds were of the national anthems and how loud 'God Save The Queen' sounded.

"People sometimes ask me why I don't sing the anthem. It's the focus thing. I go into a zone when all I can do is think about the next 90 minutes. But let's be clear: I am full of pride to play for my country, so proud that I find the sensation of pulling on the shirt with the three lions almost indescribable. That pride and emotion has to be controlled so I can get the best out of myself and the game and that's what you are watching when I stand like a statue while the anthems play out."

MONDAY JUNE 12

ON THIS DAY: Australia 3-1 Japan (Kaiserslautern); **USA 0-3 Czech Republic** (Gelsenkirchen); **Italy 2-0 Ghana** (Hanover)

Sven cancels the England training session and press conference, scheduled for 10.15am.

WAYNE SAYS: *"Every so often we're given the afternoon off and we can go into the town of Baden Baden – it's about a 20-minute car journey and the FA supply us with cars and drivers – where I can meet up with Coleen. We had a walk about, and she gave me a present. It was a Rolex watch and on the back it said 'To Wayne, Good Luck in the World Cup, Love Coleen'. It's great having her nearby. Despite what the press say, we actually see each other rarely throughout the tournament and most of the players contact with their families is by phone. But it makes a big difference knowing that your family is only a few kilometres away and that you can share the ups and downs, the frustrations and incredible highs of being an England player with them from time to time."*

TUESDAY JUNE 13

ON THIS DAY: South Korea 2-1 Togo (Frankfurt); **France 0-0 Switzerland** (Stuttgart); **Brazil 1-0 Croatia** (Berlin)

England train at 10.15am at the Mittelberg Stadium in Bühlertal, followed by a press conference with several of the players. As ever, a helicopter flies above the team coach to check the roads are kept clear and secure, while hundreds of journalists descend on the small training ground. The local regional league club SV Bühlertal have benefited from the deal with England as after the World Cup they will have gained a newly-laid pitch that has been tended to by the Wembley Stadium groundsman. The club also receives ten Euros per head for providing coffee and nibbles to the army of journalists who attend the press conferences each day. With Wayne getting ever closer to

WORLD CUP ROONEY FANS!

Leon Michael (centre), a Man United fan, went to Germany with fellow 'Red' Jesse Banister Wells (left), and Millwall fan Charlie Sean Roberts

How did you react when Wayne was injured?
Leon: "I was shocked because without him I thought that we wouldn't be able to qualify for the knock-out round."
Charlie: "I didn't think it was that bad at first."
Did you really think he'd play in the World Cup?
Charlie: "I thought he would but the newspapers and TV said he had no chance – but I'm really happy he made it."
Jesse: "It made a big difference when he finally came on."
What makes him special?
Leon: "He's got pace, stamina and a great shot."
Charlie: "Yes, he's got the lot!"

full-fitness, orthopaedic specialist Professor Angus Wallace arrives as an independent expert to assess the current fitness of Wayne.

WEDNESDAY JUNE 14

ON THIS DAY: Spain 4-0 Ukraine (Leipzig); **Tunisia 2-2 Saudi Arabia** (Munich); **Germany 1-0 Poland** (Dortmund)

England transfer from Baden Airpark to Nuremburg on a charter flight in the late morning. They have a training session at the Franken-Stadion scheduled at 4pm, and a press conference with team coach Sven-Göran Eriksson at 5pm. Sven announces that Rooney is "match-fit" for the Group B encounter against Trinidad & Tobago but that he is still uncertain about whether to play him. "Rooney has looked very good in training," said Eriksson. "Rooney told me three weeks ago he was ready – four weeks ago! He challenged everything in training. He has done full contact. I will sleep on it and then decide. I will be happy when the Rooney thing is finished – happy and relieved."

After training, the players return to the team's overnight hotel in the centre of Nuremberg. England fans gather outside and cheer for each

Hargreaves: "No, you should have danced to the Oompa band like this. I should know!"

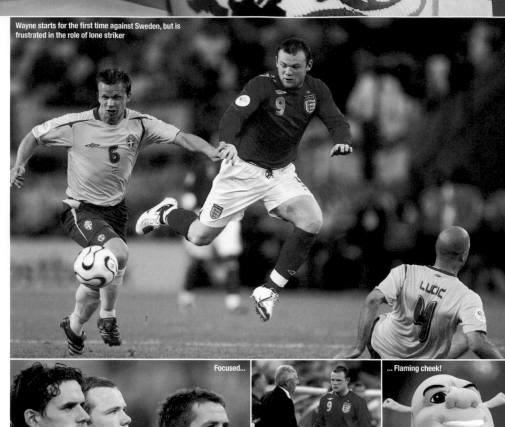
Wayne starts for the first time against Sweden, but is frustrated in the role of lone striker

player by name – and a roar goes up when a player waves back to them out of the window. Many of the squad join in the game with the fans, including Wayne, David Beckham, Steven Gerrard, Frank Lampard and Paul Robinson. Some of the players even film the scene from their windows to show their families back home.

WAYNE SAYS: *"I know that the England fans are the best and most passionate in the world. The support we've had out here has been fantastic. I think they see something of themselves in me, and I am just the same inside as them."*

THURSDAY JUNE 15

ON THIS DAY: Ecuador 3-0 Costa Rica (Hamburg); **England 2-0 Trinidad & Tobago** (Nuremberg); **Sweden 1-0 Paraguay** (Berlin)

Ahead of the match with Trinidad & Tobago independent medical advisors give their assessment on Wayne's state of fitness. "Wayne's recovery has been more rapid than expected," agree Professors Angus Wallace and Chris Moran. "The injury has healed and we are satisfied that he is as fit as he can be." The nation heaves a sign of relief and the calls grow even stronger for Wayne to start.

Wayne and the players have a pre-match stretch at 11.15am, and they attend a pre-match meeting at 2.15pm, followed by a meal. They leave the hotel at 4pm, two hours before kick-off. Once the game is underway, the team struggle to make an impact and look lethargic in the searing temperatures. Much to the delight of the crowd, who have been chanting his name, Wayne finally makes his long-awaited World Cup, replacing Michael Owen in the 58th minute. He immediately gets stuck into the match and England go on to win, thanks to late goals from Peter Crouch and Steven Gerrard.

WAYNE SAYS: *"Before the match Sven said I would be coming on and when it happened in the 52nd minute I felt fit and had no fears at all. I didn't feel worried about being clattered and getting injured again but my first touch was not good – I was probably a bit ring rusty. For a long time it didn't seem likely we'd score but we'd done what we'd set out to do and win the match. And apart from not being as sharp as I would like to have been, it did feel like I was back to normal."*

Focused...

Frustrated...

... Flaming cheek!

Mission impossible: after all the hype, Wayne finally takes to the field against Trinidad and Tobago

Out with the old and in with the new: Wayne greets former United star Dwight Yorke after the T&T game

FRIDAY JUNE 16

ON THIS DAY: Argentina v Serbia 6-0 Montenegro (Gelsenkirchen); **Holland 2-1 Ivory Coast** (Stuttgart); **Mexico 0-0 Angola** (Hanover)

It is revealed that Rooney was able to make a quick return with the England team because his injury was not a typical metatarsal break. His fracture was at the base of the metatarsal, which heals three times faster than the bone in the metatarsal shaft. The information was released by Professors Wallace and Chris Moran "Wayne had discomfort in his foot for only five days and has now been pain-free for six weeks," they say. "At his request we flew to Germany on Wednesday and carried out a very careful assessment of Wayne on Thursday. We both recognised that this was a week earlier than we had anticipated declaring him fit."

While the England players have a day-off from training, Trinidad & Tobago's Port Vale midfielder Chris Birchall states that England will struggle if they rely on Wayne Rooney too much: "Rooney's a great player but I think it will take him five or six games to get fully fit and the nation can't expect him to lift England on his own."

SATURDAY JUNE 17

ON THIS DAY: Portugal 2-0 Iran (Frankfurt); **Czech Republic 0-2 Ghana** (Cologne); **Italy 1-1 USA** (Kaiserslautern)

England hold a press conference at 3pm with Steven Gerrard and Frank Lampard, followed by training at the Mittelberg Stadium in Bühlertal an hour later.

WAYNE SAYS: *"Once the press have gone, we get down to the serious work, often in groups working on things like close control and stuff connected with the main tactical points the boss wants to get over in preparation for the next match."*

SUNDAY JUNE 18

ON THIS DAY: Japan 0-0 Croatia (Nuremberg); **Brazil 2-0 Australia** (Munich); **France 1-1 South Korea** (Leipzig)

The England squad train at 10.15am at the Mittelberg Stadium, followed by another press conference.

WAYNE SAYS: *"We always start our training session with a group stretch and warm up. For the first 15 minutes, the press are often allowed in to watch and film us. We always have a laugh and play around a bit. As I said, there is a great atmosphere in the camp and it tends to show when we're doing what we all love the most."*

MONDAY JUNE 19

ON THIS DAY: Togo 0-2 Switzerland (Dortmund); **Saudi Arabia 0-4 Ukraine** (Hamburg); **Spain 3-1 Tunisia** (Stuttgart)

England transfer from Baden Airpark to Cologne on a charter flight at 11.50am. They test tomorrow's match pitch with a 3.45pm training session at the Rhein Energie Stadium and a press conference with team coach Sven-Göran Eriksson is held at the stadium after training. Sven is finally able to field his dream strikeforce of Wayne Rooney and Micahel Owen. "The opponents do not want to hear that Rooney is going to start," said Eriksson. "He is fit and he is on fire again. In training he is tackling all over. I don't think anyone wants to meet Rooney, even if he is coming back from injury. He has learned a lot during his short career. He has become better at controlling himself. You can't take that away from him because that is one of his strengths. He has that fire inside him. He is living on the edge. Other teams maybe won't be scared, but they will be worried about Rooney."

TUESDAY JUNE 20

ON THIS DAY: Ecuador 0-3 Germany (Berlin); **Costa Rica 1-2 Poland** (Hanover); **Sweden 2–2 England** (Cologne); **Paraguay 2–0 Trinidad & Tobago** (Kaiserslautern)

Rooney starts the game against Sweden alongside Michael Owen, who suffers a serious injury in the first minute and is replaced by Peter Crouch. Wayne lasts 69 minutes of the 2-2 draw and England finish top of their group. After being substituted Wayne kicks a water bottle and punches the dug-out, before throwing his boots off. "I asked him why he did it and he said he was disappointed with himself because he thought he should have played better in the second-half," said Eriksson. "It's not a problem at all."

WAYNE SAYS: *"At half-time in the match 'Becks' asked Sven what had happened and he was told Michael was on his way to hospital. Although we really felt for Michael, there was nothing we could do so I, for one, wasn't going to let it get to me.*

"When I was subbed the TV cameras caught me giving the water bottles a good kicking as I came off, and Gary Neville offering some cooling words. It was frustration with my own performance that caused me to let fly, not at being taken off by the manager. I know I could have achieved more, but that's the way some games go."

WEDNESDAY JUNE 21

ON THIS DAY: Portugal 2-1 Mexico (Gelsenkirchen); **Iran 1-1 Angola** (Leipzig); **Holland 0-0 Argentina** (Frankfurt); **Ivory Coast 3-2 Serbia & Montenegro** (Munich)

Michael Owen is sent to the Max Grundig hospital at Buhlertal, near Baden-Baden to have a scan on his knee, but as feared the news is bad and his World Cup is over. England's dream partnership lasted just 51 seconds together at this tournament and now Wayne Rooney will have to carry the nation's hopes himself.

WAYNE SAYS: *"Michael Owen's injury was a massive loss to the team and, if I'm honest, especially to me. We've forged such a great partnership when playing for England and his absence was going to prevent us playing the way we'd planned and practised."*

THURSDAY JUNE 22

ON THIS DAY: Czech Republic 0-2 Italy (Hamburg); **Ghana 2-1 United States** (Nuremberg); **Japan 1-4 Brazil** (Dortmund); **Croatia 2-2 Australia** (Stuttgart)

England hold a press conference at 3pm, followed by training session an hour later at the Mittelberg Stadium in Bühlertal. The players are delighted to be through to the knockout stages of the tournament and can't wait for the game with Ecuador.

WAYNE SAYS: *"The spirit in the camp is fantastic, the best I've ever experienced. The players are really good mates and although we all have our particular friends – Michael before his early departure, Stevie G and me hang out together – there aren't*

any cliques. Unlike in previous tournaments, all the players from different clubs mix happily together and there are no disagreements at all – other than over the choice of music on the team bus."

FRIDAY JUNE 23

ON THIS DAY: Saudi Arabia 0-1 Spain (Kaiserslautern); **Ukraine 1-0 Tunisia** (Berlin); **Togo 0-2 France** (Cologne); **Switzerland 2-0 South Korea** (Hanover)

England train at the Mittelberg Stadium in Bühlertal at 10.15am and later there is a press conference scheduled to take place at the FA's media centre. By this time Wayne's enthusiasm for full-blooded training sessions has become well noted in the British press.

WAYNE SAYS: *"Towards the end of the session we'll usually play a short-sided game – and believe me, everyone goes in hard. After about one and half hours of training, it's back on the bus to the hotel for lunch. Afterwards you can do what you want, but I head to my room for a rest as after training I just watch a film or sleep."*

SATURDAY JUNE 24

ON THIS DAY: Germany 2-0 Sweden (Munich); **Argentina 2-1 Mexico** (Leipzig)

England make the bus journey from Baden Baden to Stuttgart for their pre-match overnight stay and at 5pm they work-out on the pitch of the Gottlieb-Daimler Stadium. Training is followed by a press conference with Sven.

SUNDAY JUNE 25

ON THIS DAY: England 1-0 Ecuador (Stuttgart); **Portugal v Holland** (Nuremberg)

A magnificent free-kick from David Beckham sees England through to the quarter-finals and Wayne completes his first full game, 57 days after he broke the bone in his foot. He plays the entire game as a lone striker. The players are delighted with Wayne's performance and Ashley Cole insists that Wayne Rooney is still the key player for England. "If we give him the ball he'll create chances or score himself," says the Arsenal defender. "The more we give it to him the more he can produce his magic. He did well against Ecuador and will get better. Playing up front on his own was going to be tough for him in these conditions but he has produced for us. He did what we know he can, he held

"Hands up who thinks Sven is a good manager!"

the ball up and gave us time to attack with him. He will be even better in the next game and he will be enjoying the stage now because he is a big game player. He is world-class and we are delighted he is fit again." After the match England return to Baden Baden by bus.

WAYNE ROONEY: *"It was difficult being up front on my own but there was a lot of support from the midfield players and it worked for me. Overall I thought it was a decent performance. Over the last 30 minutes I felt better than the first 60, so it's a positive thing for me. Hopefully that can help me for the next game. I think I have done well in the two games that I have played in. All I have missed has been a goal, but hopefully that can come."*

MONDAY JUNE 26

ON THIS DAY: Italy 1-0 Australia (Kaiserslautern); **Switzerland 0-0 Ukraine** (Cologne) *Ukraine win 3-0 on pens*

With no work scheduled for the day after the match, the backroom staff can reflect on the performances of the team so far. "Even before Sunday's match Rooney was saying he could do extra-time if needed," said Sven's assistant, Tord Grip. "Now he is saying it again but with even more confidence because he lasted a full 90 minutes for the first time since his metatarsal injury. He wants to prove he can play for two hours if needed."

WAYNE SAYS: *"The doctors made me aware that if there was contact, it wouldn't be a problem. That took an awful lot of pressure off me. In the games I've played so far I've had kicks but you've just got to stay cool and get on with it. I'm sure it'll happen again on Saturday."*

TUESDAY JUNE 27

ON THIS DAY: Brazil 3-0 Ghana (Dortmund); **Spain 1-3 France** (Hanover)

Rio Ferdinand and Owen Hargreaves face a press conference at 6pm at the Mittelberg Stadium in Bühlertal. "Anything less than the final will be a disappointment," says the Manchester United defender of his World Cup ambitions. "No one comes here to get to the quarter-final." Ferdinand also points to the talents of his Portuguese club team-mate Cristiano Ronaldo, who will be facing England at the weekend. "Cristiano is a fantastic footballer and from speaking to him beforehand he's someone who wants to make an imprint on this World Cup. He has the ability to be one of the best players in the world if he carries on improving."

The England squad seem confident that they have what it takes to get past Portugal this time around – and Wayne Rooney is looking forward to the match.

WAYNE SAYS: *"We know that we're not far away from the World Cup final, but I think this is where the competition gets really tough and we will have to be at our very best. We've had four games with three wins and a draw and I don't think the performances have been too bad. I think it's been alright and we have got the results we needed."*

England v Ecuador : Wayne the lone striker!

as that you said paintings?"

ROONEY'S VERDICT ON HIS TEAM-MATES

PAUL ROBINSON

"England's number one – he only conceded two goals in open play in five matches."

GARY NEVILLE

"He showed in the quarter-final why he was so important to the team, and how much his loss through injury meant."

JOHN TERRY

"A rock – always there when needed!"

RIO FERDINAND

"Composed as ever. He had tremendous presence and stature on the pitch throughout the tournament."

ASHLEY COLE

"He got better and better as the tournament progressed."

STEVEN GERRARD

"Excellent. Astonishing mileage over the pitch."

JOE COLE

"What a stunning goal! He had enough big moments to show how comfortably he now fits into the squad and team."

PETER CROUCH

"He showed everyone that he's a footballer, not just a big lad."

OWEN HARGREAVES

"What a revelation he was in this tournament!"

AARON LENNON

"For the amount of time he was on the pitch his contribution was outstanding."

DAVID BECKHAM

"An outstanding captain."

"Fancy penalties against Portugal?"

Shocked and stunned – the end of Wayne's World Cup. But it won't be the last red card this referee dishes out!

WAYNE'S WORLD CUP DIARY

WEDNESDAY JUNE 28

England train as usual at 10.15am at Bühlertal's Mittelberg Stadium. Wayne Rooney is among the players who attend the press conference and he reveals that a fan had sent him a healing potion to help him with his recovery. "I didn't try it though," he adds. He also discusses the process of returning after the injury and reflects on a return encounter with Portugal at the weekend, only two years after defeat to them in the quarter-finals of the European Championship.

WAYNE SAYS: *"Portugal – old friends and old rivals of mine and England's. It went to penalties in Lisbon and we were unlucky. That was disappointing, hopefully we can come out on top this time."*

THURSDAY JUNE 29

A press conference follows the usual 10.15am training session. In England Wayne Rooney's family insist that a man claiming to be his long-lost uncle is an imposter. Dr Martin Rooney boasted on German TV that he was the brother of Wayne's mum and claimed: "I always told Wayne he could be one of the greats". But Wayne's grandmother says she has never heard of him.

Alan Shearer is full of compliments for Rooney. "Wayne was awesome in the second-half against Ecaudor," says the former England striker. "He got fitter and stronger as the game went on and now I think he is ready for the match against Portugal."

WAYNE SAYS: *"If I look tired the manager will see that and he'll bring me off, and if I look okay he'll probably leave me on. With every game and every training session I'm getting better and fitter. You can see every day your touch is getting better and hopefully by the time this game comes I can be back to my best."*

FRIDAY JUNE 30

ON THIS DAY: Germany 1-1 Argentina (Berlin); *Germany win 4-2 on pens* **Italy 3-0 Ukraine** (Hamburg)

England transfer from Baden Airpark to Dusseldorf on a charter flight at 11.00am. They train at the stadium in Gelsenkirchen and afterwards Sven holds a press conference. He remains cagey about his team selection, but it is widely believed that Wayne will play up front again as a lone striker.

WAYNE SAYS: *"I have been asked to play in several positions in my career. As long as I play I don't care where it is on the pitch. I'll play in goal if that's what the manager wants. I have already played the lone-striker role for Manchester United. In the camp, the players felt that they were a much better team than in previous tournaments and we were all really happy to do exactly what we were asked by the manager. And if that meant me playing up front on my own, I was going to go out there and give it 100 per cent."*

SATURDAY JULY 1

ON THIS DAY: England 0-0 Portugal (Gelsenkirchen) *Portugal win 3-1 on pens;* **Brazil 0-1 France** (Frankfurt)

Wayne's big moment doesn't go according to the script. Giving their best performance of the World Cup, England start the match well, but after repeatedly being fouled, Wayne is stunned to be shown a red card early in the second-half. After a fine backs-to-the-wall performance by his team-mates, England eventually exit the tournament on penalties once again. Defeated and deflated, the squad fly out of Dortmund at 10pm on a charter flight, returning to their team base in Baden Baden.

WAYNE SAYS: *"I was gobsmacked and devastated when I was sent-off. In my opinion the card was completely unwarranted. I am an honest player and I tried to stay up during the challenge by the two Portuguese players. We should have had a free-kick. If I hadn't stayed up we would have been given the decision. Once Carvalho went down I had nowhere to go but over him. As for the rest of the team, all ten England players on the pitch in that quarter-final after I got sent off – it was their performance that shows what is meant by the three lions on the chest and the flag of St George."*

SUNDAY JULY 2

England stage an 11am press conference with coach Sven-Göran Eriksson and David Beckham, who resigns as England captain. The squad leave Germany in a British Airways jet at 3pm, landing at Stansted Airport. Some 200 fans have turned up to welcome the team home. Sven leads them off the plane, followed by David Beckham. Most of the players' wives and girlfriends are on the plane, but Wayne travels alone as Coleen has already been booked to return on a scheduled flight.

WAYNE SAYS: *"Little 'big moments' didn't quite happen throughout the tournament for me. As for the team, we did see brief glimpses of how it could work in maybe one and half games, but the truth is, we never got to grips with the system."*

"Stick with me kid, we'll win it next time!"

Goodbye to Germany – Rooney's coming home!

WAYNE'S

IT WAS A TOUGH DECISION BUT HER

RIO FERDINAND
CLUB: Manchester United **POSITION:** Defender

CAFU
CLUB: AC Milan **POSITION:** Defender

KAKA
CLUB: AC Milan **POSITION:** Midfielder

ZINEDINE ZIDANE
CLUB: Retired **POSITION:** Midfielder

RONALDO
CLUB: Real Madrid **POSITION:** Striker

"When I'm not playing football I spend my time watching it – everything from the Spanish and Italian leagues to the Football League Trophy, if that's what's on. But what I enjoy most is watching the really great players and here I've picked my dream team.

"It would be an all time dream to play alongside these giants of the game when they are at the peak of their talents and one of the really difficult jobs was to select the substitutes. Frankly, any one of them could walk into a World XI, never mind sit on the bench of Rooney's Dream Team!

"Playing 4-4-2, I would expect the team to have a real inner toughness and a strong, insatiable desire to win. It's a team that would excite the fans, with so much sublime skill and technical ability on show. In fact I've picked a very attacking team, even the full backs love to push on and join the attack."

SUBSTITUTES

ANDRIY SHEVCHENKO
CLUB: Chelsea
POSITION: Striker

FRANK LAMPARD
CLUB: Chelsea
POSITION: Midfielder

REAM TEAM

RE THE PLAYERS I'D LOVE TO PLAY ALONGSIDE!

IKER CASILLAS
CLUB: Real Madrid **POSITION:** Goalkeeper

JOHN TERRY
CLUB: Chelsea **POSITION:** Defender

GABRIEL HEINZE
CLUB: Manchester United **POSITION:** Defender

RONALDINHO
CLUB: Barcelona **POSITION:** Midfielder

STEVEN GERRARD
CLUB: Liverpool **POSITION:** Midfielder

WAYNE ROONEY
CLUB: Manchester United **POSITION:** Striker

GIANLUIGI BUFFON
CLUB: Juventus
POSITION: Goalkeeper

JAAP STAM
CLUB: AC Milan
POSITION: Defender

CRISTIANO RONALDO
CLUB: Manchester United
POSITION: Midfielder

IKER CASILLAS

CLUB: Real Madrid **POSITION:** Goalkeeper

Invariably the first name on Spain's team sheet, Casillas has the ability to pull off spectacular reflex saves and is regarded as near unbeatable in one-on-one situations. He first captured the imagination when, at just 18, he helped Real Madrid to victory over Valencia in the Champions League final of 2000. Since coming on as a second-half substitute in the 2002 final for Cesar Sanchez, Iker has been irreplaceable for both club and country.

WAYNE'S VERDICT: *"Over the last few years Iker has simply been the outstanding goalkeeper in Europe. Spain may have under-performed during the World Cup in Germany this summer, but I expect to see him between the Spanish goalposts for the rest of my career."*

CAFU

CLUB: AC Milan **POSITION:** Right-Back

Nicknamed 'Pendolino' (the express train), Cafu's pace and skill have maintained his position as the world's best right-back, despite turning 36 this summer. The first man to have played in the final of three World Cups, Cafu had the honour of lifting the trophy over Valencia as Brazil captain in 2002, and in the same year he also became his country's most capped player. Was one of Brazil's better performers in a disappointing World Cup in Germany.

WAYNE'S VERDICT: *"Cafu is the outstanding attacking full-back of his generation. He is fantastic defensively, but it's what he gives the team going forward that really impresses me. He is in great physical condition for his age – an example for every professional to aspire to."*

"THIS IS A TEAM THAT WOULD EXCITE THE FANS, WITH SO MUCH SUBLIME SKILL AND TECHNICAL ABILITY ON SHOW"

RIO FERDINAND

CLUB: Manchester United **POSITION:** Centre-Back

Cool under pressure and comfortable on the ball, Rio is a mobile, skilful defender and firmly established at the heart of the England team. He became the world's most expensive defender when he moved from Leeds to Man United for £30 million in July 2002, having caught the eye at that summer's World Cup. Winning a championship medal in his first season went some way to justifying the huge outlay as he performed heroically.

WAYNE'S VERDICT: *"Rio is a super guy and someone I'll be friends with long after we stop playing. He is the best thinking centre-half I've seen and is rarely caught out because he reads the game so well. Rio is totally comfortable on the ball and contributes to the team's build-up play."*

JOHN TERRY

CLUB: Chelsea **POSITION:** Centre-Back

A masterful presence in defence for Chelsea and England, Terry boasts intelligent defensive positioning and solid man-marking skills. He is dominant both on the ground and in the air and has won the respect of attacking players the world over. Appointed Blues captain in the 2003-4 season, Terry helped Chelsea win successive Premierships in 2005 and 2006, while being voted Player Of The Year by his fellow professionals in 2005.

WAYNE'S VERDICT: *"Defending is all about partnerships and in the Rio Ferdinand and John Terry pairing, I believe England has the best central defence in the world. They compliment each other brilliantly and John is as solid as a rock with a never-say-die attitude."*

GABRIEL HEINZE

CLUB: Manchester United **POSITION:** Left-Back

Heinze is an uncompromising and versatile defender who can play either in the centre of defence or on the left, offering both Manchester United and Argentina useful flexibility. Despite his nimble skills, Heinze is also a tough tackling defender with a fierce challenge. While injury blighted most of his 2005-6 season, the former Paris St Germain star fought his way back to fitness in time to make it into the Argentinian World Cup line-up.

WAYNE'S VERDICT: *"Gabriel is powerful and aggressive, and some would say a bit of a throwback in style, but he is also a very modern player, getting forward whenever he can. As a forward I know I can leave him to get on with his job – and that breeds real confidence in the team."*

WAYNE'S DREAM TEAM

RONALDO

CLUB: Real Madrid **POSITION:** Striker

He might have received criticism for his weight in recent years but the man they call 'The Phenomenon' is the nearest Brazil has come to producing a modern-day Pelé. A World Cup winner in 2002, he also won the Golden Boot and scored twice in the final, while in 2006 he broke Gerd Muller's record for the most goals in the history of the tournament. He has been voted the World Player Of The Year on three occasions.

WAYNE'S VERDICT: *"While it was obvious in Germany Ronaldo hadn't got the pace of earlier years, his movement was still excellent and his presence, touch and goalscoring talent was obvious for all to see. He is the iconic modern-day centre-forward and he looks like a good lad too."*

RONALDINHO

CLUB: Barcelona **POSITION:** Midfielder

Twice voted World Player Of The Year and a World Cup winner in 2002, Ronaldinho is blessed with almost unnatural ball control and breathtaking skill. Always smiling and ever-modest, the Brazilian finds it difficult when compared with his country's greats of the past, and yet with each passing game the feeling grows that he could become one of the finest players ever. Was instrumental in Barcelona's Champions League success in 2006.

WAYNE'S VERDICT: *"I love the way Ronaldinho uses his natural ability in the tightest situations, creating opportunities for the team and scoring outrageous goals. Right now he's the world's best footballer and if he's got a match coming up on the telly, I make sure I'm in to see it."*

KAKA

CLUB: AC Milan **POSITION:** Midfielder

The rising star of Brazilian football, Kaka is an attacking midfielder who possesses impressive ball skills and tremendous stamina. Not afraid to move into a striking role when needed, he has a great eye for goal, as demonstrated by his strike against Croatia in Brazil's opening 2006 World Cup game. In 2002, the Brazilian Player Of The Year moved to AC Milan where he established his true class, winning the Scudetto in his first season in Italy.

WAYNE'S VERDICT: *"Kaka is a player I have watched all year and it was my prediction that he would have a great World Cup. For all his aggression and forward runs, he is very disciplined and can defend when necessary. He is going to be one of Brazil's great stars for years to come."*

ZINEDINE ZIDANE

CLUB: Retired **POSITION:** Midfielder

Lethal in possession and a master of the dribble, Zidane's vision and precision passing make him one of the all-time greats. A World Cup winner in 1998, he scored twice in the final and was voted World Player Of The Year. He won the award again in 2000, before joining Real Madrid from Juventus for a world record £45 million in 2001. Retired this summer after leading France to another World Cup final, only to be sent off for butting Marco Materazzi.

WAYNE'S VERDICT: *"Friends tell me I'm constantly talking about Zidane. In my dream team, when I make runs off the ball to get behind defenders, he would always spot them and play the ball, giving it back-spin so I could run on to it without breaking my stride – a dream player."*

STEVEN GERRARD

CLUB: Liverpool **POSITION:** Midfielder

Gerrard's tackling and passing have made him a feared opponent, while he possesses the kind of shot that makes him a real threat from distance. But it is the way that he can dominate a game that marks him out as one of the world's best midfielders. Through sheer skill and determination he powered Liverpool to victory in the 2005 Champions League final and turned around the 2006 FA Cup final in much the same manner.

WAYNE'S VERDICT: *"Stevie is a great lad and one of my best mates in the England dressing room. He has really helped with my international career and is one of the least selfish people I've ever met. A footballer of world stature, he has shown you don't have to go abroad to become one."*

Think you did the business in Rooney Challenge 1? Well things are going to get a whole lot harder now! See how you get on with these tough-tackling posers and remember, the answers can be found on page 95

Come on, see if you can pick off 25 out of 25!

TEENAGE KICKS

WAYNE'S BIG MOVE TO UNITED MADE HIM ONE OF THE WORLD'S MOST VALUABLE TEENAGERS… BUT CAN YOU NAME THESE OTHER HIGH-PROFILE TEENAGE TRANSFERS?

1 This Italian striker became world's most expensive teenager when moving to Italian giants Roma from Bari, for a whopping £20m in 2001.

ANSWER

2 His last name is known throughout the world, but his first names are Luiz Nazario de Lima. Barcelona paid £16m to PSV Eindhoven for him in 1996.

ANSWER

3 Sir Alex paid Sporting Lisbon £12.24m for this youngster's services, and Wayne benefits from his superb silky skills down the right wing for United.

ANSWER

4 A Republic of Ireland star, Coventry City paid Wolves £6m when he was 19 in 1999, and then they sold him a year later to Inter Milan for £13m.

ANSWER

5 A young English talent now playing in the capital, Sir Bobby Robson once paid £5m to take him as an 18-year-old from Nottingham Forest to Newcastle.

ANSWER

SAY WHAT?

Plenty of people have said plenty of things about Wayne over the last four years. But do you know which famous figures in football said the following…

1 "He gives us something else to think about. He's a young player with remarkable physical and creative power. He has belief and determination and the physical ability to achieve what he sets out to do."

2 "Rooney can do the lot. He will eventually have all the United goalscoring records. I don't even see why he can't overtake my 46 in a season."

3 "It's the passion and aggression that people like about Wayne. He's not just a special talent, he is also very committed. And that is what you want to see in your team-mates."

4 "He does things that just can't be coached – and in that way he's like me. He is an instinctive player. I love the fact that, like me at his age, he will go straight from the training ground and have a kickabout with his mates."

5 "I know from personal experience that he's an absolute nightmare to mark. All of Europe is aware of him and I'd love to get him to Chelsea! I've not got the money to buy him but I think there are others connected with Chelsea who may be able to raise the cash!"

1	ANSWER
2	ANSWER
3	ANSWER
4	ANSWER
5	ANSWER

GOAL GRABBERS

Wayne played in some vital World Cup qualifiers to help get England to the World Cup in Germany, but can you name the missing goalscorers from these matches?

1 OCTOBER 9, 2004 ENGLAND 2 WALES 0
In just the third minute midfielder ––––– ––––––––– opens the scoring for England.
ANSWER

2 OCTOBER 9, 2004 ENGLAND 2 WALES 0
The vital second was scored by ––––– –––––– with 14 minutes left.
ANSWER

3 SEPTEMBER 3, 2005 WALES 0 ENGLAND 1
Chelsea's ––– –––– gets the only goal of the game.
ANSWER

4 MARCH 30, 2005 ENGLAND 2 AZERBAIJAN 0
––––– –––––– opens the scoring for England just before the break.
ANSWER

GUESS THE STRIKE PARTNER

Can you work out who this strike partner of Wayne is?

ANSWER

GAFFER GAFFES

Wayne's had two club managers in his time as a professional – fellow Scots Sir Alex Ferguson and David Moyes – but is it true or false that…

1 Moyes won the Scottish title as a player at Celtic?
ANSWER

2 Moyes ended his playing days at Grimsby Town?
ANSWER

3 Moyes' took over from Martin Peters as manager of Preston?
ANSWER

4 Bristol City and Shrewsbury were stops on Moyes's lower league playing career?
ANSWER

5 Moyes originally thought Wayne would make a good full-back?
ANSWER

6 Although thought of as Scottish, Sir Alex was actually born in a small South Yorkshire mining community before moving north?
ANSWER

7 As a boy, Sir Alex was a fan of Glasgow Rangers.
ANSWER

8 Sir Alex won the Scottish First Division title as manager of St Mirren?
ANSWER

9 In 1983, Aberdeen, with Sir Alex as boss, beat Barcelona in the European Cup Winners' Cup Final?
ANSWER

10 Sir Alex won the English League title during his first season in charge at Manchester United?
ANSWER

PAGE TOTAL

OUT OF 25

GROWING UP AS

There's no denying Wayne's Evertonian roots as he takes us down memory lane with a look through his family album

WAYNE ROONEY

WHAT'S IN A NAME

"I was born on October 24, 1985 at Fazakerley Hospital, Liverpool. I arrived three days early and weighed 8lb 6oz. I was named Wayne Mark Rooney but I was nearly called Adrian. That was what my dad wanted but my mum talked him out of it. His idea was to name me after Adrian Heath, one of the Everton stars, a little bloke, very quick and clever, who later went into coaching with Peter Reid at Sunderland. I was a big fan of his, but I don't think I would have fancied the name, so I was christened Wayne – after my dad."

MY BROTHERS

"Graeme, my younger brother, was born on October 15, 1987. His full name is Graeme Andrew Rooney after Graeme Sharp, the Everton striker from the 1980s, whom my dad hero-worshipped. His other hero back then was Andy Gray, a Blues legend who also played for Scotland and who is now on Sky. I also have another brother, John, born on December 17, 1990."

DAD THE BOXER

"Dad was a great boxer in his younger days growing up in Liverpool. Many of the Rooney clan were keen fighters and one of them ran a boxing club in the city called St Theresa's. My dad weighed about ten stone back then – I won't tell you how much he weighs now or he'll thump me – but he boxed as a lightweight, competing for Liverpool and then the North West Counties. This is a photo of him being presented with a cup he won when he fought in a match against the Navy, boxing for the North West Counties. He also fought in a competition in Finland and came away winning both gold and silver medals. His brothers Ritchie, John, Eugene and Alan won boxing cups as well, and football for that matter, but I think that my dad was the best of all of them when it came to boxing – he could have turned professional, or so he says. There were people talking about it to him, but I don't think he could be bothered. I don't think he fancied all the training and commitment it would have taken to get to the very top."

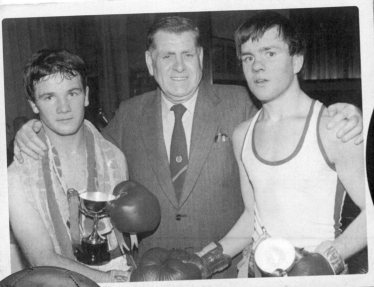

BORN A BLUE

"My family on both sides are die-hard Evertonians and my dad went to every home match possible. I attended my first Everton game when I was only six months old and dad had to carry me all the way – which involved getting on two buses – to the ground. He then had to hold me while standing at the Gwladys Street End. I was very well-behaved, apparently, so went regularly. When I got a bit older and was toddling about, I never moaned, cried or got bored. I only played up, he says, on the way home."

YOUNG BLUE

"In all the photos of me when I was little, I seem to be wearing an Everton strip of some sort. There's a snap of me, aged six months, looking very chubby with a large blue rosette which reads, 'Everton to win TODAY'. This was a free rosette, given out with the *Today* newspaper on the day of the 1986 FA Cup Final against Liverpool. Everton lost the match 3–1, a result we still don't talk about in our house."

BALL SKILLS

"It was at the age of six months that I first showed my ball skills, at least that's what my parents tell me. When a ball was put into my arms I was able to keep hold of it. At two, I was playing football and could volley the ball, so dad says, right to the end of the street where we lived. It couldn't have been a very long street! I also used to volley the ball over my nan's fence, which was about six feet high, but would then have to scramble over it to get the ball back. Usually I couldn't climb back, though, and would just stand on the other side crying my head off."

PRAYING FOR IT!

"Although I went to a Catholic primary school, as a family we didn't go to Mass very often, except on special occasions. I believed in Jesus, of course, did drawings of him at school and said my prayers most evenings. Usually, though, I was praying for Everton to win on a Saturday. I took my holy communion when I was nine. I had to wear a red sash and a red bow-tie which I hated. Once the service was over I rushed out and tore both things off."

INFANT SCHOOL

"I started out at Stonebridge Lane Infants when I was four, but have no memory of that. My mother says that on sports day I entered every race, winning every one. She has kept every school report, certificate and official document about me and my brothers, and the first of my reports dates back to 1992, when I was six. I needed 'lots of support' in my reading but in maths it reads, 'good mental skills'. In technology it says, 'enjoys making things and enjoys baking and sewing'. God knows where those skills have gone! In PE I was 'very keen and agile'. The overall report says, 'Wayne is popular with boys and girls in Year 1. He works hard and is rarely in trouble.'"

Wayne Rooney

Did you know that St. Francis built the first christmas crib and the custom continues all over the christian world today?

PLAYING FOR THE BOYS

"The first proper team I played for was a youth side, run by the Western pub where my dad used to drink, which played in an Under-12s league. Most of the pubs on our estate had boys' teams and I first started to play for them when I was seven and scored the winning goal. I also played for a number of other teams, such as Pye, while here I am playing for Copplehouse, another pub team, which I joined when I was eight and which played in an Under-9s league. I only once played for my primary school team, St Swithin's, because during all my time there they didn't have a proper team for us to play in."

BLUE OR RED?

"As a kid, I never thought about becoming a professional footballer, even for Everton. I dreamed about scoring goals, and about the Blues winning games, but it never entered my head that I could possibly become a real player. However, one day, when I was aged nine and playing for Copplehouse, scouts from both Liverpool and Everton were watching the game. After the match, the Liverpool scout approached my dad and asked if I'd like to have a trial. So two days later, after school, I went along to Melwood, Liverpool's training ground. I was wearing my Everton kit. Unfortunately, I didn't hit it off with the Liverpool coaches who were a bit funny towards me. I don't know why, perhaps it had something to do with wearing the Everton colours. I didn't wear the shirt as a defiant gesture, I just always wore it. After school, I lived in my Everton shirt."

EVERTON CALLING

"My dad received a call from Bob Pendleton, the Everton scout who had seen me play for Copplehouse. The club wanted me to attend a trial – only it was scheduled for the same evening as my second Liverpool trial. But once Everton showed interest, there was no choice and I was off to Bellefield, Everton's training ground. Dad came with me, secretly hoping to meet Joe Royle, the Everton manager. Straight after the trial, the club spoke to my dad, and asked if I would sign schoolboy forms. Of course, we said yes. I rushed home to tell mum. She wasn't in as she'd gone to church to take part in a rehearsal for Graeme's communion. She happened to be sitting next to Franny Jeffers' mother as I ran in the church, and when I told her she burst into tears. The club offered me a place for the 1995/96 season at their Centre of Excellence which later became the Everton Football Academy."

THERE'S ONLY ONE DUNCAN FERGUSON

"My bedroom was decorated with Everton memorabilia, from the bedside lampshade to the wallpaper. Posters showed off all my heroes, particularly Duncan Ferguson. He was a hard man and I liked the way he always gave his best. When Duncan went to prison, after he was involved in a fight, I wrote to him twice. I must have been about nine. I told him he shouldn't be in jail, and that me and my mates were desperate for him to come back and play for Everton. He actually wrote back, thanking me for my letter, and I was made up. He had no idea who I was, and I presume he replied to all the fans who wrote to him."

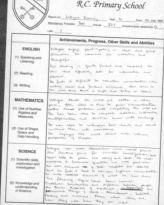

BIRTHDAY BOY

"I always had a party for my birthday, as did my two brothers. Mum did us proud, providing a sit-down tea, table-cloth, place names, ice cream and jelly, jaffa cakes, and games. There were always lots of kids invited round our house, most of them our cousins. On my first birthday, I'm told I wore the full Everton kit. For my present my dad gave me an Everton sign, in the style of a yellow car number plate. It remained in my bedroom throughout my childhood. Today, the sign takes pride of place in the glass front door at my dad's house. He kept hold of it when I moved out."

SCHOOL DAYS

"Mr primary school was Our Lady and St Swithin, a Roman Catholic school in Parkstile Lane, a ten-minute walk from our house. We had to wear a red tie, grey jumper, grey trousers and black shoes, but no trainers or football tops. Mum had gone to the same school and two of her teachers, Miss Kelly and Mrs Guy, also taught me. I liked Miss Kelly because each day she gave the best-behaved kid a creme egg. I didn't win very often – not often enough, I thought. I loved St Swithin's, liked all the teachers and got good reports. In this report, when I was nine, it says I enjoyed music, adding that I became familiar with Peer Gynt. Is he the Norwegian who once played for Manchester United?"

ACADEMY BOY

"I started with Everton, at nine, attending training three times a week after school and Sunday mornings saw us play against an Academy side from another club in the North West. Some of the kids were much bigger than me but that made me try even harder. I wanted to show off what skills I had and became very ball-greedy. The coaches would shout 'Lay it off!' while dad shouted 'Take him on!' and instead I would do neither: I'd try to score from 30 yards, which I often did. I played 29 games and scored in all but one, but the only match I remember was against Manchester United, when we hammered them 12–2 and I scored with an overhead kick from the edge of the box. When I scored, both the Everton and Mancester United parents started clapping from either side of the pitch and that's why I'll always remember that day."

SECONDARY SCHOOL

"The secondary school I went to was called De La Salle, a Roman Catholic comprehensive with about 1,000 kids, all of them boys. I didn't have much interest in academic subjects as, by then, I was so determined to succeed in football. But I was always well behaved and didn't cause trouble or muck around in class. I just didn't bother that much with things like homework, although my reports were never really bad. My Year 8 report, from July 1999, when I was 13, said I was late 51 times and my attendance was pretty poor, managing only 286 half-days out of a possible 320. The form tutor's comments mention that I have to 'improve my punctuality'. I don't think I ever did."

	EVERTON U10 – SEASON 1995-96					
1	EVERTON	4	ST HELENS	1	WAYNE	3
2	EVERTON	4	BURY	0	WAYNE	4
3	EVERTON	7	CHESTER	1	WAYNE	6
4	EVERTON	4	BLACKPOOL	2	WAYNE	2
5	EVERTON	15	PRESTON	0	WAYNE	9
6	EVERTON	5	ELSMERE PORT	2	WAYNE	2
7	EVERTON	5	LEEDS	2	WAYNE	3
8	EVERTON	8	N. FOREST	0	WAYNE	3
9	EVERTON	6	BURY	2	WAYNE	2
10	EVERTON	12	MAN. UNITED	2	WAYNE	6
11	EVERTON	2	LIVERPOOL	6	WAYNE	2
12	EVERTON	4	LIVERPOOL	3	WAYNE	5
13	EVERTON	7	N FOREST	2	WAYNE	2
14	EVERTON	2	N FOREST	1	WAYNE	
15	EVERTON	0	BURY	0	WAYNE	0
16	EVERTON	8	PRESTON	1	WAYNE	5
17	EVERTON	8	CROSBY BOYS	2	WAYNE	6
18	EVERTON	9	PRESTON	1	WAYNE	6
19	EVERTON	10	LEEDS	5	WAYNE	8
20	EVERTON	6	N. COUNTY	4	WAYNE	3
21	EVERTON	8	BLACKPOOL	1	WAYNE	3
22	EVERTON	10	PRESTON	2	WAYNE	6
23	EVERTON	13	N. FOREST	1	WAYNE	3
24	EVERTON	3	N. FOREST	0	WAYNE	1
25	EVERTON	5	TRANMERE	0	WAYNE	2
26	EVERTON	9	BURY	1	WAYNE	6
27	EVERTON	7	PETERBORO	0	WAYNE	3
28	EVERTON	13	ANGMERA	0	WAYNE	8
29	EVERTON	9	ANGMERA	3	WAYNE	4	TOTAL
30	EVERTON				WAYNE	114

GIRLFRIENDS

"I did most of the other things that the ordinary kids did on our estate, such as hanging around the chip shop and the street corners, eyeing up the girls. The girl I always really really fancied, from about 13, was Coleen McLoughlin. She was at our sister school, St John Bosco High. At De La Salle, I often had arguments with the other lads about her when we'd discuss who were the best-looking girls at St John Bosco. I always thought Coleen was the most fit and would stick up for her. I knew her brothers, and she knew my cousins, but I never seemed to get the chance to speak to her properly, let alone ask her out. I was too shy, I suppose, and too scared. I also knew she was a keen student who did her homework properly – unlike me."

IT'S A FAMILY AFFAIR

"It was great that both my younger brothers, Graeme and John, were also taken on in turn by the Everton Academy. The two of them were thrilled, of course, as was I and the whole Everton-mad Rooney clan. One day, at Bellefield, the three of us, all in our Everton kits, had our photograph taken with my hero, Duncan Ferguson. On the picture he's bending down with his arms round the three of us, and we're all so titchy compared to him. I don't think he knew who I was or had even talked to me before, but it was great to meet him. The reason we had this photograph taken was that we were three brothers, all signed as Everton schoolboys at the same time, which was unusual. Graeme and John seemed to do well, but I suppose it was hard for them with me doing particularly well in, especially when I was put up by the coaching staff by two years."

MASCOT MISCHIEF

"I was mascot when I was 10, against Liverpool, so was dead excited. I got to the stadium really early, only to find the game had been called off because the pitch was waterlogged. It was eventually played a month or so later and before kick-off me and the Liverpool mascot were pictured with the captains Dave Watson and John Barnes. Looking at the photo, I can't believe how thin and weedy I was, as well as a bit scruffy, with my socks round my ankles. As a mascot, you are allowed to score before the game begins and most usually dribble a shot in from six yards. What I did was to chip Neville Southall from outside the penalty area. Once the ball went straight over his head and another time it clipped the crossbar. I'd been practising all week, but Neville wasn't amused."

THE SPECIAL ONE

"The first time I realised I might be special as a footballer was when I was 15 and in my last year at school. It wasn't that I had done anything major, but I heard that De La Salle would be letting me off school for three days a week so I could train full-time at Everton. That 'special' treatment happened when I was in my last term at school, when I was about to leave, so I wouldn't be missing much. I was now playing for the Under-19 team and I was due to take part in some important FA Youth Cup games, along with players who had already left school and signed professional forms. I knew I was good, always keen to win, and even keener to show off how good I was. But being allowed off school for those three days a week was when it struck me most. I thought maybe I could be special, especially if they had made this arrangement, just for me."

SIGNING ON

"From the age of 14 to 16 I played in Everton's FA Youth Cup side and after two semis against Tottenham, Glenn Hoddle, then Spurs manager, asked if I was for sale. Liverpool are supposed to have tried to sign me as well and, in theory, I could have gone anywhere. Until signing pro forms at 17, a lad can go to any club, but when I turned 16, I decided to show my commitment and love for Everton by signing a pre-contract agreement meaning that, at 17, I would sign the official professional forms with them. It was a way of stopping other clubs from sniffing around. I signed during Everton's game with Derby County on December 15, 2001 – and celebrated by going onto the pitch at half-time, in front of 38,000 cheering fans."

PLAYING AWAY

"I went on my first overseas tour with Everton in 1998 when I was still 13. We played in a tournament in Switzerland against youth teams from Brazil and France, as well as the host nation; I think the French team was either Lyon or Auxerre. I was made the Everton captain, and we won the cup. We were told that playing abroad would give us an experience of foreign food and foreign places. Personally I hated all the foreign food, especially the bread. Ugh! All that lumpy brown stuff. We also flew to the USA to take part in a tournament in Dallas. We stayed there for about two weeks and each of us was homed by local families connected with the Dallas youth soccer teams. Beforehand, we each had to send off an individual letter about ourselves so we could be placed with the most suitable family. Now, when I look at my letter again, I think it's pretty clear the club must have helped us all write them. We had to list things like hobbies, so I put in fishing which I don't think I'd ever

done much. I also said I liked Oasis so that bit was true. The family I stayed with in Dallas was very nice. They had a bigger, posher home than our Croxteth council house, and had a son of my age and a younger daughter. For the first two days I was so homesick that I couldn't eat. I didn't like their sandwiches and hated the waffle things and other stuff that they had for breakfast. But it got a bit better as the time went on. They were very kind to me and one day took me to a rodeo with the other boys and girls – some of the girls were dressed as cowgirls. I enjoyed all that."

JUST

You might think that making a pair of football boots is easy, but when they're for one of the world's greatest players it's a complicated and time-consuming process

For a professional footballer like Wayne Rooney, football boots are the most important single tool of his trade. A player of Wayne's class has to have footwear that he feels comfortable with, as the right boots enable him to perform at the top of his game in every single match and help him perform the magic that the fans expect. Wayne currently wears the Nike Total 90 Supremacy football boot, but what exactly goes into designing and creating a top pair of boots for one of the world's best strikers? It's not as straight forward as you might think.

DO IT!

If Wayne needs new boots it can take up to three years to develop them.

STEP 1: RESEARCH AND DESIGN

If Wayne needs a new style of boot, the research and design process starts up to three years before they are ever seen in a game. Nike's team of footwear designers are based at the company's headquarters in Oregon, USA, and they are responsible for ensuring that the player gets the boots that will meet his needs.

First they will analyse what the player needs: Wayne's Total 90 Supremacy boots have been especially designed for power and accuracy – two key areas of Wayne's game. "We'll sit down with top players like Wayne to discuss and analyse every detail of the way they actually perform on the pitch, before we start the actual designs," says Nike's Global Football Creative Director, Peter Hudson. "With the Total 90 Supremacy boots we created a new outsole with spinal bars that transfer energy as the player's feet hit the ground, and an upper part that has laces down the side instead of the middle, so there is a bigger 'sweet-spot' when he strikes the ball to help his shots stay absolutely on-target."

Once the designers have got the fundamental requirements straight, then they will create a series of sketches and prototypes of the desired boot. The design phase often involves a team of three to four people, while the prototype team has more than ten people, and it generally takes six to eight months before they have a version they are completely happy with and are ready to test.

90

Total 90 Supremacy.

I 90 Supremacy.

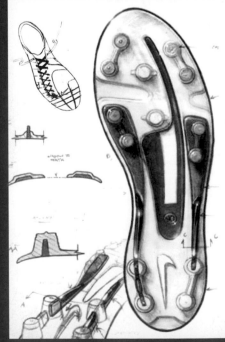

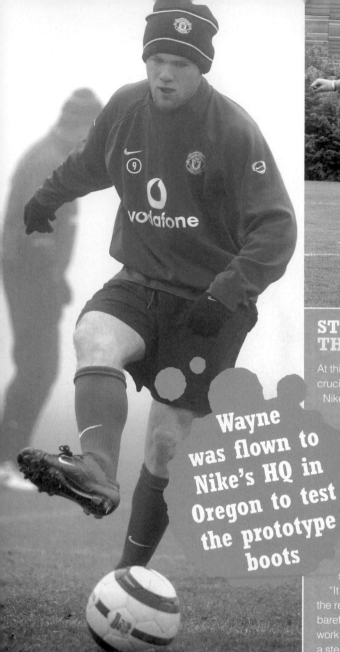

Wayne was flown to Nike's HQ in Oregon to test the prototype boots

STEP 2: TESTING THE PROTOTYPE

At this point Wayne's involvement becomes crucial again. In July 2005 Wayne visited the Nike HQ and spent time with the design team to give his input into the boot design he had discussed months earlier and to test and give feedback on the prototype boots.

As well as a Premier League-standard pitch that allows Wayne to get to grips with the boot on grass, the Nike facility also has a high-tech sport research laboratory, using computers and sensors to analyse every aspect of the way Wayne runs, turns and shoots, as well as the exact shape of his feet.

"It was really interesting to do all the tests in the research lab," says Wayne. "I had to run barefoot over pressure sensors so they could work out how my foot reacts each time I take a step, then I had to put my foot into a special

box and from that they get an exact 3-D computer reading of my feet."

After all of the tests inside the laboratory, Wayne finally gets to try the prototype boots on the pitch for the first time. He does a full hour of shooting drills, sprints, shuttles and turns. This is an important part of the process for the boot design team.

"No-one can tell you how a boot will work like the top players who will wear it," adds Hudson. "This boot is geared to Wayne's game, and getting his comments during that stage of the design process was vital. Afterwards we took his feedback and worked further on the boot to get it exactly how he wanted it."

At the end of Wayne's visit, before he went back to Manchester for pre-season training, he got the chance to meet one of his own idols, basketball star Michael Jordan. "That was fantastic, a real highlight for me," says Wayne. "We were at a big event at the Nike HQ, so I got to say hello and chat to him – I felt like any fan would do meeting one of their heroes."

STEP 3: MANUFACTURING THE BOOTS

Although the boots are designed in the USA, the actual manufacturing takes place in a factory in Montelbelluna, Northern Italy, where some of the best shoes in the world are made. Updated test models are produced and shipped to Manchester for Wayne to test in training and provide more feedback to the designers, engineers and sports research scientists.

Another important feature of the boot is its visual design. The Total 90 Supremacy features a non-symmetrical pattern to really make them stand out on the pitch. During the testing phase, Wayne uses a blacked-out version of the boots to stop the design being spotted by a photographer and leaked too early! After more feedback from Wayne, the finished boot is ready to wear and the team in Italy go into full production.

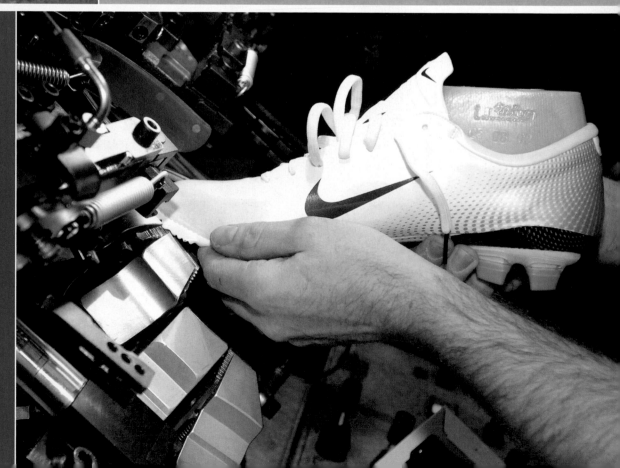

STEP 4: THE PRESS LAUNCH

Before he takes to the pitch in the Total 90 Supremacy, Wayne takes part in a photoshoot to get images of him wearing the boots that will feature in shops and magazines round the world.

There is also a launch event for the boots at Old Trafford, where media from around the world come to see the boots being revealed and to hear Wayne talking about how much he is looking forward to wearing them in the World Cup. More than 50 different organisations – radio, television, magazines and newspapers – come from places as far a-field as Brazil and Russia, showing the phenomenal interest there now is in Wayne from around the world.

"You have to talk to media a lot as a footballer, it's part of the job," says Wayne, who has blossomed in front of the flashbulbs, cameras and dictaphones. "The media who came all wanted to talk about the new boots and how I thought the World Cup would go. It was funny because the journalists from each country asked me what I knew about the players from their country and how I thought they'd do in the World Cup."

At the launch Wayne also reveals the England flag he will wear on the Total 90 Supremacy boots at the World Cup which, after his injury scare, he manages to do against Trinidad and Tobago on June 15.

Journalists from as far as Brazil and Russia came to see Wayne at the launch

STEP 5: PLAYING IN THE BOOTS

Wayne wears the boots for the first time in the Premiership game against Chelsea at the end of the 2005-6 season.

Unfortunately, he gets injured in the game, throwing his World Cup plans into confusion. But Wayne's recovery is successful and, much sooner than expected, his Total 90 boots are again unleashed on the world when he comes as a sub for Michael Owen in that Trinidad & Tobago World Cup game.

After nearly three years, Nike's designers have finally been able to see the boots in a big game. "It's always a thrill when you see a player like Wayne wearing the boots you've created and knowing that you're able to help him perform on the pitch," smiles Peter. "As a football fan, it's the best job in the world to get to work with a player like him."

So you think you've done the business in Rooney Challenges 1 & 2? And you're ready for more? If you've got a full house so far, bet you can't keep it going with these tough posers. Answers can be found on page 95

My brain is proper frazzled already!

WAYNE WONDER

REMEMBER MUCH FROM THESE ROO HIGHLIGHTS?

1 At 17 years and 317 days, Wayne became England's youngest-ever goalscorer with the equaliser in a match against...
A. Macedonia **B.** Turkey
C. Northern Ireland

ANSWER

2 Wayne scored his first ever goals at senior level for Everton with a brace in 3-0 Worthington Cup win against which lower league club?
A. Lincoln City **B.** Wrexham
C. Plymouth Argyle

ANSWER

3 In October 2002, Wayne scored a superb winner as Everton overcame champions Arsenal at Goodison Park. Who was in the Arsenal goal that day?
A. Jens Lehmann **B.** David Seaman
C. Stuart Taylor

ANSWER

4 Wayne's metatarsal injury in April 2006 is NOT the first time he's broken a bone in his foot. In Euro 2004 he was substituted after 27 minutes in the quarter-final against...
A. Holland **B.** Scotland **C.** Portugal

ANSWER

5 For the 2005-06 season, all Rooney fans know he wore the No.8 shirt, but who was in United's No.7 shirt, and who had No.9 on his back?

ANSWER

ANSWER

PLAYER SEARCH

Before the 2006 World Cup Wayne had played 29 times for England, facing 22 different teams. Can you find his international opponents hidden here?

A	W	D	E	N	M	A	R	K	P	P	O	L	Z	E	F	P	S
S	A	A	D	P	A	R	U	S	U	O	R	U	D	R	R	E	E
A	L	Z	N	E	I	G	S	S	L	O	V	A	K	I	A	D	R
M	E	E	A	S	P	E	E	P	T	U	R	K	E	Y	N	D	B
D	S	R	L	M	L	N	E	A	C	R	T	V	A	S	C	N	I
N	B	G	L	A	N	T	A	I	M	R	A	P	C	G	E	A	A
A	P	S	O	P	C	I	A	N	V	I	D	L	H	O	U	L	A
L	H	O	H	T	O	N	C	J	A	P	A	N	I	N	T	E	N
R	S	P	L	E	L	A	L	U	R	G	U	G	U	A	G	R	D
E	A	Y	A	A	N	D	U	R	U	G	U	A	Y	E	H	I	M
Z	E	D	O	C	N	E	S	T	N	T	K	N	N	O	W	N	O
T	H	O	W	T	R	D	R	O	D	D	A	T	N	N	C	R	N
I	E	T	R	A	N	O	F	N	U	R	I	S	G	S	E	E	T
W	S	P	A	G	P	H	A	T	O	N	S	T	S	W	A	H	E
S	R	A	W	B	E	L	R	T	A	Y	T	Y	H	E	N	T	N
K	L	O	A	Z	E	R	B	A	I	J	A	N	P	D	O	R	E
L	L	Q	R	C	G	R	E	E	P	A	I	X	C	E	Y	O	G
A	P	L	I	E	C	H	T	E	N	S	T	E	I	N	B	N	R
Z	M	A	C	E	D	O	N	I	A	L	L	D	E	C	A	M	O

- ☐ ARGENTINA
- ☐ AUSTRALIA
- ☐ AZERBAIJAN
- ☐ CROATIA
- ☐ DENMARK
- ☐ FRANCE
- ☐ HOLLAND
- ☐ ICELAND
- ☐ JAPAN
- ☐ LIECHTENSTEIN
- ☐ MACEDONIA
- ☐ NORTHERN IRELAND
- ☐ POLAND
- ☐ PORTUGAL
- ☐ SERBIA AND MONTENEGRO
- ☐ SPAIN
- ☐ SLOVAKIA
- ☐ SWEDEN
- ☐ SWITZERLAND
- ☐ TURKEY
- ☐ URUGUAY
- ☐ WALES

HIGHS AND LOWS

Wayne is a big player for United, standing loud and proud at a powerful 5 foot 10 inches. But can you match up these United players with their correct height?

1	RYAN GIGGS	A	5 FOOT 8 INCHES
2	JI-SUNG PARK	B	6 FOOT 1 INCHES
3	LOUIS SAHA	C	6 FOOT 2 INCHES
4	RIO FERDINAND	D	5 FOOT 11 INCHES

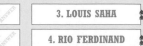
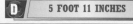

1. RYAN GIGGS	ANSWER	3. LOUIS SAHA	ANSWER
2. JI-SUNG PARK	ANSWER	4. RIO FERDINAND	ANSWER

FROM AFAR

From which country do these team-mates of Wayne come from?

1 PATRICE EVRA
ANSWER

2 CRISTIANO RONALDO
ANSWER

3 RYAN GIGGS
ANSWER

4 GIUSEPPE ROSSI
ANSWER

5 JI-SUNG PARK
ANSWER

6 TIM HOWARD
ANSWER

7 GABRIEL HEINZE
ANSWER

8 OLE-GUNNAR SOLSKJAER
ANSWER

9 WES BROWN
ANSWER

10 EDWIN VAN DER SAR
ANSWER

SWEET DEVILS

Wayne has only played for Everton and United, but since he burst onto the scene there has been a big rivalry between the clubs. How much do you remember about these games?

1 Wayne's first Everton v Man United clash saw his side lose 3-0. Which former England midfielder scored two goals that day?
ANSWER

2 Everton lost to Man United again in February 2004, with Wayne coming on at half-time in a Goodison thriller. A Frenchman and a Dutchman each scored twice as United won 4-3. Can you name them?
ANSWER

3 After signing for United, Wayne's first game against his former side was in February 2005, but in which competition?
ANSWER

4 When Wayne played against Everton in that game, which side won?
ANSWER

5 Everton beat United during in April 2005, but the Red Devils had two men sent-off that day. Who scored the only goal of the game?
ANSWER

6 Wayne scored his first goal against Everton on the opening day of the 2005-06 season. But can you remember the final score at Goodison that day?
ANSWER

7 Wayne played against his former team once more in a 1-1 draw in December 2005. Which Welshman scored United's goal?
ANSWER

GUESS THE STRIKE PARTNER

Can you work out who this strike partner of Wayne is?

ANSWER

PAGE TOTAL

OUT OF **50**

GOOOAA

MY GREATEST STF

Wayne Rooney has already hit some phenomenal strikes for Everton, Manchester United and England but here are the top ten in his very own words!

When you consider most great goalscorers don't hit the peak of their powers until at least their mid-twenties, it makes you wonder just how much better the Manchester United and England wonderkid is going to get. He may have notched 35 goals in his two seasons at Old Trafford and hit the net for England nine times in his first 13 starts – which included four at Euro 2004 – but that could be just the tip of the iceberg for a player with so much ability in front of goal. So what, exactly, makes Wayne Rooney such a brilliant goalscorer with the potential to be the very best in the world?

STRENGTH AND PACE

Not only is Rooney built like a boxer, making him very difficult to knock off the ball, but he's quick, too. Any defender who can keep pace with Wayne is always going to struggle to match his strength, while he is capable of running rings around most centre-backs, however imposing their height, weight and physique might make them appear.

POWERFUL SHOT

Rooney's best goals have all been long-range efforts – in fact, regularly banging them in from 25 or 30 yards has become something of a trademark for the Manchester United ace. He's lethal from dead ball situations, as he proved against Fenerbahçe during his memorable United debut, but is also one of the best strikers around when it comes to volleys. Hitting a ball that is falling is one of the most difficult skills a striker has to master but Rooney has proven time and again that he's adept

at it. His goal-of-the-season strike against Middlesbrough in the FA Cup in 2005, where Boro keeper Mark Schwarzer was left clutching at thin air, showed his volleying skills at their very best.

CONFIDENCE

You're 16 years old and are making your senior debut for Everton as an 80th minute substitute against league champions Arsenal. It's injury time and the ball comes to you 25 yards out. What do you do? Play it safe and pass it off to a more experienced member of the team? Keep hold of it for as long as possible to run down the clock and secure the draw? No, you thump it as hard as you can past the best goalkeeper in England like it was the most natural thing in the world. That takes extraordinary confidence in your own ability, nerves of steel and a giant helping of cheek. Wayne has all three in abundance.

WILL TO WIN

Many players claim they give 110 per cent in every game but Rooney actually does. Sometimes his will to win can lead to frustration and anger when things don't go his, or his team's, way but the odd disciplinary hiccup is more than countered by the plusses of having such a tireless, passionate worker in your side. Not only does Rooney do an excellent job as a striker or attacking midfielder, but he's usually the first to track back to help out in defence if needed, too. Rooney's never-say-die attitude is an inspiration to his team-mates, who also find themselves lifted by such a desire to win.

10 MAN UNITED 3 MIDDLESBROUGH 0

WHEN: January 29, 2005 **WHERE:** Old Trafford, Manchester **COMPETITION:** FA Cup Fourth Round

WHAT HAPPENED? United bounced back from their Carling Cup defeat to Chelsea with an emphatic win over Middlesbrough. Although John O'Shea's early goal would have been enough to see the Reds through to the famous old tournament's fifth round, Rooney was nevertheless on hand to provide a goalscoring masterclass with two fantastic goals. The first, after 67 minutes, saw Rooney receive a pass from Gary Neville some 40 yards out and, having seen Boro keeper Mark Schwarzer off his line, he struck an audacious chip which sailed over the keeper before nestling into the back of the net. Schwarzer was left gawping in amazement.

WHY WAS IT SPECIAL? While Rooney has put his Boro brace in the top ten, he rates the second as his favourite of the two, but it's doubtful he would have had the confidence to net the second without the first going in. From the moment his chip hit the net, Rooney was on fire and in complete control of the game.

TEAMS: Man United: Carroll, G Neville, Ferdinand, Brown, Heinze (Silvestre 79), Ronaldo (Miller 72), O'Shea, P Neville, Fortune, Giggs (Saha 65), Rooney. Subs not used: Howard, Scholes. Middlesbrough: Schwarzer, Reizeger, Cooper (McMahon 79), Southgate, Queudrue, Parlour, Morrison, Doriva (Job 46), Zenden, Downing, Hasselbaink (Graham 83). Subs not used: Nash, Parnaby.

"I RAN ON TO A SPINNING BALL... YOU DON'T SEE THE GOALKEEPER CHIPPED FROM 40 YARDS TOO OFTEN!"

WAYNE SAYS:
"The round before had been a real struggle with Exeter forcing a replay at their place. I added to Ronaldo's early strike with a goal in the 87th minute and that gave us a tie against Middlesbrough, which we had to win. Looking back, my two goals in this game will always rank among my favourites. My agent Paul Stretford often describes the first as an example of 'sublime skill'. Well, it was one of those moments when all the hours of practice comes together. I ran on to a spinning ball that was played over their back four and managed to chip their keeper Mark Schwarzer, who up until then had largely kept them in the game. Okay, you don't see the goalkeeper chipped from 40 yards too often!"

---

9 MAN UNITED 3 MIDDLESBROUGH 0

WHEN: January 29, 2005 **WHERE:** Old Trafford, Manchester
COMPETITION: FA Cup Fourth Round

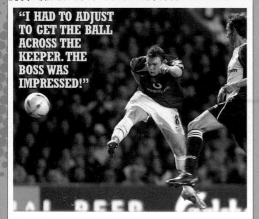

"I HAD TO ADJUST TO GET THE BALL ACROSS THE KEEPER. THE BOSS WAS IMPRESSED!"

WHAT HAPPENED? The England man's second, in the 82nd minute, was even better than the first. United keeper Roy Carroll thumped the ball upfield, feeding striker Louis Saha, who easily rose above his marker to nod down for Rooney. Without a second's pause for thought, the United striker belted the ball past Schwarzer from near the edge of the box with one of the sweetest volleys you're ever likely to see. Not for the first time, the Middlesbrough number one could only look on in amazement and admiration at the quality of strike that set United up with a fifth round clash with Rooney's former club Everton at Goodison Park.

WHY WAS IT SPECIAL? Rooney's second strike was named Goal Of The Season by BBC TV's Match Of The Day, fending off similarly terrific strikes from Liverpool's Steven Gerrard, Chelsea winger Arjen Robben and Arsenal skipper Patrick Vieira to win the accolade. The goal sent United into the fifth round and although there was a feeling the cup would again be United's, they eventually lost to Arsenal in the final.

TEAMS: Man United: Carroll, G Neville, Ferdinand, Brown, Heinze (Silvestre 79), Ronaldo (Miller 72), O'Shea, P Neville, Fortune, Giggs (Saha 65), Rooney. Subs not used: Howard, Scholes. Middlesbrough: Schwarzer, Reizeger, Cooper (McMahon 79), Southgate, Queudrue, Parlour, Morrison, Doriva (Job 46), Zenden, Downing, Hasselbaink (Graham 83). Subs not used: Nash, Parnaby.

WAYNE SAYS: "My second goal in this game was a volley and was more difficult than I had intended, because the ball came into much higher than I was expecting and I had to adjust my position to get the ball across the keeper. Apparently the boss was well impressed!"

---

8 MAN UNITED 2 ARSENAL 0

WHEN: October 24, 2004 **WHERE:** Old Trafford, Manchester **COMPETITION:** Premiership

WHAT HAPPENED? United were leading Arsene Wenger's league champions and Premiership pacesetters 1-0 with injury time well underway. Louis Saha found Alan Smith wide on the right and the former Leeds striker passed across the six-yard box for Rooney – celebrating his 19th birthday – to tap home from six yards out.

WHY WAS IT SPECIAL Rooney has and will score better goals but his injury-time tap-in to kill off Arsenal was important because it emphatically ended the 49-game unbeaten league run that the Gunners had been on since May 2003. The defeat put a big dent in Arsenal's previously unshakeable confidence and laid the groundwork for United's astounding 4-2 Premiership win at Highbury later in the season. It was the first time Sir Alex Ferguson's side had done the league double over the Gunners since the 1996/97 season.

TEAMS: Man United: Carroll, G Neville, Ferdinand, Silvestre, Heinze, Ronaldo (Smith 85), P Neville, Scholes, Giggs, Rooney, van Nistelrooy (Saha 90). Subs Not Used: Howard, Brown, Miller. Arsenal: Lehmann, Lauren, Campbell, Toure, Cole, Ljungberg, Vieira, Edu, Reyes (Pires 70), Bergkamp, Henry. Subs not used: van Persie, Taylor, Fabregas, Cygan.

"ARSENAL PLAYERS WENT MAD, SAYING I HAD DIVED WHICH I HADN'T DONE"

WAYNE SAYS:
"My first league goal for United and it came during the notorious 'Battle of the Buffet' when the boss's suit got ruined! From the beginning the atmosphere was pretty tense and nasty, and when I was brought down in the penalty area, the Arsenal players went mad, insisting I had dived which I hadn't done. I agreed with Ashley Cole and Sol Campbell, whose tackle was deemed a foul, that I'd just gone down under my own momentum, but that's not how the ref saw it. I suppose I added insult to injury with my last minute tap-in to end Arsenal's incredible unbeaten run. I say tap in, but people forget that I started the move in our half and then had to a make a lung-busting run for the finish. That's how badly we all wanted to win this one."

---

7 LEEDS UNITED 0 EVERTON 1

WHEN: November 3, 2002 **WHERE:** Elland Road, Leeds **COMPETITION:** Premiership

WHAT HAPPENED? Despite his wonder-goal against Arsenal a fortnight before, Wayne was on the bench for this game. But with the score poised at 0-0, Toffees manager David Moyes introduced the 17-year-old with just 16 minutes left. In the 80th minute, he picked up the ball 30 yards out, ran at the Leeds defence, evading two challenges, before drilling into the bottom right-hand corner of Paul Robinson's net.

WHY WAS IT SPECIAL? As well as confirming the goal against Arsenal hadn't been a fluke, Wayne's strike also bought Everton's terrible run of results at Elland Road to an abrupt end. The Toffees hadn't won there for 51 years, so it was little wonder the club's travelling fans went wild .

TEAMS: LEEDS: Robinson, Radebe, Woodgate, Viduka (Bridges 68), Kewell, Bowyer, Barmby, Lucic (Harte 46), Smith (McMaster 81), Mills, Bakke. Subs not used: Martyn, Kelly. EVERTON: Wright, Hibbert, Stubbs, Yobo, Unsworth, Carsley, Linderoth, Li Tie (Naysmith 82), Pembridge, Campbell, Radzinski (Rooney 74). Subs not used: Gerrard, Watson, Weir.

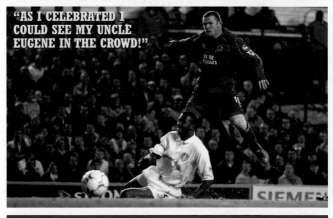

"AS I CELEBRATED I COULD SEE MY UNCLE EUGENE IN THE CROWD!"

WAYNE SAYS: "I was feeling a bit fed up with still not being started by David Moyes and we were going to Leeds knowing we hadn't got a result at Elland Road in over 50 years, so it was doubly determined to get a goal! All my family were there and when I was jumping up and down celebrating my goal in front of the travelling fans, I could clearly see my uncle Eugene in the crowd jumping up and down as well!"

6 LIVERPOOL 0 MAN UNITED 1

WHEN: January 15, 2005 **WHERE:** Anfield, Liverpool **COMPETITION:** Premiership

>> **WHAT HAPPENED?** In the 21st minute, Cristiano Ronaldo played the ball in to Wayne 30 yards out from the Liverpool goal. The former Everton hero thumped a powerful low drive into the bottom corner, embarrassing Reds keeper Jerzy Dudek in the process. Wayne ran towards the Kop to celebrate his strike – unsurprisingly the Liverpool fans didn't share the United youngster's joy, and one disgruntled supporter even lobbed a mobile phone in Rooney's direction, narrowly missing him.

>> **WHY WAS IT SPECIAL?** It was the first time Wayne had played in a match on Merseyside since his big money transfer to Old Trafford from Everton the previous summer. His goal also enabled United to record a third successive victory at Anfield – the home of their greatest rivals. More impressively still, United had to play the final 25 minutes without Wes Brown, who was sent off after picking up two yellow cards.

TEAMS: LIVERPOOL: Dudek, Carragher, Hyypia, Pellegrino, Traore, Garcia, Gerrard, Hamann (Biscan 79) Riise (Sinama-Pongolle 72), Baros, Morientes (Nunez 75). Subs not used: Warnock, Harrison. MAN UNITED: Carroll, P Neville, Brown, Silvestre, Heinze, Ronaldo (O'Shea 67), Fletcher, Keane, Scholes, Rooney (Bellion 90), Saha (Fortune 79). Subs not used: Howard, Miller.

WAYNE SAYS: "Games between Manchester United and Liverpool are huge – as big as Liverpool v Everton derbies. The rivalry meant we were in for a lot of stick from the Anfield crowd, some of it good natured, some of it not! And I really wanted to make an impact to quieten down the crowd. The tension on the pitch was just as great and when Ronaldo passed the ball I managed to unleash a bit of a piledriver that never got more than three inches off the ground before passing Dudek 25 yards away. After that, we had to defend for our lives. The boss took me off just before the whistle and even the ref said I'd be getting a lot of unnecessary aggro from the Liverpool players."

"I WANTED TO QUIETEN DOWN THE CROWD AND I MANAGED TO UNLEASH A BIT OF A PILEDRIVER THAT NEVER GOT MORE THAN THREE INCHES OFF THE GROUND."

4 FYR MACEDONIA 1 ENGLAND 2

WHEN: September 6, 2003 **WHERE:** Gradski Stadion, Skopje, Macedonia **COMPETITION:** Euro 2004 qualifier

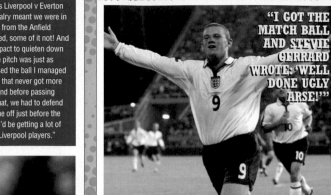

"I GOT THE MATCH BALL AND STEVIE GERRARD WROTE: 'WELL DONE UGLY ARSE!'"

>> **WHAT HAPPENED?** England had played poorly in the first period and trailed to a 27th minute goal from Macedonia's former Barnsley striker Georgi Hristov. Sven-Goran Eriksson changed things at the break, bringing on Emile Heskey for Frank Lampard to give England a more physical presence in attack. The switch paid immediate dividends as on 53 minutes David Beckham floated a long pass forward which Heskey expertly nodded into the path of Rooney. The Everton man made no mistake as he drilled the ball with his right-foot past keeper Milosevski into the bottom corner. England went on to win 2-1 and in doing so took an enormous step towards qualifying for the following year's European Championships in Portugal.

>> **WHY WAS IT SPECIAL?** Wayne's equaliser was his first goal as a senior England international, coming in his sixth appearance for his country. He also became England's youngest ever goalscorer, aged just 17 years and 317 days.

TEAMS: FYR Macedonia: Milosevski, Stavrevski, Mitreski, Stojanovski, Simulikoski, Grozdanovski (Braga 56), Trajanov, Pandev (Gjuzelov 48), Sakiri, Naumoski, Hristov (Dimitrovski 88). Subs not used: Nikoloski, Kapinkovski, Georgievski, Kumbev. England: James, G Neville, Terry, Campbell, A Cole, Beckham, Lampard (Heskey 46), Butt, Hargreaves, Owen (Dyer 86), Rooney (P Neville 74). Subs not used: Robinson, Upson, Bridge, J Cole.

WAYNE SAYS: "Although I'd started the match up front with Michael Owen, at half-time Sven said he was bringing on Emile Heskey to play with Michael, with me dropping back slightly behind the two leading strikers. He explained I'd be playing at the top of a 'diamond' formation. I'd never played there before and we hadn't even tried it in training, but I didn't mind. I like to think I can play anywhere as long as I get to play! The change worked and I latched on to a headed pass from Emile in the 53rd minute, hitting it on the half-volley. I got the match ball signed by the whole team. Michael wrote, 'That's another of my records you've broken' and Stevie Gerrard scribbled, 'Well done, Ugly Arse'."

5 ENGLAND UNDER-17s 4 SPAIN UNDER-17s 1

WHEN: May 10, 2002 **WHERE:** Gladsaxe Idrætspark, Copenhagen, Denmark **COMPETITION:** UEFA Under-17 Championship Third/Fourth Place match

>> **WHAT HAPPENED?** England had lost in the semi-finals to Switzerland so here was a chance to end the Under-17s tournament on a high by clinching the bronze medal. Wayne had already scored two goals coming into this game and produced a superb hat-trick here to make it five goals in five games. Team-mate Wayne Routledge had put England ahead but the rest of the match belonged to Rooney. He made it 2-0 after sliding in to convert a Routledge cross past keeper Roberto and 3-1 with a superb diving header from another Routledge centre. But the goal which stood out to make the top ten was the third strike where Wayne coolly slotting home when played through by England sub Mark Smyth. It was a virtuoso performance and it was little wonder he received a standing ovation when he was substituted towards the end.

>> **WHY WAS IT SPECIAL?** Wayne's three goals made European football sit up and take notice of the bright new talent in its midst. Five months later he'd announce his presence to the Premiership with that stunning strike against Arsenal and less than a year on became the youngest player to ever represent England's senior side against Australia at Upton Park.

TEAMS: ENGLAND: Drench, Biggins, Borrowdale, Gardner, Raven, Hogg, Routledge, Brown (Croft 63), Rooney (Profitt 76), Long, Doherty (Smyth 60). Subs not used: Sadler, Eyre, Mannix, Groves. SPAIN: Roberto, Molinero, Sestelo, Alexis Ruano, Garrido (Llamas 54), Aitor, Maureta (Merino 56), Silva, Gavilán, Soldado (Valero 71), David Rodríguez. Subs not used: Gonzalez, Robusté, Saura, Soriano.

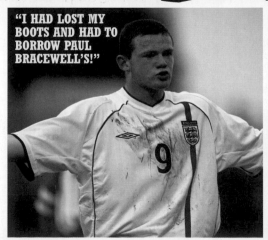

"I HAD LOST MY BOOTS AND HAD TO BORROW PAUL BRACEWELL'S!"

WAYNE SAYS: "I still have mixed feelings about playing for the Under-17s in the Euro finals that were held in Denmark that season. Of course I was, and I always am, dead proud to play for England, but I had signed official professional forms with Everton the previous December and had yet to make my first-team appearance. David Moyes had told me I'd be making my professional debut in Everton's next match against Blackburn, but instead I got the call up for the Under-17s and couldn't play in the game. Had I played for Everton that season, I would have beaten Joe Royle's record as the youngest ever Everton first-team player. Saying that, a hat-trick against Spain, giving us a 4-1 win and securing third place in the competition, was excellent compensation. The other thing about the match was I had somehow lost my boots and nobody seemed to have a spare pair. In the end I borrowed a size eight pair (I take nines) from Paul Bracewell who was part of the coaching staff. They were a bit tight, but didn't seem to do me any harm on the day!"

MAN UNITED 6 FENERBAHÇE 2

WHEN: September 28, 2004 **WHERE:** Old Trafford, Manchester **COMPETITION:** Champions League

>> **WHAT HAPPENED?** United led Fenerbahce 3-1 and were heading for three precious points in their bid to qualify for the Champions League quarter-finals. In the 54th minute, United won a free-kick 20 yards from the Turkish side's goal. Normally, Ryan Giggs would have stepped up to take the kick but he happily stepped aside to let Rooney have a try. The former Everton player – making his United debut and having already scored twice in front of the Old Trafford faithful – curled his shot round the Turks' defence, past goalkeeper Recber and into the top right-hand corner. The hat-trick was complete and the crowd erupted.

>> **WHY WAS IT SPECIAL?** Wayne's first appearance for Manchester United has been described by many Red Devils fans as the finest debut from a player in the club's history – and it's easy to see why. Not only did the teenager hit three superb goals, but he was easily the most impressive player on the pitch all night. The size of Rooney's £26 million transfer fee had caused consternation throughout the game, but in 90 perfect minutes Rooney had proved beyond any doubt that he was going to be worth every last penny.

*TEAMS: **Man United:** Carroll, G Neville, Ferdinand, Silvestre, Heinze (P Neville 82), Bellion, Djemba-Djemba, Kleberson, Giggs (Fletcher 63), van Nistelrooy (Miller 82), Rooney. Subs not used: Ronaldo, Smith, O'Shea, Ricardo. **Fenerbahçe:** Recber, Akyel (Akin 61), Luciano, Baris, Ozat, Balci, Marco Aurelio, Nobre, Sanli, De Souza, van Hooijdonk. Subs not used: Demirel, Fabiano Lima, Yozgatli, Hacioglu, Turaci, Sahin.*

"WHEN GIGGSY SHAPED TO TAKE THE FREE-KICK I GRABBED THE BALL AND TOLD HIM, 'I'M TAKING THIS, I WANT MY HAT-TRICK'!"

WAYNE SAYS: "I don't think I have ever felt my adrenaline levels so high in a match before. The move to Manchester United and the price they had paid for me made me determined to make an impact as soon as I could. I'd joined the club because I would do better as a player and win more trophies and here I was making my debut in a Champions League match! It had been 96 days since I had last played a game, back in Euro 2004 when I broke the bone in my foot, and it felt great to get my first goal for the club after 17 minutes. Ten minutes later I netted my second and now I knew a hat-trick was a real possibility. When Giggsy shaped to take the free-kick I grabbed the ball and told him, 'I'm taking this, I want my hat-trick'. Afterwards, as we were leaving the pitch the ref wouldn't give me the match ball, so Sir Alex had to go and have a word and retrieve it from the referee's dressing room."

EVERTON 2 ARSENAL 1

WHEN: October 19, 2002 **WHERE:** Goodison Park, Liverpool **COMPETITION:** Premiership

>> **WHAT HAPPENED?** As injury-time beckoned at Goodison Park, the game between Everton and Arsenal looked set to finish 1-1. The Gunners had gone ahead early on through Freddie Ljungberg but Everton hit back with a first half equaliser from Tomas Radzinski. To hold the reigning league champions would have been impressive enough as Arsene Wenger's side had been unbeaten in the Premiership since December 2001. But with time running out, Wayne expertly bought down a hopeful punt forward and with the ball at his feet ran full-tilt at the Arsenal backline. Spotting keeper David Seaman slightly off his line, Rooney lashed the ball at the goal from around 30 yards and Goodison Park erupted as it powered into the net off the underside of the crossbar. It gave Everton a 2-1 win and Wayne became an instant star around the world.

>> **WHY WAS IT SPECIAL?** Wayne's goal briefly made him the youngest goalscorer in Premiership history at 16 years and 360 days of age (this record was broken a few weeks later by James Milner, then of Leeds United). More amazingly, the young striker had only been on the pitch for ten minutes when he scored his goal, having come on as an 80th minute substitute for Radzinski. And, of course, he had netted against the champions.

*TEAMS: **Everton:** Wright, Hibbert, Yobo, Weir, Unsworth, Carsley (Stubbs 90), Gravesen, Li Tie (Linderoth 55), Pembridge, Radzinski (Rooney 80), Campbell. Subs not used: Alexandersson, Gerrard. **Arsenal:** Seaman, Lauren, Campbell, Cygan, Cole, Ljungberg (Edu 85), Silva, Vieira, Toure (Wiltord 64), Henry, Kanu (Jeffers 71). Subs not used: Luzhny, Shaaban.*

WAYNE SAYS: "Arsenal were on an incredible unbeaten run of 31 games and I'd been sitting on the bench for 80 minutes, so I was fuming and furious of course. I only had a couple of touches when Thomas Gravesen looped the ball forward in my direction – although I'm not sure it was a deliberate pass. I managed to turn my marker with one move, looked up and saw a space between Seaman and the bar. I just hit it side-footed, and a second later everything in my life changed. There's no doubt that goal helped bring about all the attention I've been getting ever since and Arsene Wenger's post-match comment still means a huge amount to me – it really kick-started my career."

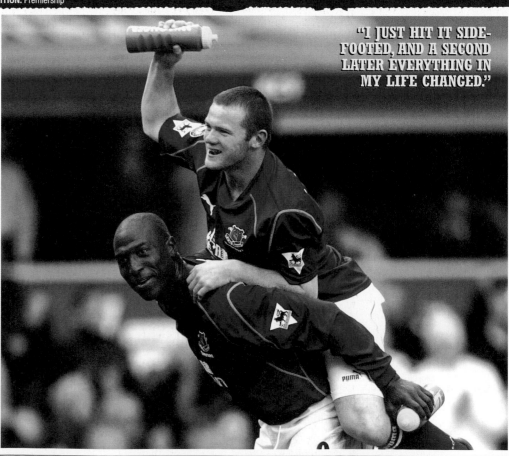

"I JUST HIT IT SIDE-FOOTED, AND A SECOND LATER EVERYTHING IN MY LIFE CHANGED."

1 MAN UNITED 2 NEWCASTLE UNITED 1

WHEN: April 24, 2005 **WHERE:** Old Trafford, Manchester **COMPETITION:** Premiership

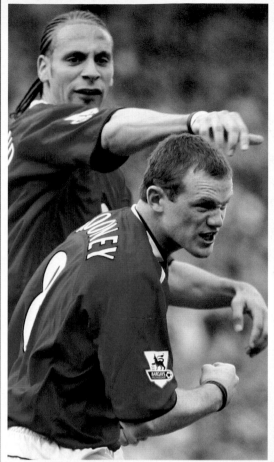

WHAT HAPPENED? Wayne wasn't enjoying the best of afternoons – he'd picked up an injury, Newcastle had gone a goal up in the first-half and he'd just been booked for a late challenge on James Milner. The youngster was a picture of frustration. Then, in the 56th minute, Newcastle midfielder Peter Ramage misdirected a header straight into his path, 25 yards out from goal. Rooney met it perfectly, hitting a screaming volley with the outside of his right boot past Shay Given and into the top left-hand corner of the net.

WHY WAS IT SPECIAL? Wayne's goal helped spark United's fightback and they eventually ran out 2-1 winners. It also illustrated the player's ability to turn a game with one moment of magic. No wonder his manager Sir Alex Ferguson called the goal "phenomenal", before adding: "I was ready to take him off because he was injured in the first half. He just hobbled on for the remainder of the game. But while he's on the pitch, he's such a threat and that's why we kept him on." Wayne was then named PFA Young Player of the Season for 2004/05 and with spectacular goals like this one, it came as no surprise.

TEAMS: Man United: Howard, P Neville, Ferdinand, Brown, Heinze (Ronaldo 37), Fletcher (Kleberson 61), Keane (Silvestre 76), Fortune, Giggs, Rooney, Smith. Subs not used: Carroll, O'Shea. **Newcastle:** Given, Carr, Boumsong, Andrew O'Brien, Elliott, Milner, Ambrose, Ramage (Robert 82), N'Zogbia, Shearer (Kluivert 66), Ameobi. Subs not used: Harper, Brittain, McClen.

WAYNE SAYS: "It was a funny sort of day and I'd had a right go at the referee because of all the rough tackles I was taking from the opposition. Eventually I got a dead leg and was really worried that Sir Alex was going to take me off. I was jogging forwards when the chance came to volley the ball. All the tension and anger I'd been feeling during the match was unleashed in that one shot, but somehow I managed to mix power with technique, which is why it was such a sweet strike."

"ALL THE TENSION AND ANGER I'D BEEN FEELING DURING THE MATCH WAS UNLEASHED IN THAT ONE SHOT!"

All quizzed-out yet? Got to the point where you can't bear the thought of another Roo-related question? If not, here's another 25 to keep you amused. And again, if you want to check your answers, they're on page 95

Don't know if I can handle much more of this!

FORWARD POWER

WILL WAYNE BECOME ENGLAND'S GREATEST EVER CENTRE FORWARD? HE HAS SOME BIG NAMES TO LIVE UP TO… BUT CAN YOU IDENTIFY WHO WE'RE DESCRIBING HERE?

1 He started his career at Leicester, made his name at Goodison Park and is now a BBC TV presenter.

ANSWER

2 Prolific for Newcastle and related to Bobby and Jackie Charlton, this man scored 10 times in 13 internationals.

ANSWER

3 Born in 1966… and still playing at the top level, this man has turned out for the likes of Man United and Millwall.

ANSWER

4 Now a racehorse trainer, he scored 21 times in 46 games for England, and won the FA Cup with Southampton.

ANSWER

5 An Everton legend, this striker once scored 60 league goals in a season and 16 in 18 games for England.

ANSWER

GREAT LIONS

We all know Wayne broke the record for being England's youngest international and youngest goalscorer… but how many more England records do you know?

1 Who scored England's fastest goal after just 27 seconds in the 1982 World Cup finals against France?

2 The country's first sending-off on home soil was by one of Wayne's current club-mates, versus Sweden, in 1999. Who was it?

3 A fellow Manchester United legend is England's all-time top goalscorer. Can you name him?

4 Although Wayne is rapidly catching up, he's still some way short of record caps-holder Peter Shilton. How many games did the goalkeeper play for England? a. 110; b. 115; c. 125

5 Wayne took the record as youngest England international, but who holds the record as the country's oldest player?

1	ANSWER
2	ANSWER
3	ANSWER
4	ANSWER
5	ANSWER

HOME FROM HOME

Wayne has played against these clubs in two seasons of Champions League football at United but can you match up the teams with their home grounds?

1	SPARTA PRAGUE	A	EL MADRIGAL
2	BENFICA	B	METROPOLE
3	VILLARREAL	C	LETNA STADIUM
4	LILLE	D	ESTADIO DA LUZ

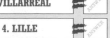

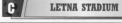

1. SPARTA PRAGUE	ANSWER	3. VILLARREAL	ANSWER
2. BENFICA	ANSWER	4. LILLE	ANSWER

GUESS THE STRIKE PARTNER

Can you work out who this strike partner of Wayne is?

ANSWER

AWAY GOALS RULE

Apart from Old Trafford and the Millennium Stadium, Wayne scored at eight different venues for United in season 2005-06. But do you know who plays at these English grounds?

1 GOODISON PARK
ANSWER

2 ST JAMES' PARK
ANSWER

3 CRAVEN COTTAGE
ANSWER

4 STADIUM OF LIGHT
ANSWER

5 UPTON PARK
ANSWER

6 VILLA PARK
ANSWER

7 ST ANDREWS
ANSWER

8 WHITE HART LANE
ANSWER

LATIN LESSON

Wayne's first club, Everton, have the motto in Latin on their club badge 'Nil Satis Nisi Optimum'. But do you know what it means?
A If they score nil, we need more.
B Only the best is good enough.
C When the going gets tough, get out of town quick smart.

ANSWER

EURO KINGS

Man United have won the European Cup twice, but in what years did they do it?
A 1961 & 1982
B 1968 & 1999
C 1969 & 1999

ANSWER

PAGE TOTAL

OUT OF **25**

GET SET

WITH ENGLAND'S WORLD CUP DISAPPOINTMENT A DISTANT MEMORY, WAYNE HAS TURNED HIS ATTENTION TO FIRING STEVE MCLAREN'S TEAM TO THE 2008 EUROPEAN CHAMPIONSHIP FINALS IN AUSTRIA AND SWITZERLAND

HAVING LOST ON PENALTIES TO Portugal at the quarter-final stage, while picking up a red card in the process, Wayne is now looking forward to England's 2008 European Championship qualifying campaign.

It was little over two years ago that Rooney's scintillating performances against Switzerland and Croatia at Euro 2004 thrust him into the world spotlight, but just as he moved into top gear, a broken foot sustained against host nation Portugal curtailed his involvement and ended any hope England had of progressing further in the competition.

Now the talisman of the side, Rooney will be looked upon to fire Steve McLaren's side to the 2008 finals in Switzerland and Austria. Standing in the way on the road to finals are Russia, Croatia, Israel, Estonia, Macedonia and Andorra, all countries of varying strengths and abilities, but all with the common goal of qualification, while beating England along the way!

Unfortunately Wayne misses the opening two fixtures against Andorra and Macedonia following his red card in Germany, but you can rest assured he'll be coming out with all guns blazing for the return home fixture against the Macedonians in October.

Make no mistake, Wayne has unfinished business to attend to, following two aborted finals in an England shirt, and he'll also been keen to show new boss McLaren and the rest of the world why he's regarded as one of the hottest strikers on the planet.

So here's to a successful Euro campaign and more goals from Mr Rooney…

FOR EURO 2008!

GROUP E

- 🏴 ENGLAND
- ⬜ CROATIA
- ⬜ RUSSIA
- ⬜ ISRAEL
- ⬜ ESTONIA
- ❄ FYR MACEDO
- ⬜ ANDORR

GROUP G

- NETHERLANDS
- ROMANIA

CH REPUBLIC
ANY
KIA
LIC OF IR
S
RUS
AN M

SAT SEPT 2 2006 ENGLAND v ANDORRA
SAT OCT 7 2006 ENGLAND v MACEDONIA
SAT SEPT 8 2007 ENGLAND v ISRAEL
WED SEPT 12 2007 ENGLAND v RUSSIA
SAT OCT 13 2007 ENGLAND v ESTONIA
WED NOV 21 2007 ENGLAND v CROATIA

WED OCT 17 2007 RUSSIA v ENGLAND

WED JUNE 6 2007 ESTONIA v ENGLAND

WED OCT 11 2006 CROATIA v ENGLAND

WED MAR 28 2007 ANDORRA v ENGLAND

WED SEPT 6 2006 MACEDONIA v ENGLAND

SAT MAR 24 2007 ISRAEL v ENGLAND

53

RUSSIA

Dmitri Bulyin celebrates his goal as Russia beat eventual champions Greece at Euro 2004

SEP. 6 2003 ▸ v FYR MACEDONIA

USUAL HOME GROUND Lokomotiv Stadium, Moscow

CAPACITY 28,800 **Manager** Guus Hiddink

FOR THE RECORD

FIRST GAME
August 16, 1992 v Mexico, Friendly, 2-0 (home)

BIGGEST WIN
6-0, June 28, 1994 v Cameroon, WC Finals

BIGGEST DEFEAT
7-1, October 13, 2004 v Portugal, WC Qualifier (away)

RECENT GAMES v ENGLAND

1992 CIS 2 England 2 *Friendly*

1991 England 3 Soviet Union 1 *Friendly*

1988 England 1 Soviet Union 3 *Euro Champs*

1986 Soviet Union 0 England 1 *Friendly*

1984 England 0 Soviet Union 2 *Friendly*

ENGLAND'S RECORD
v SOVIET UNION/CIS

P12	W5	D4	L3	F21	A15

THE OPPONENTS

WHO IS ROONEY UP AGAINST? Following Russia's failure to qualify for the World Cup finals in Germany, a young side is set to be assembled by newly-appointed coach Guus Hiddink, with 20-year-old CSKA Moscow keeper Igor Akinfeev likely to play in goal. His CSKA team-mates Alexei and Vasili Berezutski are only three years older but what they lack in defensive experience they make up for in familiarity and will be keen to test themselves against a top-quality player like Rooney and his team-mates.

HOW BIG IS THE THREAT? Hiddink has earned accolades across the globe for his coaching achievements, but taking on Russia could well be his biggest challenge yet. Russia have the quality to surprise the big nations from time to time, but lack the consistency to maintain a good level of performance over an entire qualifying campaign. A lack of experience could also count against them on this occasion.

HOW DO THEY PLAY? Russia play a rigid 4-4-2 formation but with Hiddink in control and a Dutch backroom team behind him, expect more flexibility in the team this time out. Forward Andrei Arshavin is set to become the focal point, with much of the team's attacking play coming through him.

VERDICT: Having finished third in their World Cup qualifying campaign, Russia will be keen to make amends, but with an overhaul required, Hiddink is going to have his work cut out.

THE RUSSIANS WILL BE KEEN TO TEST THEMSELVES AGAINST WAYNE ROONEY AND THE ENGLAND TEAM

JUN. 21 2004 ▸ v CROATIA

PLAYING AWAY MOSCOW

THE STADIUM The Lokomotiv Stadium in Moscow was completely rebuilt in 2002 and is the most modern of all stadia in Russia. It houses Russia's internationals, but with a capacity of less than 29,000, there is a chance the game could be switched to the 80,000 capacity Olympic Stadium.

THE FOOTBALL Following the influx of sponsorship deals, the Russian league is gaining in strength and is one of the most competitive in Europe, with ten clubs regularly fighting for the top spot. CSKA Moscow are the most successful in recent seasons, winning the title in 2003 and 2005, as well as the UEFA Cup in 2005.

THE CITY Moscow is steeped in history, so if you're off to the game, be sure to take in Red Square, home to the Kremlin, which houses the Russian government, and St Basil's Cathedral, with its elegant onion domes. Getting around is easy on a Metro system that boasts 171 stations and there are plenty of city centre bars.

PLAYERS TO WATCH

Aleksandr Kerzakov
Zenit St Petersburg

Andrei Arshavin
Zenit St Petersburg

Alexei Berezutski
CSKA Moscow

Vasili Berezutski
CSKA Moscow

Yuri Zhirkov *(below)*
CSKA Moscow

ISRAEL

USUAL HOME GROUND National Stadium, Ramat Gan

CAPACITY 41,000 **Manager** Dror Kashtan

FOR THE RECORD

FIRST GAME
September 26, 1948 v USA, Friendly, 1-3 (away)

BIGGEST WIN
9-0, March 23, 1988 v Taiwan, Friendly (neutral)

BIGGEST DEFEAT
7-1, February 13, 2002 v Germany, Friendly (away)

RECENT GAMES v ENGLAND
1988 Israel 0 England 0, *Friendly*
1986 Israel 1 England 2, *Friendly*

ENGLAND'S RECORD v ISRAEL

P2	W1	D1	L0	F2	A1

THE OPPONENTS

WHO IS ROONEY UP AGAINST? Israel are likely to feature Nir Davidovic as their number one keeper and although erratic, he is capable of breathtaking saves – Sheffield United are one club reported to be watching him. Keeping a Premiership theme, Rooney will come up against a well known opponent in Bolton centre-half Tal Ben Haim, while Shimon Gershon, the skipper of Hapeol Tel Aviv, also boasts UEFA Cup experience.

HOW BIG IS THE THREAT? Israel are not to be underestimated and will prove difficult opponents on home soil. Despite playing in a group that contained Republic Of Ireland, France and Switzerland, they remained unbeaten throughout their World Cup qualifying campaign and only missed out due to the Swiss having a better goal difference.

HOW DO THEY PLAY? Israel adopt a 4-4-1-1 formation, with the focal point being West Ham midfielder Yossi Benayoun, who plays just behind the main striker. He ended the World Cup qualifying campaign as his country's leading scorer, while former Wimbledon midfielder Walid Badir is another influential player at the heart of midfield. Israel also like to break at pace, with much of their speed coming from winger Idan Tal, who has recently signed a pre-contract agreement with Bolton.

VERDICT: Will be buoyed by their showing in the World Cup 2006 qualifiers and are likely to cause the odd upset, but a lack of goals could well be their downfall.

Avik Benado and Avi Nimni celebrate a draw in Ireland during their World Cup campaign

PLAYERS TO WATCH
Yossi Benayoun (below)
West Ham
Tal Ben Haim
Bolton
Walid Badir
Maccabi Haifa
Idan Tal
Bolton
Avi Nimni
Maccabi Tel Aviv

PLAYING AWAY RAMAT GAN

THE STADIUM The National Stadium in Ramat Gan was completed in 1951 and following a refurbishment in 1982, it now boasts a capacity of over 41,000. It is the only stadium in Israel of a standard to host FIFA World Cup games and UEFA Champions League fixtures.

THE FOOTBALL The Israeli Premier League boasts 12 teams. In recent years it has been dominated by Maccabi Haifa, who have finished top for the last six seasons and whose high-profile exports have been Yakubu and Benayoun to the Premiership.

THE CITY Ramat Gan is a suburban city in the Tel Aviv district of Israel which boasts 127,400 residents. Around 25 per cent of the city is covered in public parkland, therefore amenities for the visiting football fan are limited, so a better bet is to set up base in Tel Aviv itself.

FYR MACEDONIA

USUAL HOME GROUND Gradski Stadium, Skopje

CAPACITY 18,000 **Manager** Srecko Katanec

FOR THE RECORD

FIRST GAME
October 13, 1993 v Slovenia, Friendly, 1-4 (away)

BIGGEST WIN
11-1, Sept 9, 1996 v Liechtenstein, WC Qualifier (away)

BIGGEST DEAFEAT
6-1, June 8, 2005 v Czech Republic, WC Qualifier (away)

RECENT GAMES v ENGLAND
2003 Macedonia 1 England 2, *EC Qualifier*
2002 England 2 Macedonia 2, *EC Qualifier*

ENGLAND'S RECORD v FYC MACEDONIA

P2	W1	D1	L0	F4	A3

THE OPPONENTS

WHO IS ROONEY UP AGAINST? Macedonia, under new coach Katanec, are in the process of rebuilding following their unsuccessful World Cup qualifying campaign, and young keeper Filip Madzovski is likely to build on his recent appearances. Experience in the back-four is therefore important, so expect Eintracht Frankfurt stopper Aleksandar Vasoski to stand in Rooney's way, likewise FK Metalurg defender Igor Mitreski. Two draws against Holland in World Cup qualification suggest they can handle big occasions.

HOW BIG IS THE THREAT? Minimal. While the draws against Holland were the highlights to their World Cup 2006 qualification campaign, FYR Macedonia invariably let themselves down against lesser opposition. One point from two games against minnows Andorra typified their inconsistency, although they will be encouraged by their 2-2 draw in England during their Euro 2004 qualifying campaign.

HOW DO THEY PLAY? Katanec starred in his playing days for Sampdoria and has adopted Italian traits to his own philosophy. He usually opts for a rigid 4-4-2 formation, with much of the play targeted at Lazio striker Goran Pandev – the star of the Macedonia team – via playmaker Artim Sakiri midfield.

VERDICT: With only one or two players of proven quality, FYR Macedonia's results are again likely to be riddled with inconsistency. Technically good players they may be, but will still struggle against the stronger sides.

Ilko Naumoski goes for goal during a 0-0 World Cup qualifying draw in Holland

PLAYERS TO WATCH
Goran Pandev (below)
Lazio
Aleksandar Vasoski
Eintracht Frankfurt
Igor Mitreski
FK Metalurg
Artim Sakiri
Aalborg
Georgi Hristov
Debreceni

PLAYING AWAY SKOPJE

THE STADIUM The Gradski Stadium – or City Stadium as it is also known – in the capital Skopje, is home to two of the country's leading clubs, FK Vardar and FK Rabotnicki. It is an all-seater venue, with a large, curved, main stand and holds 18,000 spectators.

THE FOOTBALL The First League is contested by 12 clubs, who play each other three times. Rabotnicki have won the competition for the last two seasons, although Vardar boast five wins since the league's formation in 1992. Many internationals hail from these two clubs.

THE CITY Skopje's old bazaar, which dates back to the Ottoman Empire, is worth a visit. The Old Stone Bridge, across the River Vardar, is another stop off point. Expect many monuments dedicated to Mother Theresa, who was born in the country in 1910.

55

CROATIA

USUSAL HOME GROUND Maksimir Stadium, Zagreb

CAPACITY 40,000 **Manager** Zlatko Kranjcar

FOR THE RECORD

FIRST GAME
October 17, 1990 v USA, Friendly, 2-1(home)

BIGGEST WIN
7-0, June 6, 1998 v Australia, Friendly (home)

BIGGEST DEAFEAT
4-1, April 20, 1994 v Slovakia, Friendly (away)

RECENT GAMES v ENGLAND

2004: England 4 Croatia 2, *EC Finals*

2003: England 3 Croatia 1, *Friendly*

1996: England 0 Croatia 0, *Friendly*

ENGLAND'S RECORD v CROATIA

P 3	W 2	D 1	L 0	F 7	A 3

THE OPPONENTS

WHO IS ROONEY UP AGAINST? Croatia boast the experience of Stipe Pletikosa, the Hajduk Split goalkeeper, while Club Bruge's keeper Tomislav Butina will also be vying for the number one jersey for Euro 2008. Rooney can also expect a rough ride against the old warhorse and former Juventus stopper Igor Tudor at the heart of the defence, while current Juve star Robert Kovac will also be a tough proposition at the back for Croatia.

HOW BIG IS THE THREAT? Croatia are always dark horses and having won their World Cup qualifying group with ease, they have also shown their credentials with a 3-2 friendly win over Argentina in 2006. Croatia are an uncompromising side, but they also have more than their fair share of flair throughout the team. Leading the way is playmaker and rising star Niko Kranjcar, son of coach Zlatko, while the Croatian attack boasts Rangers' prolific frontman Dado Prso.

HOW DO THEY PLAY? Croatia play with a 3-5-2 formation. With two wing-backs and two holding midfielders, key man Kranjcar is allowed to get on the ball and links defence to attack by playing in the hole behind the strikers. He pulls the strings in the side, while Prso is the chief goalscorer who also brings his wide players into the game.

VERDICT: While they may not have the power of England, Croatia are good technically and should be looking for the runners-up spot in the group. They will, however, expect more.

Niko Kovac gets the better of Henrik Larsson during last year's 1-0 victory

Niko Kranjcar
Hajduk Split

Dado Prso (below)
Rangers

Robert Kovac
Juventus

Igor Tudor
Siena

Ivica Olic
CSKA Moscow

PLAYING AWAY ZAGREB

THE STADIUM The Maksimir Stadium in Zagreb received a facelift in 1997 and currently holds 40,000 spectators. However, after England have been in town in October, further work will be carried out, taking the capacity up to 55,000 with a moving roof.

THE FOOTBALL The Croatian league championship is not particularly strong, with Dinamo Zagreb regularly dominating proceedings. This point is proved by the small number of players (four) in the current squad who actually ply their trade on home soil.

THE CITY Zagreb is the capital of Croatia and therefore an important tourist centre. There are more than 3.6million exhibits in the city's countless museums, with the Archaeological Museum well worth a visit. For nightlife check out the main Ban Jelacic Square.

ESTONIA

USUAL HOME GROUND Kadriorg Stadium, Tallinn

CAPACITY 4,700 **Manager** Jelle Goes

FOR THE RECORD

FIRST GAME
October 17, 1920 v Finland, Friendly, 0-6 (home)

BIGGEST WIN
6-0, June 24, 1923 v Lithuania, Friendly (away); July 26, 1928 v Lithuania (home)

BIGGEST DEAFEAT
10-2, August 11, 1922 v Finland, Friendly (away)

RECENT GAMES v ENGLAND

Have never met

ENGLAND'S RECORD v ESTONIA

P 0	W 0	D 0	L 0	F 0	A 0

THE OPPONENTS

WHO IS ROONEY UP AGAINST? Rooney will have to get past the Arsenal reserve keeper Mart Poom if he wants to breach the Estonian defence, although Estonian-based Artur Kotenko has also been vying for the top spot of late. The centre-half pairings of Andrei Stepanov and Dmitri Kruglov are both relatively inexperienced, but having plied their trade in Russia with Torpedo Moscow and Lokomotiv Moscow respectively, they have a real physical presence.

HOW BIG IS THE THREAT? It will be minimal. Estonia finished behind Portugal, Russia and Slovakia in their World Cup qualifying group and suffered heavy 4-0 defeats against the Portuguese and Russia along the way. A Dutch coach in Jelle Goes could help the side out of its shell but the best they can hope for is points against Macedonia and Andorra.

HOW DO THEY PLAY? Estonia have historically based the game around a solid back line and they will no doubt try and adopt the same policy against the big guns in the group. When the side do venture forward, they rely heavily on Andres Oper and Kristen Viikmäe, who have amassed over 200 caps between them, and the flair of technical midfielder Maksim Smirnov.

VERDICT: Showed in World Cup 2006 qualification that they are more than a match for the smaller nations in their group, but will be out-muscled by the likes of England, Croatia and Russia. Maybe even Israel.

Urmas Rooba challenged Belgium's Peter van Houdt during Euro 2004 qualification

Mart Poom (below)
Arsenal

Liivo Leetma
TVMK

Maksim Smirnov
Levadia

Andrei Stepanov
Torpedo Moscow

Raio Piiroja
Fredrikstad FK

PLAYING AWAY TALLINN

THE STADIUM The Kadriorg Stadium in Tallinn is a multi-purpose arena and also home to leading club side Levadia Tallinn. It was built in 1926 but as it houses just 4,700 fans, there won't be many opportunities for England fans to watch the game in the flesh.

THE FOOTBALL Estonia's clubs play in the Meistriliga – a competition that boasts ten clubs. In recent seasons it has been dominated by Tallinn-based clubs, with TVMK the current holders. Many of the country's better players are attracted to the Russian league.

THE CITY Tallinn is just 80km from Finland's capital Helsinki. It boasts a picturesque old town and in Kadriorg, where the stadium is situated, the former palace of Peter The Great is worth a visit. A marina is also close by, built for the 1980 Moscow Olympics.

  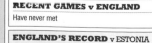

v CROATIA ◄ JUN. 21 2004

ROONEY CAN EXPECT A ROUGH RIDE AGAINST OLD WARHORSE IGOR TUDOR AT THE HEART OF THE CROATIA DEFENCE

v FYR MACEDONIA ◄ SEP. 6 2003

ANDORRA

Oscar Sonejee pulls away from Ireland's Damien Duff

USUAL HOME GROUND Estadi Communal, Andorra La Vella

CAPACITY 1311 **Manager** David Rodrigo

FOR THE RECORD

FIRST GAME

November 13, 1996 v Estonia, Friendly, 1-6 (away)

BIGGEST WIN

2-0, April 26, 2000 v Belarus, WC Qualifier (home); April 17, 2002 v Albania, Friendly (home)

BIGGEST DEAFEAT

8-1, June 4, 2005 v Czech Republic, WC Qualifier (away)

RECENT GAMES v ENGLAND

Have never met

ENGLAND'S RECORD v ANDORRA

P0	W0	D0	L0	F0	A0

THE OPPONENTS

WHO IS ROONEY UP AGAINST? Andorra's most celebrated – and most worked – player is goalkeeper Koldo Alvarez. The Spaniard, a former Atletico Madrid keeper, took out Andorran citizenship and now has over 50 caps to his name. His experience will be vital against England, likewise Ildefons Lima, who has played for Las Palmas in Spain. Another promising defender Rooney is likely to meet is Juli Fernandez from FC Santa Coloma.

HOW BIG IS THE THREAT? With just three victories in their ten-year existence, the tiny principality of Andorra will be the undoubted whipping boys of the group. Coach David Rodrigo has been at the helm since 1999 but there are signs that his side are finally coming to terms with international football after they recorded their first competitive win against FYR Macedonia during the World Cup 2006 qualifying campaign. But don't expect too much up front; their record goalscorers have a total of six goals between them!

HOW DO THEY PLAY? Not surprisingly, Rodrigo opts for a 4-5-1 system, getting as many players behind the ball as possible. Andorra also picked up more red and yellow cards than any other team during the World Cup qualifiers, so they're up for the fight!

VERDICT: Games against Andorra will be key to many teams, only as a means of improving their 'goals for' tally. They will still be looking to pull off the odd shock, with FYR Macedonia now in their sights once again.

PLAYING AWAY ANDORRA

THE STADIUM The Estadi Communal can be found in Andorra la Vella, the capital of the principality. It is also known as the Aixovall Stadium. While it is small, there are few more breathtaking arenas in football, with mountain views from every vantage point.

THE FOOTBALL The Andorran First Division comprises eight teams, making for a competitive league. Since formation in 1995, five different teams have been victorious, although Principat hold the record with four victories. FC Rangers won the title in 2006 for the first time.

THE CITY The landlocked principality of Andorra lies between France and Spain in the eastern Pyrenees. An estimated nine million tourists visit each year, so you won't be alone, and with England visiting in March 2007 you might find the time to try out one of Andorra's many ski resorts.

PLAYERS TO WATCH

Ildefons Lima *(below)*
US Triestina Calcio

Oscar Sonejee
FC Andorra

Juli Fernandez
FC Santa Coloma

Manolo Jimenez
FC Rangers

Gabi Riera
FC Andorra

THE ROONEY CHALLENGE 5

Just a few more questions to go now. If you complete these, check your answers on page 95 and if you get anywhere near the magic total of 200 you know more about Wayne and his teams that he does. Take a bow!

Bet you can't finish off with 50 out of 50!

WHO ARE YA

HERE'S WAYNE IN SOME GOAL-GETTING ACTION FOR ENGLAND, BUT CAN YOU NAME THE FIVE COUNTRIES HE'S DOING THE BUSINESS AGAINST?

1

ANSWER

2

ANSWER

3

ANSWER

4

ANSWER

5

ANSWER

PLAYER SEARCH

Wayne came on against Australia in a friendly at Upton Park to win his first cap. Can you spot his England team-mates from that game in this Rooneysearch?

V	A	S	S	E	L	L	G	M	U	R	P	H	Y	B
F	J	R	F	W	N	G	F	I	C	E	O	I	O	M
S	A	N	E	J	O	C	V	B	I	Y	K	W	E	K
F	M	I	L	L	S	G	O	R	V	D	Q	E	X	O
B	E	C	K	H	A	M	R	O	B	I	N	S	O	N
Z	S	W	I	C	I	N	S	W	S	J	E	C	M	C
E	T	I	N	V	R	B	L	N	U	B	V	H	Y	H
N	D	G	G	J	G	I	A	U	D	E	I	O	Y	E
J	E	F	F	E	R	S	M	D	F	C	L	L	I	S
E	N	O	O	C	A	M	P	B	E	L	L	E	Z	K
G	V	D	S	O	D	V	A	B	K	O	E	S	N	Y
L	L	I	D	L	G	F	R	J	O	F	K	D	S	U
G	U	O	W	E	N	N	D	B	E	A	T	T	I	E
E	H	A	R	G	R	E	A	V	E	S	N	M	O	C
S	D	G	F	E	R	D	I	N	A	N	D	O	I	K

- [ ] James
- [ ] Robinson
- [ ] Neville
- [ ] Mills
- [ ] Ferdinand
- [ ] King
- [ ] Campbell
- [ ] Brown
- [ ] Cole
- [ ] Konchesky
- [ ] Beckham
- [ ] Murphy
- [ ] Lampard
- [ ] Hargreaves
- [ ] Scholes
- [ ] Jenas
- [ ] Dyer
- [ ] Beattie
- [ ] Vassell
- [ ] Owen
- [ ] Jeffers

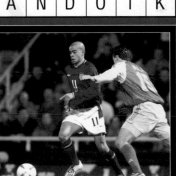

CAP THAT

Before the 2006 World Cup, Wayne had won 27 caps for England. Can you match these famous England internationals of yesteryear with the number of caps they managed to win in their careers?

A	79 CAPS
B	62 CAPS
C	59 CAPS
D	49 CAPS
E	35 CAPS
F	33 CAPS
G	26 CAPS
H	25 CAPS
I	20 CAPS
J	13 CAPS

1	STAN MORTENSEN	ANSWER	6	JOHN BARNES	ANSWER
2	PETER BEARDSLEY	ANSWER	7	GEOFF HURST	ANSWER
3	IAN WRIGHT	ANSWER	8	BRIAN LABONE	ANSWER
4	PETER REID	ANSWER	9	ALAN MULLERY	ANSWER
5	BOBBY ROBSON	ANSWER	10	CHRIS WADDLE	ANSWER

TOE NO

It's an injury he'd rather forget, but Wayne's not the only England star to have broken a metatarsal. True or False: have these stars suffered the same injury?

1 DAVID BECKHAM
ANSWER

2 JOE COLE
ANSWER

3 GARY NEVILLE
ANSWER

4 STEVEN GERRARD
ANSWER

5 JAMIE CARRAGHER
ANSWER

6 RIO FERDINAND
ANSWER

7 SCOTT PARKER
ANSWER

8 FRANK LAMPARD
ANSWER

9 ASHLEY COLE
ANSWER

10 PHIL NEVILLE
ANSWER

DOUBLE DELIGHT

Wayne was named as the PFA's Young Player of the Year again this season, but which two men did he beat into second and third?

ANSWER

ANSWER

TRIPLE TREAT

Wayne made a stunning start for Manchester United in the Champions League in September 2004, scoring a hat-trick – his first senior treble – in a 6-2 victory.
1. Which side was it against?
2. Where was the game played?

ANSWER

ANSWER

PAGE TOTAL

OUT OF 50

WAYNE'S COMPLETE CAREER GUIDE

ALL THE GAMES ALL THE GOALS

Whether it's been for Everton, Manchester United or England, WAYNE ROONEY has provided many special moments. They're all here in detail and much more!

WHILE HE REMAINS IN THE FLEDGLING years of what promises to be a fantastic career, few players can boast to have made the same impact on the top-flight stage as Wayne Rooney. Those who nurtured his precocious talent at Everton warned us that the club had a very special player in its grasp, but it wasn't until Rooney was unleashed onto the Premiership stage, some 59 days short of his 17th birthday, did the world sit up and take notice.

As the game got underway against Tottenham on the opening day of the 2002-03 season, Wayne's touch, awareness, skill and all-round power lit up Goodison Park and within six weeks he had become Everton's youngest goalscorer, netting in a Worthington Cup win at Wrexham.

But it was his scintillating first Premiership goal, sinking champions Arsenal, which really set Wayne on the road to fame and fortune. His dipping 30-yard volley on the stroke of full-time ended the Gunners' 30-match unbeaten run. It was a goal that would change Rooney's life forever.

He became the youngest ever player to represent England, making his debut against Australia aged just 17 years and 111 days, and his form at Euro 2004 – where he netted four goals before picking up a foot injury – saw his stock rise dramatically.

A move to Manchester United followed and Wayne capped his debut with a spectacular hat-trick against Turkish side Fenerbahçe in the Champions League.

Since then it's been strike after spectacular strike. Who could forget that dipping volley against Newcastle United, the 2005 'Goal of the Season' against Middlesbrough, or the brace against Wigan which helped United win the 2006 Carling Cup?

There's sure to be many more Rooney goals for us to enjoy, but for now at least let's celebrate a wonderful first four seasons: every game, every goal, every breathtaking moment…

OCT. 19   v ARSENAL

1 FA PREMIERSHIP
SATURDAY AUGUST 17, 2002

EVERTON	2
TOTTENHAM HOTSPUR	2

ATTENDANCE: 40,120

EVERTON SCORERS: Pembridge 37, Radzinski 81 **TOTTENHAM SCORERS:** Etherington 63, Ferdinand 74

After scoring two hat-tricks in pre-season against SC Weiz and Queen's Park respectively, Wayne Rooney, just 59 days short of his 17th birthday, made his Premiership debut for Everton, who were celebrating their 100th season in the top flight. Rooney, who had previously been on the bench against Southampton in April 2002, set up Mark Pembridge to give Everton the lead before the break, while his best chance was a header that produced a save from Kasey Keller early in the second-half. With the score at 1-1, coach David Moyes substituted the teenager after 67 minutes, bringing on Niclas Alexandersson.

WHAT THEY SAID ABOUT ROONEY:
"Wayne's got quick feet and plays with his head up. He has a bright future if he keeps his head together." *Glenn Hoddle (Tottenham manager)*

2 FA PREMIERSHIP
SATURDAY AUGUST 24, 2002

SUNDERLAND	0
EVERTON	1

ATTENDANCE: 37,698

EVERTON SCORER: Campbell 28

Rooney was restricted to a 16-minute substitute appearance for his second Premiership match at the Stadium of Light. With Everton leading, and shortly after goalkeeper Richard Wright had saved a penalty, Rooney came on for Alexandersson in the 74th minute but made little impact.

3 FA PREMIERSHIP
WEDNESDAY AUGUST 28, 2002

EVERTON	1
BIRMINGHAM CITY	1

ATTENDANCE: 37,197

EVERTON SCORER: Unsworth 90.
BIRMINGHAM SCORER: John (pen) 50

Rooney completed his first full 90 minutes in the Premiership as ten-man Everton – after the dismissal of Alan Stubbs early in the second-half – secured a last-gasp home draw thanks to David Unsworth's late equaliser. Several of the Everton players had goalscoring opportunities, including Rooney, who fired a shot over the bar from 25 yards out.

4 FA PREMIERSHIP
SATURDAY AUGUST 31, 2002

MANCHESTER CITY	3
EVERTON	1

ATTENDANCE: 34,835

EVERTON SCORER: Unsworth (pen) 29
MAN CITY SCORERS: Anelka 14 16 85

By the time Rooney had replaced Alexandersson in the 64th minute, Everton were trailing ten-man Manchester City 2-1. The 16-year-old did his best to equalise, combining with fellow sub Juliano Rodrigo in a neat one-two, which saw the latter shoot wide. But City defended well, while striker Nicolas Anelka completed his hat-trick and put an end to Everton's unbeaten start to the season.

5 FA PREMIERSHIP
WEDNESDAY SEPTEMBER 11, 2002

SOUTHAMPTON	1
EVERTON	0

ATTENDANCE: 29,120

SOUTHAMPTON SCORER: Pahars (pen) 73

Rooney came on as an 80th minute substitute, as Moyes tried to get Everton back into the game. It was not to be as a host of chances went begging.

6 FA PREMIERSHIP
SATURDAY SEPTEMBER 14, 2002

EVERTON	2
MIDDLESBROUGH	1

ATTENDANCE: 32,240

EVERTON SCORERS: Campbell 32 77
MIDDLESBROUGH SCORER: Nemeth 11

Once again Rooney came on as a substitute replacement for Alexandersson but on this occasion he was given his opportunity for the entire second-half. Rooney's appearance, with the score level at 1-1, gave Everton the injection they needed and he went close to scoring his first Premiership goal. Instead it was Kevin Campbell who stole the show with a brace. On a less welcome note was Rooney's first-ever yellow card shown to him by referee Matt Messias for a foul in the 49th minute.

WHAT THEY SAID ABOUT ROONEY: "Wayne gave us new energy. He made a big difference and we'll use him at the right time. But we can't expect him to carry the whole weight of the club."
David Moyes (Everton manager)

7 FA PREMIERSHIP
SUNDAY SEPTEMBER 22, 2002

ASTON VILLA	3
EVERTON	2

ATTENDANCE: 30,023

EVERTON SCORERS: Radzinski 51, Campbell 66
ASTON VILLA SCORERS: Hendrie 7 48, Dublin 85

In his third start for Everton, Rooney had a good chance of opening his goalscoring account. With the score at 0-1 in the opening half, he managed to get on the end of an Unsworth cross but the chance unfortunately went begging. Rooney picked up his second Premiership booking and after 77 minutes, with the scores level at 2-2, he was replaced again by Alexandersson.

8 WORTHINGTON CUP
SECOND ROUND
TUESDAY OCTOBER 1, 2002

WREXHAM	0
EVERTON	3

ATTENDANCE: 13,428

EVERTON SCORERS: Campbell 25, **Rooney** 82, 88

Rooney became Everton's youngest-ever goalscorer – breaking the record set by the legendary Tommy Lawton some 65 years earlier – by netting two goals in six minutes as his team easily defeated the Third Division club on a soggy night at the Racecourse Ground. Rooney replaced Tomasz Radzinski after 62

"WE LOST TO A SPECIAL GOAL FROM A SPECIAL TALENT. HE IS SUPPOSED TO BE 16, BUT I DIDN'T KNOW THAT 16-YEAR-OLDS COULD DO THINGS LIKE THAT. HE IS EVERYTHING YOU DREAM OF: INTELLIGENCE, QUICK REACTIONS, STRONG RUNNING WITH THE BALL." ARSENE WENGER

minutes and was partnering Duncan Ferguson ten minutes later. Ferguson, playing his first game since April, hit it off with the teenager who scored twice late on to make the scoreline more emphatic .

WHAT THEY SAID ABOUT ROONEY: "I'm pleased Wayne has score those goals, he had been a bit anxious about the situation over the last few games. But you expect that from a 16-year-old and now it's out of the way I'm sure they are the first of many for him at this club." *David Moyes*

⚽ **ROONEY GOAL** *(82 mins) Rooney made it 2-0 as he drove the ball home past goalkeeper Paul Whitfield after Ferguson had flicked on.*

⚽ **ROONEY GOAL** *(88 mins) Rooney raced clear down the right and then beat Whitfield with a fierce shot to make the score 3-0.*

9 **FA PREMIERSHIP**
MONDAY OCTOBER 7, 2002

MANCHESTER UNITED	3
EVERTON	0

ATTENDANCE: 67,629
MAN UNITED SCORERS: Scholes 86 90, van Nistelrooy (pen) 90

A 74th minute substitute appearance, replacing Radzinski with the score goalless, did not go acording to plan for Rooney. After Everton had contained the home side, United exploded to victory with three goals in the last four minutes of the game.

NOV. 3 v LEEDS

11 **FA PREMIERSHIP**
SUNDAY OCTOBER 27, 2002

WEST HAM UNITED	0
EVERTON	1

ATTENDANCE: 34,117
EVERTON SCORER: Carsley 70

Rooney marked his 17th birthday three days earlier by signing a three-year contract. Against West Ham he was again on the bench but made the

inevitable late second-half appearance after 64 minutes at the expense of Radzinski.
He gave his side added impetus and caused problems for the home team, but at one stage wasted a golden opportunity to score from Campbell's flick-on, which he blazed over the bar.

WHAT THEY SAID ABOUT ROONEY: "It's very exciting for Everton and English football. There were two or three times he fully stretched us… He's playing with no fear in his body. Nothing bad has ever happened to him in football. He's come in as a breath of fresh air. It's hand-brake down and let the natural talent take over." *Glenn Roeder (West Ham manager)*

12 **FA PREMIERSHIP**
SUNDAY NOVEMBER 3, 2002

LEEDS UNITED	0
EVERTON	1

ATTENDANCE: 40,161
EVERTON SCORER: Rooney 80

Moyes left it to the 75th minute to replace Radzinski this time and within five minutes Rooney had scored the match-winning goal that gave Everton their first triumph at Elland Road since 1951. It was a well deserved victory, after the side had created some good chances, and the breakthrough should have come sooner only for Radzinski to be denied three times by goalkeeper Paul Robinson.

WHAT THEY SAID ABOUT ROONEY: "Rooney's a terrific young player. He's not just a good prospect, he's a good player now." *Terry Venables (Leeds United manager)*

"I thought our performance merited a goal. Wayne does what comes naturally to him and I try to do my best to look after him. I understand that people will want him to start games, but I will use Wayne as I see fit." *David Moyes*

⚽ **ROONEY GOAL** *(80 mins) With a swift turn of speed and balance Rooney left Eirik Bakke on the floor 30 yards out. He outpaced Lucas Radebe to the ball on the right side of the penalty area and then drove a right foot shot into the far corner past goalkeeper Robinson.*

10 **FA PREMIERSHIP**
SATURDAY OCTOBER 19, 2002

EVERTON	2
ARSENAL	1

ATTENDANCE: 39,038
EVERTON SCORERS: Radzinski 22, **Rooney 90**. **ARSENAL SCORER:** Ljungberg 8

The launch of Rooneymania with his spectacular last-minute goal that came from nowhere. Rooney had started on the bench but his sensational contribution was made after coming on the field for Radzinski in the 80th minute. Rooney's first-ever Premiership goal – making him the youngest ever player to score in the Premiership – ended Arsenal's 30-game unbeaten sequence and alerted the football world to this raw yet supremely talented teenager at Goodison Park.

WHAT ROONEY SAID: "It was absolutely wonderful – a moment I will never, ever forget. Although I was some distance from the goal, I knew that time was running out; I thought it was worth me having a go. I saw a gap in the top corner of the goal and just aimed for it. When the ball went in, I couldn't contain myself."

WHAT THEY SAID ABOUT ROONEY: "It was a wonderful goal, a wonderful finish. There are special players who have graced the game down the years and Wayne can go on to become another." *David Moyes*

"We lost to a special goal from a special talent. He is supposed to be 16, but I didn't know that 16-year-olds could do things like that. He is everything you dream of: intelligence, quick reactions, strong running with the ball."
Arsene Wenger (Arsenal manager)

⚽ **ROONEY GOAL** *(90 mins) Rooney picked up the ball and there seemed no danger to Arsenal until he hit a 30-yard shot that crashed in off David Seaman's bar.*

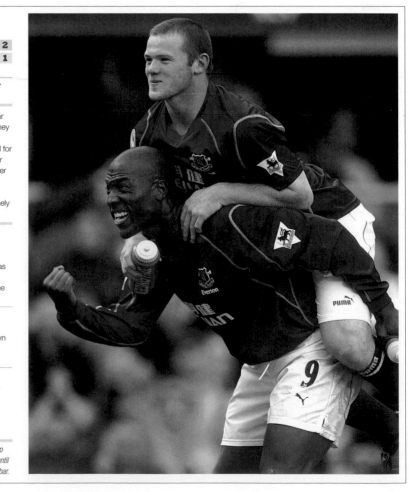

NOV. 6 ▶ v NEWCASTLE UNITED

13 WORTHINGTON CUP
THIRD ROUND
WEDNESDAY NOVEMBER 6, 2002

NEWCASTLE UNITED	**3**
EVERTON	**3**

After extra-time; Everton win 3-2 on penalties

ATTENDANCE: 13,584

EVERTON SCORERS: Campbell 11, Watson 85, Unsworth (pen) 112. **NEWCASTLE SCORERS:** Dyer 77 78, Pistone (og) 100

Everton won through to the fourth round, winning a dramatic penalty shoot-out after a thrilling 3-3 draw. Rooney, in the starting line-up, won a corner from which Campbell opened the scoring. Rooney, who later picked up a booking, could have extended the lead with a dipping shot but it was turned round the post by Newcastle goalkeeper Steve Harper. A superb cross from Rooney almost set up Campbell but Nikos Dabizas intercepted. Two goals in two minutes by Kieron Dyer put Newcastle ahead but Rooney's unstoppable run and pull back from the right flank set up Steve Watson to equalise in the 85th minute and force extra-time. Newcastle regained the lead through an Alessandro Pistone own goal but Everton levelled from the penalty spot through Unsworth as the home side were reduced to ten men. In the penalty shoot-out Watson, Campbell and Rooney, scoring what turned out to be the decisive spot-kick, were on target for Everton, while goalkeeper Richard Wright saved from Hugo Viana and Laurent Robert before Michael Chopra fired over the bar to give Everton a 3-2 shoot-out victory and their place in the fourth round of a competition they have yet to win in their history.

WHAT THEY SAID ABOUT ROONEY: "He's awesome. He's a terrific player. At 17, he's as good a player as I've seen. He's got everything - he's got strength, he's got pace, he can turn on the ball." *Sir Bobby Robson (Newcastle United manager)*

"He missed two penalties in training this morning and still walked up in front of all those people and rolled it in, which was absolutely fabulous." *Alan Irvine (Everton assistant manager)*

14 FA PREMIERSHIP
SATURDAY NOVEMBER 9, 2002

EVERTON	**1**
CHARLTON ATHLETIC	**0**

ATTENDANCE: 37,621

EVERTON SCORER: Radzinski 31

An Everton victory of good fortune and defiant defending. Rooney replaced goalscorer Radzinski after 73 minutes but, despite the expectancy of the Goodison Park faithful, the youngster could not lift his game on this occasion. The subdued sub's notable contribution was a booking from referee Rob Styles for a foul in the 82nd minute.

WHAT THEY SAID ABOUT ROONEY: "Tomasz is getting a decent turn and he is scoring, keeping going. He allows me not to play Rooney any more than I have to." *David Moyes*

15 FA PREMIERSHIP
SUNDAY NOVEMBER 17, 2002

BLACKBURN ROVERS	**0**
EVERTON	**1**

ATTENDANCE: 26,496

EVERTON SCORER: Campbell 19

Rooney was an 81st minute substitute for Gary Naysmith and apart from a couple of thwarted left-wing forays, his contribution was minimal. However, Campbell's first-half goal was enough for Everton, while Blackburn were frustrated by plenty of possession but with nothing to show for it.

16 FA PREMIERSHIP
SATURDAY NOVEMBER 23, 2002

EVERTON	**1**
WEST BROMWICH ALBION	**0**

ATTENDANCE: 40,113

EVERTON SCORER: Radzinski 35

Rooney's 87th minute appearance for match-winner Radzinski earned a standing ovation from the Goodison Park crowd but with so little time remaining, his impact on the game was negligible.

WHAT THEY SAID ABOUT ROONEY: "Having Wayne pushing for a place keeps me on my toes even if it's not easy being the one who has to give way to him every week." *Tomasz Radzinski*

17 FA PREMIERSHIP
SUNDAY DECEMBER 1, 2002

NEWCASTLE UNITED	**2**
EVERTON	**1**

ATTENDANCE: 51,607

EVERTON SCORER: Campbell 17
NEWCASTLE SCORERS: Shearer 86, Bellamy 89

Ten-man Everton looked set for an incredible yet deserved victory but two late goals from Alan Shearer and Craig Bellamy denied the visitors a seventh successive Premiership victory. Rooney, again replacing Radzinski, did not appear until the 73rd minute but he made little impression on the game as Everton were under pressure.

18 WORTHINGTON CUP
FOURTH ROUND
WEDNESDAY DECEMBER 4, 2002

CHELSEA	**4**
EVERTON	**1**

ATTENDANCE: 32,322

EVERTON SCORER: Naysmith 89 **CHELSEA SCORERS:** Hasselbaink 26 71, Petit 44, Stanic 69

Moyes put Rooney in the starting line-up in a three-man attacking strikeforce alongside Campbell and Radzinski. Unfortunately, despite early pressure, it was the home side who completely overwhelmed their opponents and progressed to the quarter-finals. Everton's 4-3-3 system was soon abandoned and the move to 4-4-2 saw Rooney switched from the left to the right flank where he made a better impression on the game. But it was Chelsea's evening and the influential Gianfranco Zola was in control and put in a virtuoso performance.

To make matters worse for Rooney he had an 81st minute penalty saved by Carlo Cudicini after William Gallas had handled the ball.

WHAT THEY SAID ABOUT ROONEY: "It was a tough night for Wayne. But he will get better for it, and I hope people will see that I am using him in the right way. I think he will cope fine with missing the penalty; I don't foresee any problems with that at all." *David Moyes*

19 FA PREMIERSHIP
SATURDAY DECEMBER 7, 2002

EVERTON	**1**
CHELSEA	**3**

ATTENDANCE: 39,396

EVERTON SCORER: Naysmith 43 **CHELSEA SCORERS:** Stanic 5, Hasselbaink 28, Gronkjaer 90

There was to be no revenge for the League Cup exit three days earlier. Rooney, back on the bench, did not enter the fray until the 63rd minute, but when he did he caused problems for Chelsea. He even burst through into the area but was denied by goalkeeper Cudicini. Despite Everton's endeavour in searching for an equaliser they were undone by Unsworth's sending-off and Jesper Gronkjaer's third.

20 FA PREMIERSHIP
SATURDAY DECEMBER 14, 2002

EVERTON	**2**
BLACKBURN ROVERS	**1**

ATTENDANCE: 36,578

EVERTON SCORERS: Carsley 12, **Rooney 25**
BLACKBURN SCORER: Cole 6

Rooney, the new BBC Sports Personality of the Year, was in the starting line-up team for his sixth start and the game saw a return to form for the young player. Everton went behind to an early goal but it was Rooney who tenaciously overturned the deficit and helped his team to victory. In the 12th minute, he hit the foot of the post with a shot from a Campbell cross, but the rebound was netted by Lee Carsley,

"HE'S AWESOME. HE'S A TERRIFIC PLAYER. AT 17, HE'S AS GOOD A PLAYER AS I'VE SEEN. HE'S GOT EVERYTHING – HE'S GOT STRENGTH, HE'S GOT PACE, HE CAN TURN ON THE BALL." SIR BOBBY ROBSON

DEC. 14 › v BLACKBURN ROVERS

who had originally instigated the attack. Rooney then gave Everton the lead 13 minutes later, which would prove to be the winner, and could have scored again but pulled his shot wide. Rooney was substituted in the last minute by Radzinski.

WHAT THEY SAID ABOUT ROONEY: "On the field it is difficult to criticise the things he does. It's all so natural to him. He's comfortable, does things in a subconscious way and has the ability to put the fear of death into people when he gets at them." *David Moyes*

⚽ **ROONEY GOAL** *(25 mins)* Goalkeeper Wright cleared the ball up field. Rooney was the quickest to react, exploiting a gap in the Blackburn defence and placed his shot to the left and beyond the reach of Brad Friedel.

21 FA PREMIERSHIP
SUNDAY DECEMBER 22, 2002

LIVERPOOL	0
EVERTON	0

ATTENDANCE: 44,025

Rooney's first Merseyside derby was a dire match and he didn't become involved until the 55th minute when replacing Radzinski. However, his arrival did get the attention from Liverpool that his reputation deserved. Steven Gerrard was intent on cutting his supply of the ball while Sami Hyypia was determined to get the ball off Rooney if he got in possession. The highlight of the match was when Rooney outwitted Hyypia on the edge of the box to fire a shot that deflected off Stephane Henchoz and clipped the bar. Rooney also had a penalty appeal turned down.

22 FA PREMIERSHIP
THURSDAY DECEMBER 26, 2002

BIRMINGHAM CITY	1
EVERTON	1

ATTENDANCE: 29,505

EVERTON SCORER: Radzinski 45
BIRMINGHAM SCORER: Kirovski 45

Rooney was sent-off after only being on the field for 15 minutes, coming on for Mark Pembridge in the 66th minute. The ball was loose between the advancing Rooney and Birmingham centre-half Steve Vickers and the sub challenged for the ball by jumping in with both feet and studs showing. Referee David Elleray was left with no option but to produce

the red card. The incident, which made Rooney the youngest player to be sent off in the history of the Premiership, grabbed all the headlines of an otherwise dull 1-1 draw.

WHAT THEY SAID ABOUT ROONEY: "To me, it looked a decent attempt to win the ball. But I think Rooney's the victim here. He's been built up as rough and tough." *David Moyes*

23 FA PREMIERSHIP
SATURDAY DECEMBER 28, 2002

EVERTON	0
BOLTON WANDERERS	0

ATTENDANCE: 39,480

A goalless draw but Rooney did his utmost not to make it so. He was on the field for the whole of the game and for most of it he tormented the Bolton defence. His runs and passing had Bolton flailing and he was able to create chances for his team-mates as well as going for goal himself, forcing the defenders into interventions and saves from goalkeeper Jussi Jaaskelainen. There were near misses too with his best chance a second-half strike that rebounded back off the crossbar.

WHAT THEY SAID ABOUT ROONEY "I told him he is a good player but that he is going to be a great player." *Ivan Campo (Bolton defender)*

"He was the only man who could have won it by himself, and Everton could never afford a player like him." *Sam Allardyce (Bolton manager)*

24 FA PREMIERSHIP
WEDNESDAY JANUARY 1, 2003

EVERTON	2
MANCHESTER CITY	2

ATTENDANCE: 40,163

EVERTON SCORERS: Watson 6, Radzinski 90
MAN CITY SCORERS: Anelka 33, Foe 82

A fourth successive draw for Everton, although Rooney got them off to a good start by setting up Watson to score after six minutes. Aside from that moment, however, Rooney had a subdued match and got himself booked. Everton fell behind with eight minutes remaining but an equaliser in stoppage time secured the Premiership point.

25 FA CUP
THIRD ROUND
SATURDAY JANUARY 4, 2003

SHREWSBURY TOWN	2
EVERTON	1

ATTENDANCE: 7,800

EVERTON SCORER: Alexandersson 60
SHREWSBURY SCORERS: Jemson 37 88

Rooney's FA Cup debut was, sadly, one of the big upsets of the third round. Third Division Shrewsbury, some 80 places below Everton, deserved their victory. Everton did not play well although Rooney did come close with a curling 20-yard effort. He also set up Radzinski who had a shot cleared off the line.

26 FA PREMIERSHIP
SATURDAY FEBRUARY 8, 2003

CHARLTON ATHLETIC	2
EVERTON	1

ATTENDANCE: 26,623

EVERTON SCORER: McBride 69
CHARLTON SCORERS: Kishishev 19, Lisbie 83

Following a four-match suspension after his sending-off at Birmingham, Rooney's return to Premiership action was restricted to a five-minute substitute cameo appearance with Everton trailing 2-1. After replacing Unsworth he did find time to fire in a powerful drive that almost found the target but it was not to be and Everton lost.

27 FA PREMIERSHIP
SATURDAY FEBRUARY 22, 2003

EVERTON	2
SOUTHAMPTON	1

ATTENDANCE: 36,569

EVERTON SCORERS: Radzinski 83 90
SOUTHAMPTON SCORER: Beattie 33

With Everton trailing 1-0, Rooney was introduced after 64 minutes, the third of Moyes's substitutes.

Rooney's presence transformed the game and put the Saints' defence on the back foot. This allowed Radzinski to finally find the net, as he headed home Rooney's 83rd minute cross from the left. Rooney created a similar chance for Campbell but he failed to score. With the Southampton defence panicking, Radzinski blasted home the winner after 92 mins and 51 seconds.

WHAT THEY SAID ABOUT ROONEY: "They dropped back and were afraid of Wayne from the moment he came on the pitch." *Tomasz Radzinski*

28 FA PREMIERSHIP
SATURDAY MARCH 1, 2003

MIDDLESBROUGH	1
EVERTON	1

ATTENDANCE: 32,473

EVERTON SCORER: Watson 23
MIDDLESBROUGH SCORER: Juninho 74

Not the most thrilling Premiership match ever witnessed but Everton did lead for a long time until Juninho grabbed the equaliser. Four minutes later Rooney replaced Thomas Gravesen but not even his presence could change the tone of the game. However, Rooney almost got a last-gasp winner but he guided his effort just wide.

29 FA PREMIERSHIP
SATURDAY MARCH 15, 2003

EVERTON	0
WEST HAM UNITED	0

ATTENDANCE: 40,158

Neither goalkeeper was bothered in the first half of this match and Moyes's response was a triple substitution on 55 minutes, with Li Tie, Campbell and Rooney on for Scot Gemmill, Naysmith and Brian McBride. Rooney began attacking down the wing, causing problems to the West Ham flank. However, Everton's finishing was poor and the closest Rooney came was a cross-shot that Hammers defender Ian Pearce deflected wide.

DEC. 22 › v LIVERPOOL

"HE WAS THE ONLY ONE MAN WHO COULD HAVE WON IT BY HIMSELF, AND EVERTON COULD NEVER AFFORD A PLAYER LIKE HIM." SAM ALLARDYCE

30 FA PREMIERSHIP
SUNDAY MARCH 23, 2003

ARSENAL	2
EVERTON	1

ATTENDANCE: 38,042

EVERTON SCORER: Rooney 56
ARSENAL SCORERS: Cygan 8, Vieira 64

Rooney completed his fourth full Premiership match of the season and was in wonderful form. He caused all sorts of problems for Pascal Cygan and Giovanni van Bronckhorst and created chances for his team-mates. In the 56th minute he cancelled out Cygan's first-half goal but it was the influential Patrick Vieira who was to edge the game for Arsenal.

 ROONEY GOAL *(56 mins) Rooney moved forward with Cygan fatally backing off. Rooney's subsequent low angled shot beat goalkeeper Stuart Taylor and the ball also went through Cygan's legs.*

31 FA PREMIERSHIP
SUNDAY APRIL 6, 2003

EVERTON	2
NEWCASTLE UNITED	1

ATTENDANCE: 40,031

EVERTON SCORERS: Rooney 18, Unsworth (pen) 65. **NEWCASTLE SCORER:** Robert 40

Although Rooney's contribution was sporadic throughout the game, whenever he did get himself involved it was invariably a contribution of significance. He brought moments of panic to a Newcastle defence in disarray, running at them down the middle or attacking down the left flank. It was from one of these forays that he fed Campbell, who was brought down by Jonathan Woodgate in the area, and Unsworth stepped up to convert the match-winning penalty.

ROONEY GOAL *(18 mins) David Weir flicked on a corner for Rooney to head past Shay Given into the net.*

32 FA PREMIERSHIP
SATURDAY APRIL 12, 2003

WEST BROMWICH ALBION	1
EVERTON	2

ATTENDANCE: 27,039

EVERTON SCORERS: Weir 23, Campbell 45
WEST BROM SCORER: Balis (pen) 18

Moyes was sent from the dugout after his sustained outburst following the award of a dubious penalty from which West Brom took the lead, along with poor challenges on Gravesen and Rooney. Back in the starting line-up because Radzinski was suffering with a groin injury, Rooney was sent clear but his attempted chip was charged down and then he was shoved but no penalty awarded. It set Moyes off again and the referee sent him to the stands. Aside from that it was an exciting opening period, with chances created including one in the 13th minute by Rooney who perhaps should have set up Campbell instead of wasting the opportunity himself. On the stroke of half-time he made amends when Albion goalkeeper Russell Hoult, who had been at fault for Weir's equaliser, dropped a cross and Rooney gifted Campbell the winner when he could have easily gone for goal himself.

33 FA PREMIERSHIP
SATURDAY APRIL 19, 2003

EVERTON	1
LIVERPOOL	2

ATTENDANCE: 40,162

EVERTON SCORER: Unsworth (pen) 58
LIVERPOOL SCORERS: Owen 31, Murphy 64

This bitter Merseyside derby did not end well for the home side, who finished the game with only nine men. Rooney started and finished the game alongside Campbell in attack. However, it was to be Michael Owen and Danny Murphy's day as Everton sought to win the physical battle and picked up six yellow cards in all, with Weir and Naysmith both dismissed for second bookable offences. Liverpool played the better football and deserved the win.

APR. 4 >> v NEWCASTLE UNITED

34 FA PREMIERSHIP
MONDAY APRIL 21, 2003

CHELSEA	4
EVERTON	1

ATTENDANCE: 40,875

EVERTON SCORER: Carsley 77
CHELSEA SCORERS: Gudjohnsen 25, Hasselbaink 48, Gronkjaer 62, Zola 90

Everton's policy for this game appears to have been, unsuccessfully, to avoid defeat. On occasions both Rooney, starting in the place of the injured Radzinski, and strike partner Campbell joined the rest of the side behind the ball. It was a quiet game for Rooney, while Chelsea were rampant in attack.

WHAT THEY SAID ABOUT ROONEY: "He has perhaps a problem with the standard he has set himself." *David Moyes*

35 FA PREMIERSHIP
SATURDAY APRIL 26, 2003

EVERTON	2
ASTON VILLA	1

ATTENDANCE: 40,167

EVERTON SCORERS: Campbell 59, **Rooney 90**
ASTON VILLA SCORER: Allback 49

Rooney scored a dramatic injury-time winner after Everton had overcome a one-goal deficit to clinch the points. Rooney, only starting because Radzinski failed a fitness test, was the game's man of the match. Marcus Allback put Villa ahead just after the re-start but Campbell, Rooney's strike partner, headed home an equaliser. Rooney, back to his dangerous self, struck his eighth goal of the season in dramatic fashion two minutes into stoppage time and then earned an ovation by being immediately substituted by Gemmill.

WHAT THEY SAID ABOUT ROONEY: "I came very close to bringing him off because it was one of those days when some of the things he did inspired us and others made him look like a boy who needed to put his feet up. But I always felt that he might be able to do something to turn the game." *David Moyes*

"It was a good strike by Rooney and Everton showed again that they're a difficult team to beat. David has

turned them into a tight, competitive unit."
Graham Taylor (Aston Villa manager)

 ROONEY GOAL *(90 mins) Rooney fired home a left foot shot, sending the ball past Villa goalkeeper Peter Enckelman to make it 2-1 and the game safe.*

36 FA PREMIERSHIP
SATURDAY MAY 3, 2003

FULHAM	2
EVERTON	0

ATTENDANCE: 18,385

FULHAM SCORERS: Stubbs (og) 34, Wright (og) 43

Not the best day for Everton where things didn't go right and they ultimately lost because of two own-goals. Boss Moyes said, "You'll do well to find two worse goals than that in the Premiership this season." Neither Rooney nor Campbell had any real opportunity to force a breakthrough in a poor game for the visitors.

37 FA PREMIERSHIP
SUNDAY MAY 11, 2003

EVERTON	1
MANCHESTER UNITED	2

ATTENDANCE: 40,168

EVERTON SCORER: Campbell 8. **MAN UNITED SCORERS:** Beckham 43, van Nistelrooy (pen) 79

Rooney received a knock in the first-half that was aggravated by a second-half challenge by Laurent Blanc. He stayed on until the end of the game but it was later discovered that medial ligaments had been damaged. During the game Rooney had missed and created some decent chances for Everton, including missing the target from a Naysmith cross. He was then denied by the legs of United goalkeeper Roy Carroll and he also picked up his eighth booking of the season. Captain Campbell gave Everton an early lead but a David Beckham free-kick and a Ruud van Nistelrooy penalty ended Everton's hopes of a UEFA Cup place. After the full-time whistle the visitors were presented with the FA Premiership trophy.

WAYNE ROONEY'S STRIKE RATE	SEASON 02/03		
PREMIERSHIP	33 GAMES/6 GOALS		18%
FA CUP	1 GAMES/0 GOALS		0%
LEAGUE CUP	3 GAMES/2 GOALS		67%
EUROPE	N/A		N/A
OVERALL	8 GOALS IN 37 GAMES		22%

38 FA PREMIERSHIP
SATURDAY AUGUST 16, 2003

| ARSENAL | 2 |
| EVERTON | 1 |

ATTENDANCE: 38,014

EVERTON SCORER: Radzinski 84
ARSENAL SCORERS: Henry (pen) 35, Pires 38

Deservedly beaten by Arsenal, Everton only appeared to threaten at the start and at the end of the game, notably after Rooney, now recovered from a ligament injury sustained by a tackle on him in a pre-season friendly against Rangers, had replaced Tobias Linderoth as a 57th minute substitute. Before then Arsenal were reduced to ten men after the dismissal of Sol Campbell, but they found themselves 2-0 up by the break. Rooney was later booked and team-mate Li Tie was sent-off in the 87th minute for a second bookable offence, just minutes after Radzinski gave Everton undeserved hope of a point.

WHAT THEY SAID ABOUT ROONEY: "The things that Wayne does in training are amazing and he will be quicker and stronger this season."
David Unsworth (Everton)

39 FA PREMIERSHIP
SATURDAY AUGUST 23, 2003

| EVERTON | 3 |
| FULHAM | 1 |

ATTENDANCE: 37,604

EVERTON SCORERS: Naysmith 7, Unsworth 20, Watson 35. **FULHAM SCORER:** Hayles 69

With Ferguson suspended and Campbell out with a hamstring injury, Rooney was in the starting line-up and he provided the inspiration for a stunning first-half performance by Everton that had the points tied up by the break. Rooney helped set up Radzinski who had his shot blocked, but Naysmith seized the ball to fire home from 22 yards after just seven minutes. Rooney almost set up Naysmith again before beginning another move that let Pembridge send in an angled pass for Unsworth to net 13 minutes later. The third goal came from an Alan Stubbs free-kick, which Naysmith nodded on for Rooney to bring under control and set up Watson to score. Fulham rallied after the break but Rooney and Everton still had chances. Rooney was injured in the 74th minute and was replaced by Nick Chadwick, and left the field to a standing ovation.

40 FA PREMIERSHIP
TUESDAY AUGUST 26, 2003

| CHARLTON ATHLETIC | 2 |
| EVERTON | 2 |

ATTENDANCE: 26,336

EVERTON SCORERS: Watson 26, **Rooney 72**
CHARLTON SCORERS: Euell (pen) 25, (pen) 45

Watched by England coach Sven-Göran Eriksson, Everton twice fell behind to conceded penalties but managed to level the score on each occasion, firstly through Watson and then spectacularly through Rooney. For all their endeavours, the home side created few chances, while Everton, led by Radzinski

SEP. 28 ▸ v LEEDS

"EVERYONE HAS BEEN TELLING US FOR WEEKS AND WEEKS THAT ROONEY CAN BE WHATEVER HE WANTS TO BE AND I BELIEVE THAT IN AT LEAST ONE RESPECT, THE EVERTON 17-YEAR-OLD IS TEN YEARS AHEAD OF HIS TIME." MARK LAWRENSON

and partner Rooney, regularly tested the resilient Charlton defence. Although not fully match fit Rooney completed the game.

WHAT THEY SAID ABOUT ROONEY: "I felt he was flagging a bit in the second-half and looked like he was on his knees again. The goal gave him that extra incentive and dragged him on. So we stuck with him, he got the goal and we're pleased we got 90 minutes out of him. It was a great touch and he finished the way Alan Shearer finishes in front of goal – he made sure he scored." *David Moyes*

"Everyone has been telling us for weeks and weeks that Rooney can be whatever he wants to be and I believe that in at least one respect, the Everton 17-year-old is ten years ahead of his time."
Mark Lawrenson (BBC pundit)

⚽ **ROONEY GOAL** *(72 mins) Naysmith's cross didn't look dangerous until Rooney got the ball and quickly turned Charlton defender Mark Fish before he blasted the ball past goalkeeper Dean Kiely and into the net.*

41 FA PREMIERSHIP
SATURDAY AUGUST 30, 2003

| EVERTON | 0 |
| LIVERPOOL | 3 |

ATTENDANCE: 40,200

LIVERPOOL SCORERS: Owen 39 52, Kewell 80

In the cold light of day the simple fact was Liverpool's Owen found the net while Everton's Rooney was

denied by superb saves from keeper Jerzy Dudek. Each time Owen scored, Rooney had a goalscoring opportunity. In the first instance, Dudek raced from his line and parried away. At 2-0 Rooney got in a header that proved to be too close to the Liverpool goalkeeper. On another occasion a surging run was ended when Igor Biscan legitimately bundled him off the ball. Then later on he saw a header that failed to find the net. To complete another miserable Merseyside derby for Rooney, he was booked.

WHAT THEY SAID ABOUT ROONEY: "It's obvious Wayne Rooney is a special talent."
Michael Owen (Liverpool)

42 FA PREMIERSHIP
SATURDAY SEPTEMBER 13, 2003

| EVERTON | 2 |
| NEWCASTLE UNITED | 2 |

ATTENDANCE: 40,228

EVERTON SCORERS: Radzinski 67, Ferguson (pen) 88. **NEWCASTLE SCORERS:** Shearer (pen) 59 (pen) 82

Rooney, a hero for England in midweek, lasted only 30 minutes of this encounter. Injury forced him to limp off the pitch, to be replaced by Francis Jeffers. He went down after a challenge from Olivier Bernard who, unseen by the referee, also gave Rooney another kick while the Everton player was on the ground. The game itself turned out to be a thrilling event-filled spectacle, with three penalties (all converted) and two red cards. Everton once again fell

behind twice and only secured the draw in the closing minutes of the match.

WHAT THEY SAID ABOUT ROONEY: "He is a good lad who wants to learn and wants to listen. He is an exceptionally talented footballer and we are trying to make sure he remains that and becomes better in the future." *David Moyes*

43 FA PREMIERSHIP
SUNDAY SEPTEMBER 21, 2003

| MIDDLESBROUGH | 1 |
| EVERTON | 0 |

ATTENDANCE: 28,113

MIDDLESBROUGH SCORER: Job 6

Middlesbrough's first win of the season was achieved by an early goal and a protection strategy based on clearing the ball from their own area as quickly and as often as possible. In the last quarter of the game, Rooney, who picked up another yellow card, and Radzinski were bolstered in attack by substitutes Ferguson and James McFadden, but none of the quartet could manage the breakthrough as the Boro defence held steadfast in the closing stages.

44 CARLING CUP
SECOND ROUND
WEDNESDAY SEPTEMBER 24, 2003

| EVERTON | 3 |
| STOCKPORT COUNTY | 0 |

ATTENDANCE: 19,807

EVERTON SCORERS: Ferguson (pen) 26 56, Chadwick 44

A McFadden-inspired Everton had this Carling Cup tie against Second Division Stockport sewn up by the time Rooney came on as a 60th minute substitute for Gravesen. Rooney, playing behind Ferguson – who grabbed a brace – and fellow goalscorer Chadwick, went close to adding a fourth goal in the 77th minute with 25-yard left foot shot that narrowly flew over the crossbar.

NOV. 1 ▸ v CHELSEA

"ROONEY IS A MASSIVE TALENT… WHEN YOU TALK ABOUT TOUCH, TECHNIQUE AND ABILITY, HE'S GOT THE LOT. HE CAN SCORE AND MAKE GOALS AS WELL, BUT UNLESS YOU ARE DIEGO MARADONA YOU CAN'T EXPECT AN 18-YEAR-OLD TO BE WINNING GAMES WEEK-IN WEEK-OUT – AND THERE WAS ONLY ONE LIKE MARADONA." ALAN HANSEN

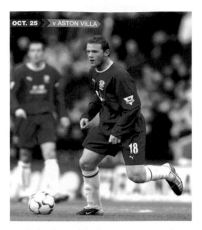

OCT. 25 > v ASTON VILLA

45 FA PREMIERSHIP
SUNDAY SEPTEMBER 28, 2003

| EVERTON | 4 |
| LEEDS UNITED | 0 |

ATTENDANCE: 39,151

EVERTON SCORERS: Watson 27 37 52, Ferguson 39

By the time Rooney replaced Watson – a defender by trade – in the 76th minute, the latter had effectively sealed the victory for Everton with his first professional hat-trick. Leeds, who included World Cup winner Roque Junior in their back four, were poor, as Everton completely overran them and could have easily won by a greater score.

46 FA PREMIERSHIP
SATURDAY OCTOBER 4, 2003

| TOTTENHAM HOTSPUR | 3 |
| EVERTON | 0 |

ATTENDANCE: 36,137

TOTTENHAM SCORERS: Kanoute 43, Poyet 46, Robbie Keane 49

Three goals in six minutes spread either side of the half-time break sunk Everton. It was an easy win for Tottenham and even the appearance of Rooney, as a 55th minute substitute for McFadden, could not lift the visitors. To make matters worse Rooney got himself booked for dissent. It was yellow card number five for him in the 2003-4 season and meant an automatic one-match suspension.

WHAT ROONEY SAID: "It's a bit disappointing when you're not in all the time. But, if the other lads are in the side doing a job, you have to accept it – it's the manager's decision."

47 FA PREMIERSHIP
SATURDAY OCTOBER 25, 2003

| ASTON VILLA | 0 |
| EVERTON | 0 |

ATTENDANCE: 36,146

Rooney, back after serving his suspension and a day after turning 18, was below par in this goalless encounter at Villa Park. In the second-half he did go close with a shot from Kilbane's low cross but the effort was wide. Later Rooney tried a speculative 40-yard lob to beat keeper Thomas Sorensen but the goal attempt was well wide of the target. For much of the game Dion Dublin had the better of Rooney, as did Villa over Everton.

WHAT ROONEY SAID: "I know I haven't played as well as I can this season."

WHAT THEY SAID ABOUT ROONEY: "Nobody has had a talent like Wayne Rooney in this country for a long, long time." *David Moyes*

48 CARLING CUP
THIRD ROUND
WEDNESDAY OCTOBER 29, 2003

| EVERTON | 1 |
| CHARLTON ATHLETIC | 0 |

ATTENDANCE: 24,863

EVERTON SCORER: Linderoth 41

A Linderoth goal was enough to send Everton through to the fourth round but the home side could have won by a greater margin. Rooney had several chances, including one effort set up by a Gravesen

cross that hit the crossbar and the resulting rebound was headed home by Linderoth. Rooney hit the post with another shot and also went close, shooting into the side-netting. On other occasions Rooney was denied by visiting keeper Kiely, including a chipped effort that was well saved.

49 FA PREMIERSHIP
SATURDAY NOVEMBER 1, 2003

| EVERTON | 0 |
| CHELSEA | 1 |

ATTENDANCE: 40,189

CHELSEA SCORER: Mutu 49

In a week when Everton revealed £13 million losses, another defeat was exactly what they didn't want. Despite an edgy first-half, Everton did match Chelsea for much of the game as both sides wasted goalscoring opportunities. Rooney's best effort was a chip that was just a little too high, much to the relief of Chelsea goalkeeper Carlo Cudicini. But it was Adrian Mutu's goal that decided the game shortly after the break.

50 FA PREMIERSHIP
SATURDAY NOVEMBER 22, 2003

| EVERTON | 2 |
| WOLVERHAMPTON WANDERERS | 0 |

ATTENDANCE: 40,190

EVERTON SCORERS: Radzinski 16, Kilbane 19

Everton recorded their first league win in six matches, largely thanks to the effective Gravesen and skilful Rooney. The game was virtually over by the 20th minute. Radzinski opened the scoring and within three minutes Rooney had crossed for Kevin Kilbane to score with a looping header past goalkeeper

Michael Oakes. Wolves worried Everton little and it was not until the end that they made a serious effort on the home side's goal, which goalkeeper Nigel Martyn repelled with his legs.

51 FA PREMIERSHIP
SATURDAY NOVEMBER 29, 2003

| BOLTON WANDERERS | 2 |
| EVERTON | 0 |

ATTENDANCE: 27,350

BOLTON SCORERS: Frandsen 26, Djorkaeff 46

Bolton deservedly won this fixture as they outplayed Everton and were largely untroubled themselves. Rooney, who spent his day off the previous Wednesday filming a Coca-Cola commercial in Madrid, looked out of form and was substituted after 54 minutes by manager Moyes. Rooney was less than happy with the decision and expressed his feelings to Moyes as he left the pitch. Rooney had lobbed over the crossbar with Everton's only real chance of the first-half but even his replacement Jeffers fared little better.

WHAT THEY SAID ABOUT ROONEY: "Maybe we have been playing him too much, maybe we have to look at it and say he's starting too many games and we are expecting too much of him… I think we all expect too much and maybe even Wayne, on occasions, feels he has to live up to that but in the main he is a terrific player and he is going to become a great player." *David Moyes*

52 CARLING CUP
FOURTH ROUND
WEDNESDAY DECEMBER 3, 2003

| MIDDLESBROUGH | 0 |
| EVERTON | 0 |

After extra-time; Middlesbrough won 5-4 on penalties

ATTENDANCE: 18,568

Everton bowed out of the Carling Cup following a goalless 120 minutes and a penalty shoot-out that was decided by Gaizka Mendieta's successful spot-kick. The tense 5-4 defeat for Everton was watched from the sidelines by Rooney, who had been substituted in the 98th minute. Rooney, marshalled by Gareth Southgate and Chris Riggott, had a subdued first-half and only had a 20th minute free-kick that went wide and a 42nd minute tame shot that was comfortably dealt with by keeper Mark Schwarzer to show for his efforts. In the second-half he was fortunate not to be booked after several players got involved in a mêlée during which, unseen

by the referee, Rooney pushed Jonathan Greening. Everton did well to survive extra-time but the penalty shoot-out proved too much.

53 FA PREMIERSHIP
SUNDAY DECEMBER 7, 2003

| EVERTON | 0 |
| MANCHESTER CITY | 0 |

ATTENDANCE: 37,871

Rooney was the casualty of a half-time tactical substitution by Moyes but the player was reportedly unhappy at the decision. Moyes had selected Rooney to play just behind twin strikers Radzinski and Jeffers in a bold formation. The plan, unfortunately, did not work and Rooney did not re-emerge for the second-half. Chances were few and far between, although Gravesen did hit the woodwork for the Toffees.

WHAT THEY SAID ABOUT ROONEY: "Rooney is a massive talent. When you talk about touch, technique and ability, he's got the lot. He can score and make goals as well, but unless you are Diego Maradona you can't expect an 18-year-old to be winning games week-in week-out – and there was only one like Maradona." *Alan Hansen (BBC pundit)*

"I tried to play Wayne behind Francis Jeffers and Tomasz Radzinski, but it didn't work… I'm not overly concerned about Wayne. As I keep saying he's the best 18-year-old in the country and he will have peaks and troughs. Maybe he is trying too hard, but he is important to us and that's why I keep picking him." *David Moyes*

AUG. 23 > v FULHAM

JAN. 17 ▸ v CHARLTON ATHLETIC

54 FA PREMIERSHIP
SATURDAY DECEMBER 13, 2003

PORTSMOUTH	1
EVERTON	2

ATTENDANCE: 20,101

EVERTON SCORERS: Carsley 27, **Rooney 42**
PORTSMOUTH SCORERS: Roberts 15

Against Portsmouth, Rooney was match-winner for Everton and also experienced a phantom dismissal in the club's first away win of the season. The visitors were trailing when Rooney came on as a 24th minute substitute for the unfortunate Watson, who was returning from injury. The player then gave fans plenty to talk about, not least the impetus he gave Everton from his position wide on the right. Within three minutes of Rooney's appearance Everton had equalised through Carsley. Then shortly before the break Rooney scored what turned out to be the winner with his first goal since August. In the 71st minute, however, Steve Stone's challenge saw Rooney lose his composure and he retaliated by shoving Stone on the floor. Immediately Rooney headed for an early bath but referee Uriah Rennie brandished only a yellow card. Manager Moyes was less than happy with Rooney's reaction and also gave him a tongue-lashing on the touchline.

WHAT THEY SAID ABOUT ROONEY: "Wayne knows he was very lucky today. I saw him push him [Stone] and normally when you do that you have to face the consequences." *David Moyes*

"Wayne Rooney needs to learn to control himself but I've got more to worry about than him." *Harry Redknapp (Portsmouth manager)*

"This is his first real season where the scrutiny has been on him because he made such an impact last season… I'd like him to just keep doing what he has been doing, keep playing his football, he's young and he's learning, leave it at that." *Kevin Campbell*

ROONEY GOAL *(42 mins) Portsmouth goalkeeper Pavel Srnicek flailed at Naysmith's cross and Rooney turned and fired home a deflected left-foot shot.*

55 FA PREMIERSHIP
SATURDAY DECEMBER 20, 2003

EVERTON	3
LEICESTER CITY	2

ATTENDANCE: 37,007

EVERTON SCORERS: Howey (og) 33, **Rooney 71**, Radzinski 79. **LEICESTER SCORERS:** Ferdinand 45, Scowcroft 58

On the hour, just after Everton had squandered a lead and found themselves trailing, boss Moyes called Rooney from the bench to replace McFadden and get the home side back on track. In the 71st minute he duly obliged with a spectacular equaliser and raced to the dug-out in celebration. Radzinski then gave Everton a match-winning lead eight minutes later in this seesaw game.

WHAT ROONEY SAID: "I do not really think this season is more difficult, I think there is just a bit more expectation this season and that goes not just for me but the rest of the squad."

WHAT THEY SAID ABOUT ROONEY: "You can see by his face and his body language that he is enjoying things more at present. We have eased the pressure and expectations on him by putting him back on the bench. He is now doing the job he did for us last season by coming on and either helping us win or draw games." *David Moyes*

ROONEY GOAL *(71 mins) Radzinski raced forward and his pass was touched on by Campbell for Rooney to unleash a thunderous shot beyond the dive of Ian Walker and high into the roof of the net.*

56 FA PREMIERSHIP
FRIDAY DECEMBER 26, 2003

MANCHESTER UNITED	3
EVERTON	2

ATTENDANCE: 67,642

EVERTON SCORERS: G Neville (og) 13, Ferguson 90 **MAN UNITED SCORERS:** Butt 9, Kleberson 44, Bellion 68

Rooney and Tony Hibbert had a tough time on Everton's right as they were both outclassed by Manchester United's Ronaldo in an entertaining game. Rooney's frustration at not being able to keep up with the Brazilian resulted in a booking for a foul. Ronaldo had been involved in all three of United's goals and after the third one went in, Rooney found himself replaced by substitute McFadden.

57 FA PREMIERSHIP
SUNDAY DECEMBER 28, 2003

EVERTON	1
BIRMINGHAM CITY	0

ATTENDANCE: 39,631

EVERTON SCORER: Rooney 69

Rooney proved to be a match-winning half-time substitute for Everton. After a dire goalless first-half, he replaced Carsley and went on to score the only goal of the game following a corner. Throughout the second-half Rooney was a menace to the Birmingham defence and almost added a second with a rising, angled shot that produced a brilliant save from Maik Taylor.

WHAT THEY SAID ABOUT ROONEY "If you cast your mind back to last season, you will recall that Wayne had his best impact coming off the bench, and he seems to be doing that again this season. We are not going to call him 'Supersub', though, because he has far too much talent for that. When he comes on, he gives the crowd a lift and he gives the team a lift." *Alan Irvine (Everton assistant manager)*

ROONEY GOAL *(69 mins) From Naysmith's corner goalkeeper Taylor appeared to have beaten Everton's Ferguson and Stubbs with a catch but the ball dropped from his hands and Rooney smashed the loose ball into the net.*

58 FA CUP
THIRD ROUND
SATURDAY JANUARY 3, 2004

EVERTON	3
NORWICH CITY	1

ATTENDANCE: 29,955

EVERTON SCORERS: Kilbane 14, Ferguson (pen) 37 (pen) 69 **NORWICH SCORER:** Brennan 26

Everton overcame top-of-the-table Championship side Norwich City to progress to the fourth round. Two penalties – one in each half – from Ferguson made it a clear win for Everton but the winning margin could have been greater but for the wasted chances, with Rooney, in the starting line-up, among the culprits. Rooney went close on several occasions but all his efforts were just too wide or too high.

59 FA PREMIERSHIP
WEDNESDAY JANUARY 7, 2004

EVERTON	1
ARSENAL	1

ATTENDANCE: 38,726

EVERTON SCORER: Radzinski 75
ARSENAL SCORER: Kanu 29

Both teams had opportunities to win this game but in the end the spoils were shared. Arsenal led from the 29th minute through Kanu but Radzinski equalised with 15 minutes left. However, both sides created chances throughout the game. Rooney was chosen to play on the right with Radzinski and Ferguson the main strikers. Rooney missed a golden opportunity on 15 minutes when six yards out he headed Kilbane's superb cross well wide of the target. Later, Rooney fired in a free kick that visiting goalkeeper Jens Lehmann did well to fist away.

60 FA PREMIERSHIP
SATURDAY JANUARY 10, 2004

FULHAM	2
EVERTON	1

ATTENDANCE: 17,013

EVERTON SCORER: Kilbane 81 **FULHAM SCORERS:** Saha (pen) 45, Malbranque 46

With Everton trailing 2-0 thanks to goals in the last minute of the first-half and the opening minute of the second-half, Rooney was one of a triple substitution made by Moyes after 56 minutes to try and turn the tide. It nearly worked with a Rooney header only stopped by Edwin Van der Sar's outstretched foot. Kilbane did cut the deficit but an equaliser could not be found. Everton could have celebrated a victory as they created a host of first-half chances that would have won them the game by the break.

61 FA PREMIERSHIP
SATURDAY JANUARY 17, 2004

EVERTON	0
CHARLTON ATHLETIC	1

ATTENDANCE: 36,322

CHARLTON SCORER: Stuart 41

Everton put a massive amount of second-half pressure on Charlton, but could not find the breakthrough for an equaliser. Rooney carved out chances for his team-mates but opportunities such as his cross for Ferguson and the free-kick for Kilbane resulted in goal attempts that were off target. Ex-Evertonian Graham Stuart scored Charlton's winner in the 41st minute but Rooney and Co could not beat goalkeeper Kiely and his defence.

62 FA CUP
FOURTH ROUND
SATURDAY JANUARY 31, 2004

EVERTON	1
FULHAM	1

ATTENDANCE: 27,862

EVERTON SCORER: Jeffers 90
FULHAM SCORER: Davis 49

Everton managed to stay in the FA Cup thanks to Jeffers. An 85th minute substitute, he notched a dramatic last-minute equaliser to cancel Sean Davis's earlier goal. It was a scrappy first-half but Everton had the majority of the possession. Even after going behind, Everton appeared to have the edge and were doing everything but put the ball in the net. Then coach Moyes made the late substitution that saved Everton from defeat.

63 FA PREMIERSHIP
SATURDAY JANUARY 31, 2004

LIVERPOOL	0
EVERTON	0

ATTENDANCE: 44,056

A breathless Merseyside derby that served up plenty of action but couldn't provide a goal, largely thanks to goalkeepers Martyn and Dudek. Rooney and Ferguson led the attack for Everton and caused problems for the home side. Rooney proved to be the creator, with one right-wing cross leaving Ferguson to head just wide. Another cross resulted in a Stubbs header that Dudek pushed over the bar. Everton kept searching for the opener after the break, while at the other end they had to thank Martyn for keeping Liverpool out too.

64 FA CUP
FOURTH ROUND REPLAY
WEDNESDAY FEBRUARY 4, 2004

FULHAM	2
EVERTON	1

After extra-time

ATTENDANCE: 11,551

EVERTON SCORERS: Jeffers 90 **FULHAM SCORERS:** Inamoto 62, Malbranque 102

Rooney almost gave Everton a half-time lead in stoppage time, with a close range header from a Radzinski cross, but the effort was headed off the line by Fulham's Carlos Bocanegra. It was one of several good chances squandered by Everton. As in the first match, Fulham took the lead in the second-half and Jeffers had to equalise in injury time to force an extra period of play. Sadly for Rooney and Everton, the winning goal came from Steed Malbranque in the 102nd minute, sending Fulham through to the fifth round.

FEB. 4 ▸ v FULHAM

65 FA PREMIERSHIP
SATURDAY FEBRUARY 7, 2004

EVERTON	3
MANCHESTER UNITED	4

ATTENDANCE: 40,190

EVERTON SCORERS: Unsworth 49, O'Shea (og) 65, Kilbane 75. **MAN UNITED SCORERS:** Saha 9, 29, van Nistelrooy 24 89

Half-time substitute Rooney inspired Everton to a sensational comeback after his team were trailing 3-0 at the break. However, Rooney's good work was undone by a dramatic 89th minute winner from van Nistelrooy. Rooney nearly scored an injury time equaliser but his touch to a Radzinski low cross went inches wide. Everton got a goal back early in the second-half and Rooney almost reduced the deficit further but was kept out by goalkeeper Tim Howard with a blocked save and then a tip over the crossbar. The latter effort led to a corner from which O'Shea put into his own net. Ten minutes later and Everton were all square, thanks to Kilbane. But football showed it can be a cruel game when van Nistelrooy netted his second before Rooney's last-gasp effort went wide of the post.

WHAT THEY SAID ABOUT ROONEY: "We just couldn't handle Rooney. He was getting the ball from everywhere and we couldn't stop him. We knew they would come at us in the second-half and would get the ball up to Duncan Ferguson as much as they could, but it was Rooney who made the difference. It was thanks to him Everton dominated the second-half and we didn't expect that." *Ruud van Nistelrooy*

66 FA PREMIERSHIP
WEDNESDAY FEBRUARY 11, 2004

BIRMINGHAM CITY	3
EVERTON	0

ATTENDANCE: 29,004

BIRMINGHAM SCORERS: Johnson 8, Lazaridis 39, Forssell 49

Defensive frailties allowed Everton to concede three goals and suffer a deserved defeat that left them just four points above the relegation zone. Rooney was lacking in creative inspiration, while his team suffered an inability to contain or seriously bother the home side.

67 FA PREMIERSHIP
SATURDAY FEBRUARY 21, 2004

SOUTHAMPTON	3
EVERTON	3

ATTENDANCE: 31,875

EVERTON SCORERS: Rooney 7 78, Ferguson 32 **SOUTHAMPTON SCORERS:** Phillips 58, Beattie (pen) 82, Fernandes 90

Rooney, partnered in attack with Ferguson, was back to form, demonstrated by his seventh minute goal that gave Everton an early lead. Ferguson's header from a Gravesen cross made it 2-0 just after half an hour. Both Rooney and Ferguson constantly threatened and could have made Everton's half-time lead even greater. Although Kevin Phillips halved the deficit in the 58th minute, Rooney restored the two-goal advantage with 12 minutes left. However, although Everton were superb in attack their defensive deficiencies were never far from the surface and were the reason why the visitors had to settle for a point. A needless penalty was conceded and despatched by James Beattie

and then Farbrice Fernandes equalised in stoppage time with a curling shot.

WHAT THEY SAID ABOUT ROONEY: "In my seven or eight years of directing youth football I've not seen a better talent. He's a genius." *Steve Wigley (Southampton caretaker manager)*

"Wayne played an exceptional game considering he returned at 5.30am on Thursday and was training the same afternoon." *David Moyes*

"Wayne was sensational all day and that was certainly the best he's played for a long time. Considering he didn't get a lot of the ball, he was brilliant in the first-half and fantastic in the second." *Steve Watson (Everton)*

⚽ **ROONEY GOAL** *(7 mins) Rooney seized onto a loose ball after David Prutton had lost possession and then fired in a shot that spun off Michael Svensson and into the net to make the score 1-0.*

⚽ **ROONEY GOAL** *(78 mins) Rooney and Watson exchanged passes allowing Rooney to fire home with a right foot shot to bring the score to 3-1.*

68 FA PREMIERSHIP
SATURDAY FEBRUARY 28, 2004

EVERTON	2
ASTON VILLA	0

ATTENDANCE: 39,353

EVERTON SCORERS: Radzinski 78, Gravesen 84

Everton at last ended a nine-game run without a win with a 2-0 victory over Aston Villa. However, they had to survive a tough first-half and it wasn't until late in the game that the deadlock was broken and the three points assured. With the introduction of sub Radzinski, Rooney was pushed out wide.

> ## "WE JUST COULDN'T HANDLE ROONEY. HE WAS GETTING THE BALL FROM EVERYWHERE AND WE COULDN'T STOP HIM. WE KNEW THEY WOULD COME AT US IN THE SECOND HALF AND WOULD GET THE BALL UP TO DUNCAN FERGUSON AS MUCH AS THEY COULD, BUT IT WAS ROONEY WHO MADE THE DIFFERENCE. IT WAS THANKS TO HIM EVERTON DOMINATED THE SECOND-HALF AND WE DIDN'T EXPECT THAT." RUUD VAN NISTELROOY

He was his tenacious self, battling for everything and attacking at will. Villa kept him at bay while his goal attempts did not hit the target. He appealed for a penalty after he was bundled off the ball but referee Matt Messias waved it aside. He did have an altercation with Lee Hendrie, retaliating to the Villa player's challenge. He got off with a warning but was booked later. It was Rooney, however, who carved out the opportunity to give Everton the lead: his ball into the area was headed home by Radzinski in the 78th minute. Six minutes later Gravesen's individual goal secured the points.

WHAT THEY SAID ABOUT ROONEY: "The idea was to play Rooney as a right-sided forward, to play him against JLloyd Samuel. We were short in the final third today and we knew that if we could give Wayne a little more space he could pick a pass out. In the end it worked a little bit like that." *David Moyes*

69 FA PREMIERSHIP
SATURDAY MARCH 13, 2004

EVERTON	1
PORTSMOUTH	0

ATTENDANCE: 40,105

EVERTON SCORER: Rooney 78

Not the best football match to be played in the Premiership, with chances squandered by poor finishing. A goalless draw looked the most likely outcome until Rooney broke the deadlock with a match-winning goal 12 minutes from the end. The strike gave Everton a much-needed lift as they took

all three points. The scoreline could have been even more comfortable had Rooney found the net with his two attempts before the final whistle.

WHAT THEY SAID ABOUT ROONEY: "The quality came at the end from Wayne. He had been finding things a bit tough out there until that moment. He had found it hard to make an impact, but that is what good players do. They produce a little bit of magic when it is needed." *David Moyes*

"We did deserve at least a point, but they had Rooney and that was the difference." *Harry Redknapp*

"He plays from the heart but has the ability to play with his brain as well." *Alex Nyarko (Everton)*

⚽ **ROONEY GOAL** *(78 mins) Radzinski's square pass allowed Rooney to turn and beat defender John Curtis before firing home a low shot past Hislop's right.*

70 FA PREMIERSHIP
SATURDAY MARCH 20, 2004

LEICESTER CITY	1
EVERTON	1

ATTENDANCE: 31,650

EVERTON SCORER: Rooney 75
LEICESTER SCORER: Bent 90

Rooney found himself booked for a foul on Nikos Dabizas but within a minute he had beaten Dabizas fairly in the air and finished a move that gave ten-man Everton the lead. Rooney's striking partner and captain Ferguson had been sent-off in the first-half but Rooney was not left isolated upfront and manager Moyes partnered him up with Radzinski. The positive ploy almost paid maximum dividends but in injury time Marcus Bent equalised for the home side just minutes after Rooney had been take off and replaced by substitute Campbell.

⚽ **ROONEY GOAL** *(75 mins) Rooney beat Dabizas in the air and directed the ball to Radzinski who centred the ball back for Rooney to blast his shot past goalkeeper Walker.*

71 FA PREMIERSHIP
SATURDAY MARCH 27, 2004

EVERTON	1
MIDDLESBROUGH	1

ATTENDANCE: 38,210

EVERTON SCORER: Radzinski 78
MIDDLESBROUGH SCORER: Job 83

Rooney partnered Radzinski in attack, with Ferguson ruled out by injury. However, the pair of them had a tough time, often being isolated up front and lacking a decent supply. The few chances that came Rooney's way ended in frustration: he fired a 25-yard shot wide, while his other efforts were either blocked or simply lacked the power to cause problems. Radzinski finally got a breakthrough with a low drive 12 minutes from time, but again Everton conceded a stoppage-time equaliser, this time it was Joseph-Desire Job who took full advantage.

WHAT THEY SAID ABOUT ROONEY: "What really strikes you when you play with him is that his movement's so intelligent for someone his age. He takes up positions into which defenders are reluctant to go, and that unnerves you. He's strong, he's prepared to shoot from anywhere and he's not afraid to miss." *Gareth Southgate (Middlesbrough)*

72 FA PREMIERSHIP
TUESDAY APRIL 13, 2004

LEEDS UNITED	1
EVERTON	1

ATTENDANCE: 39,835

EVERTON SCORER: Rooney 13
LEEDS SCORER: Milner 50

Everton dominated the first part of the game and took a deserved lead through Rooney, who netted his ninth goal of the season. Only good goalkeeping by Robinson and frantic defending, notably by Michael Duberry, kept Everton from scoring more than that one goal. Leeds battled and became the superior team, equalising early in the second-half. Everton – save for Rooney screwing a shot wide and failing to find the unmarked Radzinski – found themselves on the back foot for rest of the game.

⚽ **ROONEY GOAL** *(13 mins) Rooney latched on to a Watson through ball then and fired a low shot past goalkeeper Robinson.*

73 FA PREMIERSHIP
SATURDAY APRIL 17, 2004

CHELSEA	0
EVERTON	0

ATTENDANCE: 41,169

The two teams played out a goalless draw in which Everton looked to Rooney to produce a breakthrough, while Chelsea relied on Wayne Bridge's forward forrays. Rooney had a curling free-kick scrambled away, then was denied by the foot of goalkeeper Marco Ambrosio, and stopped by defender Robert Huth after breaking clear of Marcel Desailly. Everton survived with help from the woodwork, but were happy to have secured an invaluable point.

74 FA PREMIERSHIP
SATURDAY APRIL 24, 2004

EVERTON	0
BLACKBURN ROVERS	1

ATTENDANCE: 38,884

BLACKBURN SCORER: Stead 81

On another disappointing day for the Goodison Park faithful, Everton had plenty of possession but failed to create any decent chances. Rooney was as

"WHAT REALLY STRIKES YOU WHEN YOU PLAY WITH HIM IS THAT HIS MOVEMENT'S SO INTELLIGENT FOR SOMEONE HIS AGE. HE TAKES UP POSITIONS INTO WHICH DEFENDERS ARE RELUCTANT TO GO, AND THAT UNNERVES YOU. HE'S STRONG, HE'S PREPARED TO SHOOT FROM ANYWHERE AND HE'S NOT AFRAID TO MISS." GARETH SOUTHGATE

anonymous as the rest of his team and ultimately Everton were undone by 21-year-old Jonathan Stead's headed winner nine minutes from full-time.

75 FA PREMIERSHIP
SATURDAY MAY 1, 2004

WOLVERHAMPTON WANDERERS	2
EVERTON	1

ATTENDANCE: 29,395

EVERTON SCORER: Osman 3
WOLVES SCORERS: Camara 55, Cort 84

Everton got off to a bright start with Rooney hitting a long ball that McFadden picked up and hit into the area for Leon Osman to head home. Everton could easily have been 3-0 up by the sixth minute and continued to create further chances with Rooney going close a couple of times himself. Wolves themselves were also going for goal but did not find it until after the break, when they kept Martyn busy. After Henri Camara had equalised Rooney was booked for a lunge on Wolves goalkeeper Paul Jones. Three minutes later Carl Cort scored the winner for the home team and the visitors were left to rue not taking advantage of their early chances.

WHAT THEY SAID ABOUT ROONEY: "Rooney's 18 years old and he will make mistakes… He was just being enthusiastic. If you take that away from him then you will take away a part of his special talent." *David Weir (Everton captain)*

76 FA PREMIERSHIP
SATURDAY MAY 8, 2004

EVERTON	1
BOLTON WANDERERS	2

ATTENDANCE: 40,190

EVERTON SCORER: Ferguson 68
BOLTON SCORER: Djorkaeff 14 87

Youri Djorkaeff scored twice for Bolton and effectively ran the game. Bolton were the more confident team, while Everton floundered. Despite Ferguson's goal, the team could have no complaints about the outcome, including Rooney who played throughout.

77 FA PREMIERSHIP
SATURDAY MAY 15, 2004

MANCHESTER CITY	5
EVERTON	1

ATTENDANCE: 47,284

EVERTON SCORER: Campbell 60
MAN CITY SCORERS: Wanchope 16 30, Anelka 41, Sibierski 89, Wright-Phillips 90

Rooney's last match for Everton was a woeful affair although he did set up his side's consolation goal for Campbell and also got himself booked. Everton were appalling on the day and the size of Manchester City's winning margin was completely justified as they rubbed salt into the wounds with two late goals.

FEB. 28 › v ASTON VILLA

78 CHAMPIONS LEAGUE
GROUP D
TUESDAY SEPTEMBER 28, 2004

| MANCHESTER UNITED | 6 |
| FENERBAHÇE | 2 |

ATTENDANCE: 67,128

MAN UNITED SCORERS: Giggs 7, **Rooney 17 28 54**, van Nistelrooy 78, Bellion 81

FENERBAHÇE SCORERS: Marcio Nobre 47, Sanli 60

Making his debut for Manchester United following his £27 million move from Everton, the clash with Fenebahçe also marked Rooney's debut in European club football and his first appearance since the injury that had wrecked his Euro 2004 campaign. Putting in a fantastic performance, Wayne justified his price tag by scoring his first-ever hat-trick. Partnering van Nistelrooy, who also scored, he was brilliant and could only have been bolstered by Ryan Giggs's opening goal. From then on Rooney had the Fenerbahçe defence on the back foot as United were majestic in attack. Rooney not only scored goals, he also created United's sixth, setting up David Bellion despite tiring in the closing stages. Rooney's debut number 8 shirt ended up being an exalted exhibit in the Manchester United museum.

WHAT THEY SAID ABOUT ROONEY: "That's why we signed him as he's got great potential…

I think he can only get stronger. The important thing for me as a coach is to allow the boy to develop naturally without too much public attention. I want him to be as ordinary as he can."
Sir Alex Ferguson

"To get a hat-trick is unbelievable, fairytale stuff. I do not think he knows what pressure is."
Rio Ferdinand (Man United)

"If I was to pick out one thing to praise it would be his attitude. He is only 18, it is his debut and he knows all eyes are on him – yet he just goes out and does his own thing."
Ruud van Nistelrooy (Man United)

"Rooney is still very young and maybe he will become the player of the century. He is at the beginning now though."
Christoph Daum (Fenerbahçe coach)

 ROONEY GOAL (17 mins) Rooney latched on to van Nistelrooy's defence-splitting pass and fired home from the edge of the area to make it 2-0.

 ROONEY GOAL (28 mins) Gabriel Heinze and Giggs combined to set up Rooney who fired a powerful shot from the edge of the box that ended in the bottom corner of the net, making the score 3-0.

ROONEY GOAL (54 mins) Rooney fired home a curling free-kick that beat goalkeeper Rustu Recber to send the Old Trafford crowd into raptures.

"TO GET A HAT-TRICK IS UNBELIEVABLE, FAIRYTALE STUFF. I DO NOT THINK HE KNOWS WHAT PRESSURE IS." RIO FERDINAND

79 FA PREMIERSHIP
SUNDAY OCTOBER 3, 2004

| MANCHESTER UNITED | 1 |
| MIDDLESBROUGH | 1 |

ATTENDANCE: 67,988

MAN UNITED SCORER: Smith 81
MIDDLESBROUGH SCORER: Downing 33

After the fairytale European antics of midweek both Rooney and Manchester United were brought down to earth by Steve McClaren's injury-hit Middlesbrough. Rooney found himself contained by fair means or foul by George Boateng, while United really didn't galvanise themselves until the final half an hour. Alan Smith did head home an equaliser and both sides had chances to win, but both Gaizka Mendieta and Gary Neville made glaring misses.

WHAT THEY SAID ABOUT ROONEY: "Young Wayne was maybe a bit tired after that game in midweek." *Sir Alex Ferguson*

80 FA PREMIERSHIP
SATURDAY OCTOBER 16, 2004

| BIRMINGHAM CITY | 0 |
| MANCHESTER UNITED | 0 |

ATTENDANCE: 29,221

Rooney came on as a 59th minute substitute for Kleberson and became one of a four-strike forward line alongside van Nistelrooy, Smith and Louis Saha. Unfortunately, all four failed to score. To their credit, Birmingham never allowed United to get into their stride and prevented them from settling and were perhaps unlucky not to win.

81 CHAMPIONS LEAGUE
GROUP D
TUESDAY OCTOBER 19

| SPARTA PRAGUE | 0 |
| MANCHESTER UNITED | 0 |

ATTENDANCE: 20,654

It was hard work for the visitors, showing seven changes from the Premiership clash with Birmingham, as they secured a point in Prague. Rooney tried his best to break the deadlock. He had a shot that was a whisker away from the post and then another effort found the side netting. O'Shea and van Nistelrooy benefited from Rooney's creativity but were unable to exploit it with goals. Rooney and Giggs were replaced after 78 minutes by Saha and Ronaldo, who briefly gave United further impetus but not enough to break the resilient Sparta defence.

82 FA PREMIERSHIP
SUNDAY OCTOBER 24, 2004

| MANCHESTER UNITED | 2 |
| ARSENAL | 0 |

ATTENDANCE: 67,862

MAN UNITED SCORERS: van Nistelrooy (pen) 73, **Rooney 90**

Rooney celebrated his 19th birthday by winning a dubious-looking penalty and scoring his first Premiership goal for United. In so doing he ended Arsenal's record unbeaten sequence at 49 games. For much of the game Sol Campbell appeared to have Rooney under control but then in a flash Rooney turned and fell under the challenge of the Arsenal man, with referee Mike Riley pointing to the spot without hesitation. Van Nistelrooy duly converted the kick and as Arsenal poured forward in an attempt to find the equaliser, Rooney made it 2-0 in injury time to halt the Gunners in their tracks for the second time in his career. As always in United-Arsenal clashes there was a degree of ill feeling, particularly from Arsenal, aggrieved at the penalty decision, and the arguing continued in the tunnel at the end of the match.

WHAT THEY SAID ABOUT ROONEY: "Rooney didn't exactly have the best of games but he made

OCT. 3 · v MIDDLESBROUGH

one goal and scored another and made sure that his side got something out of it." *Alan Hansen*

"I don't think there was any contact at all. Even Rooney told our players that no one touched him. In a game like that, to see how lightly the referee gave a penalty is difficult to take." *Arsene Wenger*

 ROONEY GOAL (90 mins) Saha and Smith combined with a pass to the right side, then Smith directed the ball across the box for Rooney to fire past Jens Lehmann from ten yards out.

83 FA PREMIERSHIP
SATURDAY OCTOBER 30, 2004

| PORTSMOUTH | 2 |
| MANCHESTER UNITED | 0 |

ATTENDANCE: 20,190

PORTSMOUTH SCORERS: Unsworth (pen) 53, Yakubu 72

Manchester United started brightly and looked likely to pick up three away points. However, towards the end of the first half, and despite the loss of Diomansy Kamara, Portsmouth began to get the upper hand. Rooney became frustrated and was guilty of a late tackle on Nigel Quashie, receiving a yellow card for his challenge. United's mood didn't improve after the break. They conceded a penalty and fell behind, then 19 minutes later Yakubu made it 2-0 to wrap up a convincing win for the home side.

84 CHAMPIONS LEAGUE
GROUP D
WEDNESDAY NOVEMBER 3, 2004

| MANCHESTER UNITED | 4 |
| SPARTA PRAGUE | 1 |

ATTENDANCE: 66,706

MAN UNITED SCORERS: van Nistelrooy 14 (pen) 25 60 90 **SPARTA PRAGUE SCORER:** Zelenka 53

Rooney was cast as striking sidekick as van Nistelrooy netted all four goals in the 4-1 drubbing of Sparta Prague. Rooney did get the ball in the net in the 82nd minute but it was disallowed for offside. The scoreline was convincing, although United were not completely unthreatened and on several occasions goalkeeper Roy Carroll was required to deal with the Sparta threat. But the headlines belonged to van Nistelrooy who turned in a sublime European display and not for the first time.

85 FA PREMIERSHIP
SUNDAY NOVEMBER 7, 2004

| MANCHESTER UNITED | 0 |
| MANCHESTER CITY | 0 |

ATTENDANCE: 67,863

A typical Manchester derby that Rooney didn't get to experience until the 76th minute when he replaced Paul Scholes. However, it was a day when United failed to fire and City had the upper hand. In such contest a point was the best the home side could hope for, although Sir Alex Ferguson felt his side were denied a penalty.

OCT. 24 › v ARSENAL

86 FA PREMIERSHIP
SUNDAY NOVEMBER 14, 2004

NEWCASTLE UNITED	1
MANCHESTER UNITED	3

ATTENDANCE: 52,320

MAN UNITED SCORERS: Rooney 7 90,
van Nistelrooy (pen) 73
NEWCASTLE SCORER: Shearer 71

Manchester United deservedly beat their hosts with Rooney scoring twice and helping to win the penalty for his side's all-important second goal. Ferguson outwitted his opposite number Graeme Souness with superior tactics: Manchester United packed the midfield and then sent players racing forward beyond lead striker van Nistelrooy. Rooney was positioned in the hole behind the Dutchman but in front of the recognised four-man midfield. At the start and at various times either Scholes, Darren Fletcher, Rooney or Ronaldo all surged forward, with Roy Keane playing the holding role. The Newcastle defence was unable to cope and Rooney gave the visitors the perfect start in the seventh minute. However, the lead was cancelled out by Alan Shearer's 71st minute left foot shot that set up a grandstand finish. Within two minutes United restored the lead from the penalty spot after Rooney and Newcastle defender Andy O'Brien chased a through ball. Rooney outmuscled his opponent and then attempted to chip into the area, but as goalkeeper Shay Given attempted to secure the loose ball, he brought down Scholes. A penalty was awarded and van Nistelrooy made no mistake as he

fired home. Rooney put the matter beyond doubt with another goal in the last minute of the game.

WHAT ROONEY SAID: "With Chelsea and Arsenal winning, it's a big win. It keeps us in the race. No one should write us off."

⚽ **ROONEY GOAL** *(7 mins) A counter-attack following a Shearer free-kick saw the ball moved quickly out to the right from Keane, to Gary Neville and on to Fletcher. Fletcher sent the ball into the Newcastle area where Rooney met it first time and fired it past Given to make the score 1-0.*

⚽ **ROONEY GOAL** *(90 mins) Smith nipped in quicker than Newcastle defenders Ronny Johnsen and Olivier Bernard to set up van Nistelrooy, but his shot was blocked on the line by Titus Bramble. Rooney was on hand to shoot home the rebound from close range.*

87 FA PREMIERSHIP
SATURDAY NOVEMBER 20, 2004

MANCHESTER UNITED	2
CHARLTON ATHLETIC	0

ATTENDANCE: 67,704

MAN UNITED SCORERS: Giggs 41, Scholes 50

A predictably comfortable win for United. Rooney was restrained but reliable following the midweek events in Madrid with England, and United demonstrated patience knowing that inevitably they would find the net and earn the expected three points. Giggs gave them the lead four minutes before the break and then Scholes got a second goal in the 50th minute.

NOV. 20 › v CHARLTON ATHLETIC

88 CHAMPIONS LEAGUE
GROUP D
TUESDAY NOVEMBER 23, 2004

| MANCHESTER UNITED | 2 |
| OLYMPIQUE LYONNAIS | 1 |

ATTENDANCE: 66,398

MAN UNITED SCORERS: G Neville 19, van Nistelrooy 53. LYONNAIS SCORER: Diarra 40

Sir Alex's 1,000th match in charge of Manchester United was marked by a 2-1 win over French champions Lyon. Gary Neville opened the scoring but Mahamadou Diarra was to equalise as a result of goalkeeper Carroll's handling blunder before the break. Rooney was in fine form, as was his team. He hit the woodwork in the 14th minute and later quickly turned and fired from inside the area after a Smith flick on, but the 26th minute shot went wide of the far post. Four minutes later Rooney linked up with Scholes and Keane to drive a low shot just wide of the post again. A 51st minute corner saw Rooney come close to scoring but his attempt was cleared off the line. The ball was chipped back into the area from the byline by Ferdinand, enabling van Nistelrooy to head home the winner in a game that saw United qualify for the knock-out stages.

89 FA PREMIERSHIP
SATURDAY NOVEMBER 27, 2004

| WEST BROMWICH ALBION | 0 |
| MANCHESTER UNITED | 3 |

ATTENDANCE: 27,709

MAN UNITED SCORERS: Scholes 53 82, van Nistelrooy 72

Bottom-of-the-table West Brom were simply outclassed by Manchester United, who cruised to the most comfortable of victories. The home side's

cause was not helped by the loss of two key players in the first-half through injury – defensive lynchpin Darren Moore and Cosmin Contra. Two goals from Scholes sandwiched van Nistelrooy's goalbound header and the scoreline was never in doubt. Rooney went close with a powerful drive in the second-half that thudded against the advertising hoardings, but it was Scholes's day.

90 FA PREMIERSHIP
SATURDAY DECEMBER 4, 2004

| MANCHESTER UNITED | 3 |
| SOUTHAMPTON | 0 |

ATTENDANCE: 67,921

MAN UNITED SCORERS: Scholes 53, ROONEY 58, Ronaldo 87

A fourth successive Premiership victory for Manchester United as the Red Devils proved too good for the Saints. Rooney played his part starting on the left of a five-man midfield behind lone striker Alan Smith (van Nistelrooy was out injured). Rooney would turn defence into attack from deep and helped to create a host of chances for the home side. Southampton resisted the inevitable up to half-time but then superior talent and thinking shone through. Scholes opened the scoring and then Rooney made it 2-0 in the 58th minute. Towards the end of the game Cristiano Ronaldo deservedly got a third goal with a well-taken volley. A 3-0 win for Manchester United, who had amazingly kicked-off on a Saturday afternoon at 3pm for the first time all season.

⚽ **ROONEY GOAL** *(58 mins)* With a quick change of pace Rooney latched on to an excellent Giggs pass and then chipped the ball over goalkeeper Kasey Keller and into the roof of the Southampton net.

JAN. 15 ▷ v LIVERPOOL

91 FA PREMIERSHIP
MONDAY DECEMBER 13, 2004

| FULHAM | 1 |
| MANCHESTER UNITED | 1 |

ATTENDANCE: 21,940

MAN UNITED SCORER: Smith 33
FULHAM SCORER: Bouba Diop 87

Manchester United looked set for another victory but Fulham's Papa Bouba Diop snatched an equaliser towards the end. United had been the better side throughout the first-half and perhaps should have had more than Smith's 33rd minute goal to show for

it. With Rooney playing on the left, each time he or Ronaldo got the ball there was tangible expectation from the crowd and a sense of concern in the Fulham defence. Rooney went close to scoring when he fired a Smith pass against a post. Keane also hit the woodwork. Fulham goalkeeper Edwin van der Sar also kept United out with some marvellous saves. The failure to add to Smith's goal was to cost United two valuable points in their race with Chelsea and Arsenal for the Premiership title.

92 FA PREMIERSHIP
SATURDAY DECEMBER 18, 2004

| MANCHESTER UNITED | 5 |
| CRYSTAL PALACE | 2 |

ATTENDANCE: 67,814

MAN UNITED SCORERS: Scholes 22 49, Smith 35, Boyce (og) 48, O'Shea 90
PALACE SCORERS: Granville 27, Kolkka 46

Rooney had the unnerving experience of having an eighth minute penalty saved by Palace goalkeeper Gabor Kiraly after Fletcher had been brought down by Danny Granville. It was a fraught situation for United until early in the second-half when United twice took the lead. Rooney's corner led to Scholes breaking the deadlock after 22 minutes and then Smith netted in the 35th minute with a header from a Scholes corner. United's goals were cancelled out by Granville and Joonas Kolkka respectively, the latter arriving within a minute of the second-half kick-off. Parity was short-lived as Rooney was released by Scholes and his shot was saved by Kiraly's legs. Gary Neville hit the ball back into the area towards Scholes and it went over the line with the unfortunate Boyce getting the final touch. United's lead was extended moments later by Scholes and in the last moments John O'Shea scored United's fifth.

DEC. 26 ▷ v BOLTON WANDERERS

93 FA PREMIERSHIP
SUNDAY DECEMBER 26, 2004

| MANCHESTER UNITED | 2 |
| BOLTON WANDERERS | 0 |

ATTENDANCE: 67,867

MAN UNITED SCORERS: Giggs 10, Scholes 89

A consistent performance with moments of magic that earned Manchester United their sixth win in seven league games. Giggs gave the home side an early lead, which could have increased on several occasions, but it wasn't until the penultimate minute of the match that Scholes found the net again. Rooney showed flashes of his ability but largely had a quiet game, except when Bolton's Israeli international Tel Ben I laim suggested he had dived when trying to win a free-kick. Rooney shoved him away, to which Ben Haim overreacted and fell to the floor. Fortunately for Rooney, referee Gallagher chose not to show a card.

WHAT THEY SAID ABOUT ROONEY: "There was a bit of play-acting but Rooney pushed his hand in his face and under today's rules and regulations, the referee had to send him off if he saw it. He was pretty lucky to get away with it." *Sam Allardyce*

"No matter what we say, Wayne is going to get a three-match ban and be done for violent conduct. Even our most severe critic would say that is unfair. The central issue to me is the system. We are getting done because we are on TV and highlighted so much because it is Manchester United and Wayne Rooney." *Sir Alex Ferguson*

94 FA PREMIERSHIP
TUESDAY DECEMBER 28, 2004

| ASTON VILLA | 0 |
| MANCHESTER UNITED | 1 |

ATTENDANCE: 42,593

MAN UNITED SCORER: Giggs 41

Rooney and Giggs were deployed on the flanks by boss Ferguson in a 4-3-3 formation. Both players switched flanks at will but they had different matches. Giggs was undoubtedly the man of the match and scorer of the winning goal after 41 minutes. Rooney came close to giving away a penalty after a 12th minute tackle on Nolberto Solano, but the referee waved in his favour. He also suffered a thigh injury to his right leg after landing awkwardly and he had to limp off after 61 minutes, to be replaced by Ronaldo.

95 CARLING CUP
SEMI-FINAL, FIRST LEG
WEDNESDAY JANUARY 12, 2005

| CHELSEA | 0 |
| MANCHESTER UNITED | 0 |

ATTENDANCE: 41,492

Rooney made his first appearance of United's Carling Cup campaign in an exciting tie that had plenty of action but lacked the goals. Both teams felt they should have had penalties. It was a fast and furious first-half in which Rooney saw a header tipped round the post by Carlo Cudicini. It was hard for Rooney as both John Terry and Gallas kept a close eye on him. There was further controversy after the game when Chelsea boss José Mourinho suggested Sir Alex Ferguson had influenced the referee at half-time, believing the official favoured United after the break.

96 FA PREMIERSHIP
SATURDAY JANUARY 15, 2005

| LIVERPOOL | 0 |
| MANCHESTER UNITED | 1 |

ATTENDANCE: 44,183

MAN UNITED SCORER: Rooney 21

A superb 25-yard strike made Rooney the match-winner as Manchester United won at Anfield. Success was derived from the outstanding performances of Keane, Scholes and Fletcher, where United tilted the balance in midfield talent and thought in their favour. However, United were forced to rethink after Wes Brown was sent-off midway through the second-half. With the extra-man Liverpool began to attack with more conviction and

United protected their slender lead through a combination of tenacity and tactical fouling. Rooney was booked for a needless foul on Luis Garcia and was substituted in the last minute as Ferguson sought to ensure victory, and eleven men on the pitch, against their fierce north-west rivals.

WHAT THEY SAID ABOUT ROONEY: "There was a lot of hostility towards him. He did very well not to react." *Steve Bennett* (referee)

 ROONEY GOAL *(21 mins) Rooney exchanged passes with Ronaldo and unleashed a 25-yard shot that flew past Dudek at his near post and into the net.*

97 FA CUP
THIRD ROUND REPLAY
WEDNESDAY JANUARY 19, 2005

| EXETER CITY | 0 |
| MANCHESTER UNITED | 2 |

ATTENDANCE: 9,033

MAN UNITED SCORERS: Ronaldo 9, **Rooney 87**

After the embarrassment of being held to a goalless draw at Old Trafford by non-league Exeter City, Sir Alex Ferguson added more stars, including Rooney, to his side for the replay. Ronaldo opened the scoring after nine minutes and then followed a constant period of pressure on the Conference side's goal. Rooney and United had plenty of chances but Exeter keeper Paul Jones was outstanding and his defence managed to keep the ball out. Occasionally Exeter threatened the United goal but any hopes of taking the game to extra-time were ended by Rooney's 87th-minute goal.

 ROONEY GOAL *(87 mins) Rooney was put clear and he coolly rounded heroic goalkeeper Jones before slotting the ball home.*

JAN. 12 ▸ v CHELSEA

98 FA PREMIERSHIP
SATURDAY JANUARY 22, 2005

| MANCHESTER UNITED | 3 |
| ASTON VILLA | 1 |

ATTENDANCE: 67,859

MAN UNITED SCORERS: Ronaldo 8, Saha 69, Scholes 70 **ASTON VILLA SCORER:** Barry 53

Two goals in two second-half minutes confirmed the victory that Manchester United richly deserved after leading for so much of the game. From the outset United, and Rooney, were in excellent form. Rooney gave early warning with a dipping cross that Saha headed over. Keane set up Ronaldo who backed up that warning with a goal for United after eight minutes. Villa kept fighting but United went in search of more goals, with Rooney firing a vicious shot over the bar. Then eight minutes after the break Villa equalised through Gareth Barry – it was the first goal United had conceded in 816 minutes of football. This aberration of equality lasted 15 minutes until a Rooney cross was turned in by Saha and within a minute Scholes headed home Ronaldo's long ball. Rooney was not to complete the match. He had been the victim of a flying tackle from Lee Hendrie, for which the Villa man was booked, and after 73 minutes he was replaced by Giggs.

99 CARLING CUP
SEMI-FINAL SECOND LEG
WEDNESDAY JANUARY 26, 2005

| MANCHESTER UNITED | 1 |
| CHELSEA | 2 |

Chelsea win 2-1 on aggregate

ATTENDANCE: 67,000

MAN UNITED SCORER: Giggs 67
CHELSEA SCORERS: Lampard 29, Duff 85

An exciting Carling Cup tie in which Rooney was introduced on the hour for Quinton Fortune, who had a legitimate penalty appeal turned down as a battling Manchester United trailed 1-0. Rooney re-invigorated United and their dogged determination was rewarded when Giggs equalised shortly afterwards. However it was not to be United's night as Damien Duff scored an incredible winning goal with five minutes remaining and inflicted upon Ferguson his first domestic semi-final defeat.

WHAT THEY SAID ABOUT ROONEY: "I thought in the second-half we were a threat to them all the time, particularly when we brought Wayne Rooney on. He got into some great scoring positions and the keeper made some fantastic saves from Ronaldo, including one cleared off the line." *Sir Alex Ferguson*

WAYNE ROONEY'S STRIKE RATE	SEASON 04/05		
PREMIERSHIP		29 GAMES/11 GOALS	38%
FA CUP		6 GAMES/3 GOALS	50%
LEAGUE CUP	2 GAMES/0 GOALS		0%
EUROPE		6 GAMES/3 GOALS	50%
OVERALL		17 GOALS IN 43 GAMES	40%

"HE'S A PHENOMENAL TALENT AND HE'LL GET BETTER AND BETTER. I SAW HIM WHEN HE WAS 16. I SAID HE'LL BE ONE OF THE GREATS AND I HAVEN'T CHANGED MY MIND." GEORGE BEST

100 FA CUP
FOURTH ROUND
SATURDAY JANUARY 29, 2005

| **MANCHESTER UNITED** | 3 |
| **MIDDLESBROUGH** | 0 |

ATTENDANCE: 67,251

MAN UNITED SCORERS: O'Shea 10, **Rooney 67 82**

Rooney led the Manchester United charge to the fifth round with a magnificent performance that included two stunning goals. Rooney was uncontainable and could have finished with a bigger individual goal tally but for Middlesbrough keeper Mark Schwarzer. O'Shea had given the home side the lead after ten minutes and from that point on the seal was set, with Rooney in daring form.

WHAT THEY SAID ABOUT ROONEY: "In Wayne Rooney they had the difference on the day. He is a magnificent player." *Steve McClaren (Middlesbrough manager)*

"The boy has exceptional talent. The volley reminded me of van Basten but it was a marvellous overall performance from him and will do him the power of good." *Sir Alex Ferguson*

"You can't teach that kind of ability. To lob the keeper from so far out for the first one was amazing and then for the volley to go in as well, it's just great to see." *Roy Keane (Man United)*

WHAT ROONEY SAID: "Those are two of the best goals I've scored in my career. I'm really pleased with them."

⚽ **ROONEY GOAL** *(67 mins) From a staggering 40 yards out Rooney, having received a pass from Gary Neville, successfully lobbed Middlesbrough goalkeeper Schwarzer to score.*

⚽ **ROONEY GOAL** *(82 mins) The Boro goalkeeper was left with no chance against Rooney's spectacular volley from the edge of the area after Saha had flicked on Carroll's clearance.*

101 FA PREMIERSHIP
TUESDAY FEBRUARY 1, 2005

| **ARSENAL** | 2 |
| **MANCHESTER UNITED** | 4 |

ATTENDANCE: 38,164

MAN UNITED SCORERS: Giggs 18, Ronaldo 54 58, O'Shea 89. **ARSENAL SCORERS:** Vieira 8, Bergkamp 35

A high-tension, high-profile match that lived up to its billing with goals, poor tackling, ill-discipline, gamesmanship, haranguing the referee, the Keane-

FEB. 13 v MANCHESTER CITY

Patrick Vieira confrontation and good football too. Vieira gave Arsenal the lead that lasted ten minutes when Rooney pulled the ball back for Giggs to score with a half-volley that deflected off Ashley Cole. Dennis Bergkamp gave the Gunners a half-time lead but United battled back after the break, with Ronaldo equalising. Rooney was denied by the legs of goalkeeper Manuel Almunia before the break and then, in the second-half, he nearly gave United the lead with a shot that hit the post before Ronaldo struck again. Rooney, who was booked for persistent fouling, was perhaps fortunate not to be dismissed after swearing at referee Graham Poll. As it turned out, his team-mate Mikael Silvestre was shown the red card in the 69th minute after a tussle with Freddie Ljungberg. However, United's ten men hung on and O'Shea added a fourth goal in the 89th minute as the visitors ran out deserving winners.

102 FA PREMIERSHIP
SATURDAY FEBRUARY 5, 2005

| **MANCHESTER UNITED** | 2 |
| **BIRMINGHAM CITY** | 0 |

ATTENDANCE: 67,838

MAN UNITED SCORERS: Keane 55, **Rooney 78**

Manchester United appeared to be in sluggish mood in the first-half and the closest they came to scoring was when Rooney met Ferdinand's 35-yard floated pass with a header that Birmingham keeper Maik Taylor deflected onto the post. After the break captain Keane set up his side for victory with a goal after 55 minutes. Despite having a quiet game, Rooney popped up with 12 minutes remaining with a goal that assured the win.

⚽ **ROONEY GOAL** *(78 mins) Ronaldo intercepted Kenny Cunningham's poorly executed backpass, goalkeeper Taylor managed to knock the ball away but only into the path of Rooney who chipped the ball home.*

103 FA PREMIERSHIP
SUNDAY FEBRUARY 13, 2005

| **MANCHESTER CITY** | 0 |
| **MANCHESTER UNITED** | 2 |

ATTENDANCE: 47,111

MAN UNITED SCORERS: Rooney 68, Dunne (og) 75

Rooney was the difference in this Manchester derby, as he was responsible for both United goals, albeit aided by the unlucky Richard Dunne. Despite the high emotional intensity and expectancy of this fixture, Rooney was the epitome of calm, even when referee Steve Bennett appeared, to United fans, to be favouring the home side with his decisions. United persisted and duly gained their reward with a Rooney goal in the 68th minute, which glanced off Dunne on the way in. Shortly afterwards, Rooney was in sight of David James's goal and his attempt this time was inadvertently turned into the net by Dunne.

WHAT THEY SAID ABOUT ROONEY: "Like all great players, Wayne raises his game when it really matters." *Sir Alex Ferguson*

"He's a phenomenal talent and he'll get better and better. I saw him when he was 16. I said he'll be one of the greats and I haven't changed my mind." *George Best (Manchester United legend)*

WHAT ROONEY SAID: "I was upfront on my own, which is my preferred position."

⚽ **ROONEY GOAL** *(68 mins) Scholes and Keane combined to send Gary Neville clear on the right. Neville's cross created a near-post header by Rooney that glanced off City defender Dunne and into the net.*

WAYNE'S AWAY DAYS
The complete away record in English club competitions

BLACKBURN ROVERS
EWOOD PARK

FOR EVERTON
| 15 | 02/03 | Prem | Won 1-0 |
FOR MAN UNITED
| 149 | 05/06 | Lge Cup | Drew 1-1 |
| 154 | 05/06 | Prem | Lost 4-3 |

RECORD **W1 D1 L1 F0**

MANCHESTER UNITED
OLD TRAFFORD

FOR EVERTON
| 9 | 02/03 | Prem | Lost 3-0 |
| 56 | 03/04 | Prem | Lost 3-2 |

RECORD **W0 D0 L2 F0**

WIGAN ATHLETIC
JJB STADIUM

FOR MAN UNITED
| 159 | 05/06 | Prem | Won 2-1 |

RECORD **W1 D0 L0 F0**

LIVERPOOL
ANFIELD

FOR EVERTON
| 21 | 02/03 | Prem | Drew 0-0 |
| 63 | 03/04 | Prem | Drew 0-0 |
FOR MAN UNITED
96	04/05	Prem	Won 1-0
127	05/06	Prem	Drew 0-0
157	05/06	FA Cup	Lost 1-0

RECORD **W1 D3 L1 F1**

EVERTON
GOODISON PARK

FOR MAN UNITED
104	04/05	FA Cup	Won 2-0
114	04/05	Prem	Lost 1-0
122	05/06	Prem	Won 2-0

RECORD **W2 D0 L1 F1**

WREXHAM
THE RACECOURSE

FOR EVERTON
| 8 | 02/03 | Lge Cup | Won 3-0 |

RECORD **W1 D0 L0 F2**

BURTON ALBION
PIRELLI STADIUM

FOR MAN UNITED
| 148 | 05/06 | FA Cup | Drew 0-0 |

RECORD **W0 D1 L0 F0**

WOLVERHAMPTON WANDERERS
MOLINEUX

FOR EVERTON
| 75 | 03/04 | Prem | Lost 2-1 |
FOR MAN UNITED
| 153 | 05/06 | FA Cup | Won 3-0 |

RECORD **W1 D0 L1 F0**

SHREWSBURY TOWN
GAY MEADOW

FOR EVERTON
| 25 | 02/03 | FA Cup | Lost 2-1 |

RECORD **W0 D0 L1 F0**

NEUTRAL (CARDIFF)
MILLENIUM STADIUM

FOR MAN UNITED
113	04/05	FA Cup SF	Won 4-1
120	04/05	FA Cup F	Drew 0-0
			(lost on pens)
158	05/06	Lge Cup F	Won 4-0

RECORD **W2 D1 L0 F2**

ASTON VILLA
VILLA PARK

FOR EVERTON
| 7 | 02/03 | Prem | Lost 3-2 |
| 47 | 03/04 | Prem | Drew 0-0 |
FOR MAN UNITED
| 91 | 04/05 | Prem | Won 1-0 |
| 142 | 05/06 | Prem | Won 2-0 |

RECORD **W2 D1 L1 F1**

BIRMINGHAM CITY
ST ANDREWS

FOR EVERTON
| 22 | 02/03 | Prem | Drew 1-1 |
| 66 | 03/04 | Prem | Lost 3-0 |
FOR MAN UNITED
80	04/05	Prem	Drew 0-0
143	05/06	Lge Cup	Won 3-1
145	05/06	Prem	Drew 2-2

RECORD **W1 D3 L1 F1**

EXETER CITY
ST JAMES PARK

FOR MAN UNITED
| 97 | 04/05 | FA Cup | Won 2-0 |

RECORD **W1 D0 L0 F1**

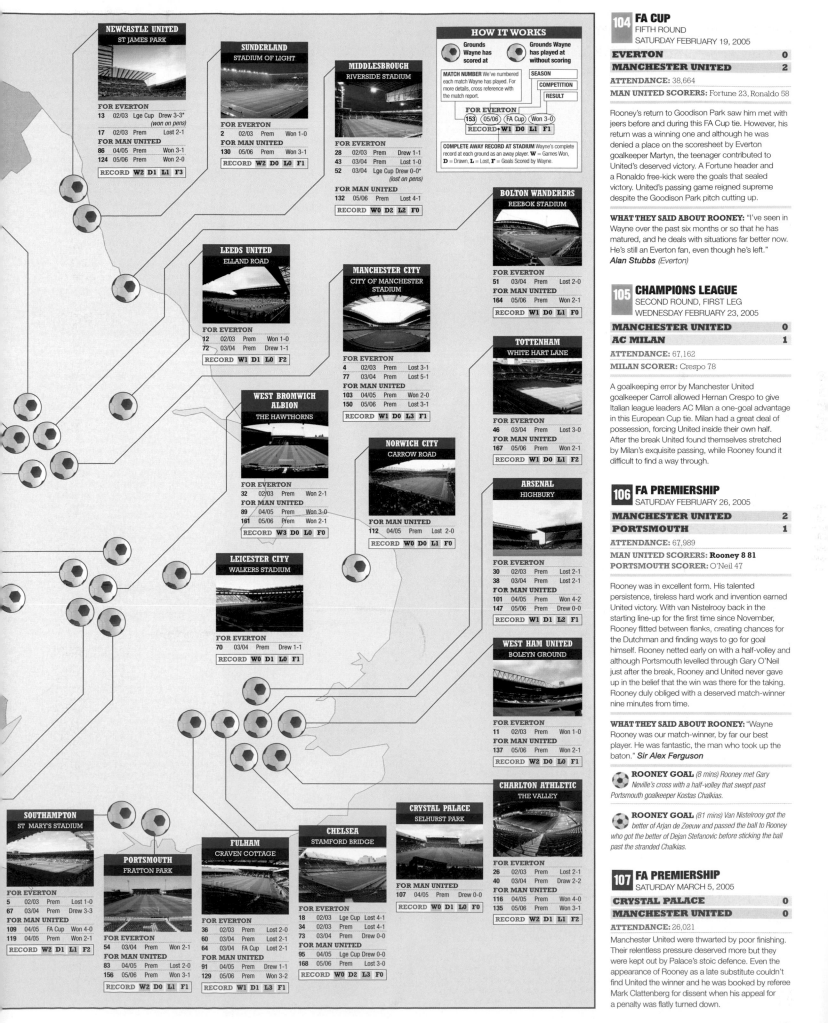

NEWCASTLE UNITED
ST JAMES PARK

FOR EVERTON

13	02/03	Lge Cup	Drew 3-3*
			(won on pens)
17	02/03	Prem	Lost 2-1

FOR MAN UNITED

| 86 | 04/05 | Prem | Won 3-1 |
| 124 | 05/06 | Prem | Won 2-0 |

RECORD W2 D1 L1 F3

SUNDERLAND
STADIUM OF LIGHT

FOR EVERTON

| 2 | 02/03 | Prem | Won 1-0 |

FOR MAN UNITED

| 130 | 05/06 | Prem | Won 3-1 |

RECORD W2 D0 L0 F1

MIDDLESBROUGH
RIVERSIDE STADIUM

FOR EVERTON

28	02/03	Prem	Drew 1-1
43	03/04	Prem	Lost 1-0
52	03/04	Lge Cup	Drew 0-0*
			(lost on pens)

FOR MAN UNITED

| 132 | 05/06 | Prem | Lost 4-1 |

RECORD W0 D2 L2 F0

HOW IT WORKS

⚽ Grounds Wayne has scored at
⚽ Grounds Wayne has played at without scoring

MATCH NUMBER We've numbered each match Wayne has played. For more details, cross reference with the match report.

SEASON
COMPETITION
RESULT

FOR EVERTON

| 153 | 05/06 | FA Cup | Won 3-0 |

RECORD W1 D0 L1 F1

COMPLETE AWAY RECORD AT STADIUM Wayne's complete record at each ground as an away player. **W** = Games Won, **D** = Drawn, **L** = Lost, **F** = Goals Scored by Wayne.

BOLTON WANDERERS
REEBOK STADIUM

FOR EVERTON

| 51 | 03/04 | Prem | Lost 2-0 |

FOR MAN UNITED

| 164 | 05/06 | Prem | Won 2-1 |

RECORD W1 D0 L1 F0

LEEDS UNITED
ELLAND ROAD

FOR EVERTON

| 12 | 02/03 | Prem | Won 1-0 |
| 72 | 03/04 | Prem | Drew 1-1 |

RECORD W1 D1 L0 F2

MANCHESTER CITY
CITY OF MANCHESTER STADIUM

FOR EVERTON

| 4 | 02/03 | Prem | Lost 3-1 |
| 77 | 03/04 | Prem | Lost 5-1 |

FOR MAN UNITED

| 103 | 04/05 | Prem | Won 2-0 |
| 150 | 05/06 | Prem | Lost 3-1 |

RECORD W1 D0 L3 F1

TOTTENHAM
WHITE HART LANE

FOR EVERTON

| 46 | 03/04 | Prem | Lost 3-0 |

FOR MAN UNITED

| 167 | 05/06 | Prem | Won 2-1 |

RECORD W1 D0 L1 F2

WEST BROMWICH ALBION
THE HAWTHORNS

FOR EVERTON

| 32 | 02/03 | Prem | Won 2-1 |

FOR MAN UNITED

| 89 | 04/05 | Prem | Won 3-0 |
| 161 | 05/06 | Prem | Won 2-1 |

RECORD W3 D0 L0 F0

NORWICH CITY
CARROW ROAD

FOR MAN UNITED

| 112 | 04/05 | Prem | Lost 2-0 |

RECORD W0 D0 L1 F0

ARSENAL
HIGHBURY

FOR EVERTON

| 30 | 02/03 | Prem | Lost 2-1 |
| 38 | 03/04 | Prem | Lost 2-1 |

FOR MAN UNITED

| 101 | 04/05 | Prem | Won 4-2 |
| 147 | 05/06 | Prem | Drew 0-0 |

RECORD W1 D1 L2 F1

LEICESTER CITY
WALKERS STADIUM

FOR EVERTON

| 70 | 03/04 | Prem | Drew 1-1 |

RECORD W0 D1 L0 F1

WEST HAM UNITED
BOLEYN GROUND

FOR EVERTON

| 11 | 02/03 | Prem | Won 1-0 |

FOR MAN UNITED

| 137 | 05/06 | Prem | Won 2-1 |

RECORD W2 D0 L0 F1

CHARLTON ATHLETIC
THE VALLEY

FOR EVERTON

| 26 | 02/03 | Prem | Lost 2-1 |
| 40 | 03/04 | Prem | Draw 2-2 |

FOR MAN UNITED

| 116 | 04/05 | Prem | Won 4-0 |
| 135 | 05/06 | Prem | Won 3-1 |

RECORD W2 D1 L1 F2

CRYSTAL PALACE
SELHURST PARK

FOR MAN UNITED

| 107 | 04/05 | Prem | Drew 0-0 |

RECORD W0 D1 L0 F0

CHELSEA
STAMFORD BRIDGE

FOR EVERTON

18	02/03	Lge Cup	Lost 4-1
34	02/03	Prem	Lost 4-1
73	03/04	Prem	Drew 0-0

FOR MAN UNITED

| 95 | 04/05 | Lge Cup | Drew 0-0 |
| 168 | 05/06 | Prem | Lost 3-0 |

RECORD W0 D2 L3 F0

FULHAM
CRAVEN COTTAGE

FOR EVERTON

| 36 | 02/03 | Prem | Lost 2-0 |
| 60 | 03/04 | FA Cup | Lost 2-1 |

FOR MAN UNITED

| 91 | 04/05 | Prem | Drew 1-1 |
| 129 | 05/06 | Prem | Won 3-2 |

RECORD W1 D1 L2 F1

PORTSMOUTH
FRATTON PARK

FOR EVERTON

| 54 | 03/04 | Prem | Won 2-1 |

FOR MAN UNITED

| 83 | 04/05 | Prem | Lost 2-0 |
| 156 | 05/06 | Prem | Won 3-1 |

RECORD W2 D0 L1 F1

SOUTHAMPTON
ST MARY'S STADIUM

FOR EVERTON

| 5 | 02/03 | Prem | Lost 1-0 |
| 67 | 03/04 | Prem | Drew 3-3 |

FOR MAN UNITED

| 109 | 04/05 | FA Cup | Won 4-0 |
| 119 | 04/05 | Prem | Won 2-1 |

RECORD W2 D1 L1 F2

---

104 FA CUP
FIFTH ROUND
SATURDAY FEBRUARY 19, 2005

| EVERTON | 0 |
| MANCHESTER UNITED | 2 |

ATTENDANCE: 38,664

MAN UNITED SCORERS: Fortune 23, Ronaldo 58

Rooney's return to Goodison Park saw him met with jeers before and during this FA Cup tie. However, his return was a winning one and although he was denied a place on the scoresheet by Everton goalkeeper Martyn, the teenager contributed to United's deserved victory. A Fortune header and a Ronaldo free-kick were the goals that sealed victory. United's passing game reigned supreme despite the Goodison Park pitch cutting up.

WHAT THEY SAID ABOUT ROONEY: "I've seen in Wayne over the past six months or so that he has matured, and he deals with situations far better now. He's still an Everton fan, even though he's left." *Alan Stubbs (Everton)*

105 CHAMPIONS LEAGUE
SECOND ROUND, FIRST LEG
WEDNESDAY FEBRUARY 23, 2005

| MANCHESTER UNITED | 0 |
| AC MILAN | 1 |

ATTENDANCE: 67,162

MILAN SCORER: Crespo 78

A goalkeeping error by Manchester United goalkeeper Carroll allowed Hernan Crespo to give Italian league leaders AC Milan a one-goal advantage in this European Cup tie. Milan had a great deal of possession, forcing United inside their own half. After the break United found themselves stretched by Milan's exquisite passing, while Rooney found it difficult to find a way through.

106 FA PREMIERSHIP
SATURDAY FEBRUARY 26, 2005

| MANCHESTER UNITED | 2 |
| PORTSMOUTH | 1 |

ATTENDANCE: 67,989

MAN UNITED SCORERS: Rooney 8 81
PORTSMOUTH SCORER: O'Neil 47

Rooney was in excellent form. His talented persistence, tireless hard work and invention earned United victory. With van Nistelrooy back in the starting line-up for the first time since November, Rooney flitted between flanks, creating chances for the Dutchman and finding ways to go for goal himself. Rooney netted early on with a half-volley and although Portsmouth levelled through Gary O'Neil just after the break, Rooney and United never gave up in the belief that the win was there for the taking. Rooney duly obliged with a deserved match-winner nine minutes from time.

WHAT THEY SAID ABOUT ROONEY: "Wayne Rooney was our match-winner, by far our best player. He was fantastic, the man who took up the baton." *Sir Alex Ferguson*

⚽ **ROONEY GOAL** *(8 mins) Rooney met Gary Neville's cross with a half-volley that swept past Portsmouth goalkeeper Kostas Chalkias.*

⚽ **ROONEY GOAL** *(81 mins) Van Nistelrooy got the better of Arjan de Zeeuw and passed the ball to Rooney who got the better of Dejan Stefanovic before sticking the ball past the stranded Chalkias.*

107 FA PREMIERSHIP
SATURDAY MARCH 5, 2005

| CRYSTAL PALACE | 0 |
| MANCHESTER UNITED | 0 |

ATTENDANCE: 26,021

Manchester United were thwarted by poor finishing. Their relentless pressure deserved more but they were kept out by Palace's stoic defence. Even the appearance of Rooney as a late substitute couldn't find United the winner and he was booked by referee Mark Clattenberg for dissent when his appeal for a penalty was flatly turned down.

MAY. 15   ▸ v SOUTHAMPTON

108 CHAMPIONS LEAGUE
SECOND ROUND, SECOND LEG
TUESDAY MARCH 8, 2005

AC MILAN	**1**
MANCHESTER UNITED	**0**

AC Milan win 2-0 on aggregate

ATTENDANCE: 78,957

MILAN SCORER: Crespo 61

Manchester United bowed out of the European Cup despite fielding a team weighted with attackers as Rooney, Ronaldo, Scholes and Giggs all supported targetman van Nistelrooy. Unfortunately, like all good Italian sides, Milan knew how to defend. When United did break through, the rare goalscoring opportunity was wasted. As in the first leg, Crespo scored for Milan and United, never looking likely to score three goals, were out – their dreams of repeating their 1999 triumph shattered.

109 FA CUP
QUARTER-FINAL
SATURDAY MARCH 12, 2005

SOUTHAMPTON	**0**
MANCHESTER UNITED	**4**

ATTENDANCE: 30,971

MAN UNITED SCORERS: Keane 2, Ronaldo 45, Scholes 48 87

Rooney was in superb form as Manchester United sailed their way into the semi-finals. Rooney helped create three of United's four goals and also hit the woodwork twice himself. Keane had given United the ideal start after two minutes. Further chances were created, including a shot from Rooney that was turned onto the bar. He also missed with a header from the rebound. Another Rooney shot was touched on to the post shortly before the break, but just when Southampton felt they were within reach of half-time with only a single goal deficit, Rooney powered forward, beating two defenders. He then passed to van Nistelrooy who set up Ronaldo to shoot home before the whistle was blown. Rooney and van Nistelrooy combined to present Scholes with a successful shot at goal after the break and the goalscoring was complete in the 87th minute when Rooney found van Nistelrooy on the wing and the Dutchman's cross was headed in by Scholes.

110 FA PREMIERSHIP
SATURDAY MARCH 19, 2005

MANCHESTER UNITED	**1**
FULHAM	**0**

ATTENDANCE: 67,959

MAN UNITED SCORER: Ronaldo 21

Manchester United were the better team and deserved the win but the overall performance was no great shakes with all but Ronaldo playing below their best for United. The home side were guilty of surrendering possession and not exploiting chances when they came their way, including a Rooney effort that he flicked wide of the mark from Ronaldo's cross. An average day for United but they won thanks to a couple of crucial saves by goalkeeper Howard and a first-half goal from Ronaldo, who scored from 20 yards out after Keane and Rooney had combined to set up the chance.

111 FA PREMIERSHIP
SATURDAY APRIL 2, 2005

MANCHESTER UNITED	**0**
BLACKBURN ROVERS	**0**

ATTENDANCE: 67,939

Flashes of brilliance from Rooney illuminated this frustrating goalless draw for Manchester United and the highlight was his spectacular 30-yard shot that thumped against the post. Skipper Keane also hit the woodwork later in the game but the visitors managed to hold on for a draw. They were helped in no small part by goalkeeper Brad Friedel, who was called upon to make a number of significant saves, among them a Rooney header that he managed to tip away. However, towards the end even Rooney's talented light began to fade and some of the crowd showed their dissatisfaction at the final whistle.

> **"IT WAS A FANTASTIC GOAL THAT CHANGED THE COURSE OF THE GAME. I WAS READY TO TAKE HIM OFF BECAUSE HE TOOK A KNOCK IN THE FIRST-HALF AND HE LOOKED LIKE HE WAS STRUGGLING. BUT HE IS ALWAYS A GOAL THREAT AND IT WAS A PHENOMENAL STRIKE CONSIDERING HE WAS INJURED AT THE TIME. I KEPT HIM ON AFTER THAT BECAUSE YOU NEVER KNOW WHEN HE MIGHT DO SOMETHING LIKE THAT AGAIN."** SIR ALEX FERGUSON

112 FA PREMIERSHIP
SATURDAY APRIL 9, 2005

| NORWICH CITY | 2 |
| MANCHESTER UNITED | 0 |

ATTENDANCE: 25,522

NORWICH SCORERS: Ashton 55, McKenzie 66

A goalless first-half against bottom-of-the-table Norwich saw Rooney brought on in the hope of giving United the lift they needed but, unfortunately, it was not to be his day. A foul on Tomas Helveg led to Dean Ashton heading home the resulting free-kick from David Bentley. Later Rooney was dispossessed by Youssef Safri, who instigated an attack that ended with Leon McKenzie volleying home. Rooney never gave up, tenaciously trying to turn the tide United's way, but an under-powered shot and a failed chip were not up to standard. In stoppage time Rooney did force goalkeeper Robert Green into a superb save, touching his shot over the bar.

113 FA CUP
SEMI-FINAL
SUNDAY APRIL 17, 2005

| MANCHESTER UNITED | 4 |
| NEWCASTLE UNITED | 1 |

ATTENDANCE: 69,280 (Millennium Stadium)

MAN UNITED SCORERS: van Nistelrooy 19 58, Scholes 45, Ronaldo 76
NEWCASTLE SCORER: Ameobi 59

Manchester United won through to the FA Cup Final without too much trouble. After Ronaldo had scored United's fourth goal, Ferguson rested Rooney, Ronaldo and Scholes with a 78th minute triple substitution. Rooney had chances to get on the scoresheet but Newcastle's over-worked goalkeeper Given kept him out.

114 FA PREMIERSHIP
WEDNESDAY APRIL 20, 2005

| EVERTON | 1 |
| MANCHESTER UNITED | 0 |

ATTENDANCE: 37,160

EVERTON SCORER: Ferguson 55

A disappointing return to Goodison for Rooney. Aside from the obvious jeering, United were also defeated and saw two of his team-mates – Gary Neville and Scholes – sent-off. Everton handled themselves well with Joseph Yobo having the measure and speed to deal with Rooney. In the eighth minute Rooney fired in a 25-yard shot that goalkeeper Martyn parried away. Ferguson, Rooney's former strike partner, scored the only goal of the game as United's patchy league form continued.

115 FA PREMIERSHIP
SUNDAY APRIL 24, 2005

| MANCHESTER UNITED | 2 |
| NEWCASTLE UNITED | 1 |

ATTENDANCE: 67,845

MAN UNITED SCORERS: **Rooney 57**, Brown 74
NEWCASTLE SCORER: Ambrose 27

Rooney scored another one of his spectacular strikes that was the outstanding highlight of this match by far. The goal was a prime example why he was to be

presented the PFA Young Player of the Year Award later that evening. Unfortunately, Manchester United's overall performance was not as spectacular as it was when the two side met in the FA Cup. They fell behind to a first-half Darren Ambrose goal and Rooney, himself, suffered a dead leg and boss Ferguson was preparing to substitute him just as he unleashed his unbelievable equaliser. Brown scored the winner from a Giggs corner and although Newcastle had looked the better outfit, it was the home side that earned the points.

WHAT THEY SAID ABOUT ROONEY: "It was a fantastic goal that changed the course of the game. I was ready to take him off because he took a knock in the first-half and he looked like he was struggling a bit. But he is always a goal threat and it was a phenomenal strike considering he was injured at the time. I kept him on after that because you never know when he might do something like that again."
Sir Alex Ferguson

 ROONEY GOAL (57 mins) *A fantastic goal. Rooney ran onto a Peter Ramage clearance and volleyed home from 25 yards. The ball dipped and swerved as it flew in.*

116 FA PREMIERSHIP
SUNDAY MAY 1, 2005

| CHARLTON ATHLETIC | 0 |
| MANCHESTER UNITED | 4 |

ATTENDANCE: 26,789

MAN UNITED SCORERS: Scholes 34, Fletcher 44, Smith 62, **Rooney 67**

Another easy victory for Manchester United with Rooney persistently causing all sorts of problems for the Charlton defence. From the kick-off, he had goalkeeper Stephan Andersen under pressure; it was a Rooney shot into a crowded goalmouth that caught Andersen off guard, the ball bounced off the keeper and Scholes ruthlessly exploited the error to give United the lead. Rooney and Scholes were both denied by Andersen before Fletcher made it 2-0 a minute before half-time. Smith and Rooney added further second-half goals and Rooney, with the FA Cup Final in mind, was immediately substituted to the relief of the Charlton defence.

 ROONEY GOAL *(67 mins) An excellent build up of neat passing ended with Rooney flicking the ball past stranded goalkeeper Andersen.*

117 FA PREMIERSHIP
SATURDAY MAY 7, 2005

| MANCHESTER UNITED | 1 |
| WEST BROMWICH ALBION | 1 |

ATTENDANCE: 67,827

MAN UNITED SCORER: Giggs 21
WEST BROM SCORER: Earnshaw (pen) 62

This draw meant that Manchester United were unlikely to secure the runners-up spot they craved. United, who took the lead from a Giggs free-kick, squandered many chances and were made to pay when Robert Earnshaw converted a controversially awarded penalty for West Brom. Rooney, who started on the bench, was brought on and he was determined to find a winner, trying an over-ambitious

goal attempt from inside his own half and then forcing goalkeeper Tomasz Kuszczak into two fine saves before the final whistle.

118 FA PREMIERSHIP
TUESDAY MAY 10, 2005

| MANCHESTER UNITED | 1 |
| CHELSEA | 3 |

ATTENDANCE: 67,832

MAN UNITED SCORER: van Nistelrooy 8
CHELSEA SCORERS: Tiago 18, Gudjohnsen, J Cole 80

Rooney and the Manchester United team formed a guard of honour for the new Premiership champions Chelsea at the end of this game. Chelsea's 3-1 win had broken United's record for the most Premiership points and the most Premiership wins. Rooney was as busy as ever in this game, helping to give United the lead early on and went close to scoring himself. But the visitors were confident and competent enough to overturn a single goal deficit and ran out worthy 3-1 winners.

119 FA PREMIERSHIP
SUNDAY MAY 15, 2005

| SOUTHAMPTON | 1 |
| MANCHESTER UNITED | 2 |

ATTENDANCE: 32,066

MAN UNITED SCORERS: Fletcher 19, van Nistelrooy 63
SOUTHAMPTON SCORER: O'Shea (og) 10

United's Premiership season ended with a 2-1 win at Southampton, leaving them in third place in the final Premiership table. United started slowly, gifting the home side a goal, before their own quality took control. With the FA Cup Final just a week away, Rooney was substituted in the 73rd minute by Saha and United went through the motions for an expected victory as Saints were relegated.

120 FA CUP
FINAL
SATURDAY MAY 21, 2005

| ARSENAL | 0 |
| MANCHESTER UNITED | 0 |

After extra-time; Arsenal win 5-4 on penalties

ATTENDANCE: 71,826 (Millennium Stadium)

Penalties (Manchester United first):
Van Nistelrooy 0-1; Lauren 1-1; Scholes (saved) 1-1; Ljungberg 1-2; Ronaldo 2-2; van Persie 2-3; Rooney 3-3; Cole 3-4; Keane 4-4; Vieira 4-5

An FA Cup Final in which Manchester United dominated, hitting the woodwork twice. Rooney was Man of the Match but Arsenal ended up winning the trophy after a penalty shoot-out. Rooney was involved in all the key action and was soon fouled by Ashley Cole, who got the first booking of the afternoon. Rooney then had a shot blocked by goalkeeper Lehmann, and although Ferdinand was on hand to shoot home the rebound, the goal was ruled offside. Rooney tested Lehmann again after good work by van Nistelrooy and was proving a menace to Arsenal as he beat two defenders before being brought down. The resulting free-kick saw him fire the dead ball over the bar. United had thrown everything at Arsenal, but a combination of Lehmann, the woodwork and poor finishing prevented them getting onto the scoresheet. Extra-time saw more goalmouth action and ended up with the sending-off of Arsenal's Jose Antonio Reyes. As the match went to penalties, Scholes saw Manchester United's second spot kick saved by Lehmann. All the other penalties were converted, including Rooney's effort which was blasted into the top corner of the net, sending Lehmann the wrong way.

WHAT THEY SAID ABOUT ROONEY: "You could toss a coin for Man of the Match out of Wayne Rooney and Cristiano Ronaldo, because they were great, the pair of them. There's a great future for those boys." *Sir Alex Ferguson*

121 CHAMPIONS LEAGUE
THIRD QUALIFYING ROUND FIRST LEG
TUESDAY AUGUST 9, 2005

MANCHESTER UNITED	3
DEBRECENI VSC	0

ATTENDANCE: 51,701

MAN UNITED SCORERS: Rooney 7, van Nistelrooy 49, Ronaldo 63

Manchester United, playing 4-3-3 with Rooney, van Nistelrooy and Ronaldo forming a three-man attack of width and movement, easily overcame the Hungarian champions. Rooney was as excellent as ever, giving United the lead after seven minutes and then helping to create a goal each for his attacking colleagues. He set up van Nistelrooy for a low shot into the bottom corner shortly after half-time and the two players combined in the 63rd minute for Ronaldo to net from close range.

WHAT THEY SAID ABOUT ROONEY: "You always hope to get an early start and Wayne took it very well. He got a little break off the defender but nonetheless you've got to put it away." *Sir Alex Ferguson*

ROONEY GOAL *(7 mins): The ball moved fluently from Keane on to Ronaldo and then to Rooney. Rooney's short pass for van Nistelrooy saw an attempted clearance deflect back to Rooney who fired a right foot shot past goalkeeper Norbert Csernyanski.*

122 FA PREMIERSHIP
SATURDAY AUGUST 13, 2005

EVERTON	0
MANCHESTER UNITED	2

ATTENDANCE: 38,610

MAN UNITED SCORERS: van Nistelrooy 43, **Rooney 46**

Rooney was key to inflicting a 2-0 defeat upon his former club at Goodison Park. He created a goal just before half-time for van Nistelrooy, when he played in the forward-running O'Shea whose cross was blasted home from six yards out. After just 29 seconds of the second-half Rooney scored the easiest of goals himself to kill the game for United.

WHAT THEY SAID ABOUT ROONEY: "He's a fantastic player at a fantastic club and it's frightening to say it but he can only get better. He's already achieved a lot but there's definitely more to

come. I think he's starting to believe he's one of the best players in the world and he's putting in the performances to justify that."
David Weir (Everton captain)

"Wayne was the Man of the Match as far as I'm concerned. They didn't give him the award simply because this was his return to Everton – and I don't think that's fair. He was fantastic. He took his goal well and I was pleased with his performance because it can be tricky going back to your old club." *Sir Alex Ferguson*

WHAT ROONEY SAID: "It was probably the easiest goal I've ever scored and it was a goal that killed them off really. We were just so keen to get off to a winning start."

ROONEY GOAL *(46 mins): Yobo bizarrely played a pass across his own area behind unsighted centre-half Weir. Rooney then dashed in and slid the ball home past stranded goalkeeper Martyn.*

123 FA PREMIERSHIP
SATURDAY AUGUST 20, 2005

MANCHESTER UNITED	1
ASTON VILLA	0

ATTENDANCE: 67,934

MAN UNITED SCORER: van Nistelrooy 66

Manchester United were in unstoppable form and perhaps should have won by a greater margin than a single van Nistelrooy goal in the second-half. United goalkeeper van der Sar had very little to do as Rooney, who was later subbed by Smith, and his fellow attackers, sought to break through Villa's dense defence. They did, finally, and should have had more than just the one goal.

124 FA PREMIERSHIP
SUNDAY AUGUST 28, 2005

NEWCASTLE UNITED	0
MANCHESTER UNITED	2

ATTENDANCE: 52,327

MAN UNITED SCORERS: Rooney 66, van Nistelrooy 90

Rooney and van Nistelrooy were the key figures behind a Manchester United win of perseverance and determination. Although Newcastle were a minimal threat, the visitors still had to work hard for

their victory. Rooney broke the deadlock in the second-half with a route-one goal and then in the last minute van Nistelrooy seized on a loose ball, after Jean-Alain Boumsong failed to control, to fire home.

WHAT THEY SAID ABOUT ROONEY: "Wayne is world class and there is still a lot to come from him, but the team is not only Rooney. He played well at Newcastle by scoring the first and making the second." *Edwin van der Sar*

"The second goal was a great example for any young person who wants to get to the very top. He defended in the right-back position, won the ball, played the pass and continued a 50-yard run to play Ruud in. He showed great work ethic, and any young, great player who can do that is a great example for others." *Sir Alex Ferguson*

ROONEY GOAL *(66 mins) Goalkeeper van der Sar's long punt downfield saw the ball bounce behind defender Boumsong and Rooney set off at pace to latch onto the ball and fire the shot beyond Given.*

125 FA PREMIERSHIP
SATURDAY SEPTEMBER 10, 2005

MANCHESTER UNITED	1
MANCHESTER CITY	1

ATTENDANCE: 67,839

MAN UNITED SCORER: van Nistelrooy 45
MAN CITY SCORER: Barton 76

This Manchester derby was sedated by a City side that knew how to blunt the United attack. United had plenty of possession and spent the majority of the time in the City half but with little to show in the final third. There was a dependence on Rooney to make something happen and he was United's best player but with minimum goalscoring success. Partner van Nistelrooy had given United the lead on the stroke of half-time and it looked enough until Joey Barton equalised in the final quarter. City striker Andy Cole could have scored the winner with the game's last attack in stoppage time, but van der Sar came to the rescue to deny the former United man.

126 CHAMPIONS LEAGUE
GROUP D
WEDNESDAY SEPTEMBER 14, 2005

VILLARREAL	0
MANCHESTER UNITED	0

ATTENDANCE: 22,000

Rooney was sent off in the 64th minute for two bookable offences. The first was for a foul on Villarreal centre-back Quique Alvarez, where the defender's theatrical response to Rooney's contact certainly contributed to the yellow card. This riled the 19 year old, who questioned the referee's decision and followed it up with a sarcastic clap of the hands that led the Danish official to produce a second yellow card for dissent. The dismissal came at a time when United were finally bringing the home side under control but that went as ten-man United were forced to defend with resilience for the point.

WHAT THEY SAID ABOUT ROONEY: "Wayne reacts to what he considers are injustices. He felt it was a wrongful booking but the fact is you can't applaud a referee like that. He's a young lad, 19 years old – we hope that, with maturity, these things will evaporate. The important thing is to retain his good points and eradicate all the bad ones, and that's our job." *Sir Alex Ferguson*

127 PREMIERSHIP
SUNDAY SEPTEMBER 18, 2005

LIVERPOOL	0
MANCHESTER UNITED	0

ATTENDANCE: 44,917

With so much talent on the field it was disappointing that this match saw both teams effectively cancel each other out. There were glimpses of the gifted players such as Rooney but the reality was that goalkeepers Jose Manuel Reina and van der Sar had little to bother them.

WHAT THEY SAID ABOUT ROONEY: "It's normal for someone like Rooney to have that passion if you have a player with this quality. Normally he has a strong character because you can't play at this level as a teenager without one. I had Raul at Real Madrid when he was 17. He wasn't the quickest, not the best in the air, nor the strongest. But he had a very strong mentality. A strong character. So you need to support the player."
Rafael Benitez (Liverpool manager)

128 FA PREMIERSHIP
SATURDAY SEPTEMBER 24, 2005

MANCHESTER UNITED	1
BLACKBURN ROVERS	2

ATTENDANCE: 67,765

MAN UNITED SCORER: van Nistelrooy 67
BLACKBURN SCORERS: Pedersen 33 81

Rooney, who did not finish the previous game at Liverpool, found himself on the bench until the 54th minute of this match. Blackburn had taken a 33rd minute lead through Morten Pedersen and towards the end of the half the disgruntled Old Trafford crowd were chanting Rooney's name. When he did appear, in place of Fletcher, he went on to create an equaliser for van Nistelrooy midway through the second-half. However, it was not to be a complete transformation in United's fortunes as Pedersen struck again with nine minutes remaining.

129 FA PREMIERSHIP
SATURDAY OCTOBER 1, 2005

FULHAM	2
MANCHESTER UNITED	3

ATTENDANCE: 21,862

MAN UNITED SCORERS: van Nistelrooy (pen) 17 45, **Rooney 18**. **FULHAM SCORERS:** John 2, Jensen 28

Manchester United's attack won the day, covering the frailties of their defensive play. A five-goal first-half saw United overcome an early goal but it wasn't until the all-important fifth goal that the game was decided in favour of United. Rooney, who played superbly throughout, and van Nistelrooy spearheaded a 4-4-2 formation, but the immediate success of this was not apparent when Collins John opened the scoring after two minutes. Two quick goals in the 17th and 18th minutes showed United's offensive power with van Nistelrooy converting a penalty and Rooney also finding the net to give United the lead. Ten minutes later Fulham midfielder Claus Jensen levelled, but on the stroke of half-time van Nistelrooy struck again to net what proved to be the winner after a scintillating move from defence to attack.

WHAT THEY SAID ABOUT ROONEY: "He's a young player and he has an exceptional talent as everybody knows. But his temperament is always

OCT. 15 v SUNDERLAND

there to be questioned by people as he plays his football on the edge... It's a cliché but it's true that Wayne wouldn't be the same player if you took the edge away. I would rather have the player we have now. It's not as though he is not making an effort. He is." *Rio Ferdinand*

 ROONEY GOAL *(18 mins) A neat passing build-up culminated in Rooney firing home past Mark Crossley.*

130 FA PREMIERSHIP
SATURDAY OCTOBER 15, 2005

SUNDERLAND	1
MANCHESTER UNITED	3

ATTENDANCE: 39,085

MAN UNITED SCORERS: Rooney 40, van Nistelrooy 76, Rossi 87
SUNDERLAND SCORER: Elliott 82

Sunderland's approach was to play a high tempo game but it was ultimately unsustainable. United, inspired by Rooney, proved to be the better side over the game despite a frustrating first-half. Rooney opened the scoring in the 40th minute and then set up van Nistelrooy to make it 2-0 late in the second-half. Sunderland did briefly halve the deficit until substitute Giuseppe Rossi, who had replaced the Dutchman, made it 3-1 near the end.

WHAT THEY SAID ABOUT ROONEY: "England are looking for Rooney to win the World Cup for them and you can see why." *Mick McCarthy (Sunderland manager)*

ROONEY GOAL *(40 mins): Ji-Sung Park delivered a penetrative pass for Rooney to pick up just inside his own half. He then raced forward leaving Sunderland defenders in his wake before rounding Sunderland goalkeeper Kelvin Davis and turning the ball into the net.*

131 FA PREMIERSHIP
SATURDAY OCTOBER 22, 2005

MANCHESTER UNITED	1
TOTTENHAM HOTSPUR	1

ATTENDANCE: 67,856

MAN UNITED SCORERS: Silvestre 7
TOTTENHAM SCORER: Jenas 72

Despite all of United's endeavours they produced an ordinary performance in a run-of-the-mill scoring draw against a difficult-to-beat Spurs. Silvestre gave the home side an early lead and Jermaine Jenas equalised in the 72nd minute. United out-manned Spurs in midfield but appeared to be reliant on Rooney to produce something out of the blue.

On this occasion, he popped up infrequently and the match played out to an inevitable draw, which delighted the visiting supporters.

132 FA PREMIERSHIP
SATURDAY OCTOBER 29, 2005

MIDDLESBROUGH	4
MANCHESTER UNITED	1

ATTENDANCE: 30,579

MAN UNITED SCORER: Ronaldo 90
MIDDLESBROUGH SCORERS: Mendieta 2 78, Hasselbaink 25, Yakubu (pen) 45

A crushing, disappointing defeat for Manchester United in which only Rooney and substitute Ronaldo came out with any credit. Ronaldo's stoppage time consolation was United's 1,000th Premiership goal, but the result sent shockwaves through the League.

133 CHAMPIONS LEAGUE
GROUP D
WEDNESDAY NOVEMBER 2, 2005

LILLE	1
MANCHESTER UNITED	0

ATTENDANCE: 65,000

LILLE SCORER: Acimovic 38

A rather anaemic game decided by Milenko Acimovic's 38th minute drive. It was Lille's first win of the group. United's best chance came 20 minutes later when a Rooney corner was met by Ronaldo's shoulder and directed off the underside of the bar before being cleared off the line. Near the end of a frustrating game Rooney was booked for dissent as United's season threatened to implode.

134 FA PREMIERSHIP
SUNDAY NOVEMBER 6, 2005

MANCHESTER UNITED	1
CHELSEA	0

ATTENDANCE: 67,864

MAN UNITED SCORER: Fletcher 31

Fletcher's first goal of the season was enough to earn Manchester United victory and end Chelsea's 40-match unbeaten run. Rooney was as hard-working as ever and United gave a solid team performance of concentration and diligence in a match of intense atmosphere and variable quality. Chelsea created almost twice as many goal attempts as the home side but they didn't create any goals.

WHAT THEY SAID ABOUT ROONEY: "He has the potential to be a legendary player. One of Pelé's great

qualities was that he could take any situation in his stride. From what I have seen of Wayne, I think he can too." *Zico (Japan coach)*

"Wayne is a fantastic player... and he's going to be a massive player for Manchester United and England for years to come. There are so many positives about him, so many more positives to come out. He's a real natural talent. I love him as a player and he's a great man, too." *Frank Lampard (Chelsea)*

135 FA PREMIERSHIP
SATURDAY NOVEMBER 19, 2005

CHARLTON ATHLETIC	1
MANCHESTER UNITED	3

ATTENDANCE: 26,730

MAN UNITED SCORERS: Smith 37, van Nistelrooy 70 85
CHARLTON SCORER: Ambrose 65

In the first match of the post-Keane era, it was Rooney who inspired United to a 3-1 victory. The visitors were more fluid in their performance and Charlton couldn't cope. Smith and Scholes established a foothold in midfield, leaving Rooney to roam and inflict damage. As early as the eighth minute he played a superb pass that had van Nistelrooy through but the Dutchman's shot was cleared off the line by Hermann Hreidarsson. When the first goal came, Rooney was involved; Ronaldo opened up the left giving Rooney possession of the ball and universal defensive attention from the Charlton defensive. This allowed him to feed the ball to the unmarked Fletcher, who set up Smith to score. Ambrose equalised in the 65th minute but it was a short-lived glimmer of hope as Rooney unleashed his talent again with a devastating run down the left from inside his own half, eluding four opponents as he did so. In space he chipped the ball to van Nistelrooy who chested it down before thumping it home. The Dutchman struck again with five minutes remaining but Rooney was the Man of the Match.

136 CHAMPIONS LEAGUE
GROUP D
TUESDAY NOVEMBER 22, 2005

MANCHESTER UNITED	0
VILLARREAL	0

ATTENDANCE: 67,471

Manchester United managed just two attempts on target throughout the game – this was no reflection on Rooney and van Nistelrooy but on a midfield that seemed bereft of ideas. The result seriously put United's continued presence in Europe's elite competition in doubt.

WHAT THEY SAID ABOUT ROONEY: "He's undoubtedly one of the most talented young players in the world. Rooney has shown at Euro 2004 and in the Champions League that he can perform on football's major stages."
Jurgen Klinsmann (Germany coach)

137 FA PREMIERSHIP
SUNDAY NOVEMBER 27, 2005

WEST HAM UNITED	1
MANCHESTER UNITED	2

ATTENDANCE: 34,755

MAN UNITED SCORERS: Rooney 47, O'Shea 56
WEST HAM SCORER: Harewood 2

The sad death of former Manchester United legend George Best was marked by one minute of heartfelt applause. Then followed a performance of a modern genius in the form of the gifted Rooney. West Ham took an early lead but then allowed the United striker to dominate the game. Hungry for the ball, he drove United forward but he and his team-mates were

denied by former goalkeeping colleague Carroll. The equaliser, just after the break, inevitably came from Rooney while the winning goal also came from his corner that O'Shea headed home. It was the United number eight's day again.

WHAT ROONEY SAID: "George [Best] was one of the best players in the world, if not the best. I'm sure I've a long way to go before I get to those heights, but hopefully one day people will talk about me like that."

ROONEY GOAL *(47 mins): Tomas Repka's attempted clearance was blocked and the ball came to Park who slipped the ball through to Rooney. He evaded Danny Gabbidon's challenge before shooting home.*

138 FA PREMIERSHIP
SATURDAY DECEMBER 3, 2005

MANCHESTER UNITED	3
PORTSMOUTH	0

ATTENDANCE: 67,684

MAN UNITED SCORERS: Scholes 20, **Rooney 79**, van Nistelrooy 84

Portsmouth were no problem for Rooney and Manchester United. Ferguson's men showed moments of exquisite one-touch play and mesmerising movement that left the visitors floundering. Once Scholes opened the scoring after 20 minutes the outcome was never in doubt, although in terms of goals, that was not confirmed until Rooney and van Nistelrooy decided the clash in a six-minute spell late in the game.

ROONEY GOAL *(79 mins): Rooney pounced on an error by Andy O'Brien before hitting the ball past rookie goalkeeper Jamie Ashdown.*

139 CHAMPIONS LEAGUE
GROUP D
WEDNESDAY DECEMBER 7, 2005

BENFICA	2
MANCHESTER UNITED	1

ATTENDANCE: 61,000

MAN UNITED SCORER: Scholes 6
BENFICA SCORERS: Geovanni 16, Beto 31

Manchester United bowed out of the European Cup and also missed out on the consolation of a UEFA Cup spot following this disappointing 2-1 defeat by Benfica. Despite the ideal start of Scholes's sixth-minute goal, it was to be a below-par performance, with even Rooney lacking the invention to get his side out of trouble. He was presented with a couple of half-chances but they were blocked by Luisao. Goals from Geovanni and Beto won it for the Portuguese side.

140 FA PREMIERSHIP
SUNDAY DECEMBER 11, 2005

MANCHESTER UNITED	1
EVERTON	1

ATTENDANCE: 67,831

MAN UNITED SCORER: Giggs 15
EVERTON SCORER: McFadden 7

The failure to take the abundance of chances they created resulted in Manchester United dropping two points at Old Trafford. United dominated, particularly in the first-half, with Rooney among the culprits unable to beat Everton goalkeeper Richard Wright. Everton had taken a surprise lead early on, Giggs then equalised after 15 minutes but, despite the driving play of Rooney, the one-way traffic reaped nothing more. After the break United still held the edge although their play never returned to the heights of the first-half.

"HE'S UNDOUBTEDLY ONE OF THE MOST TALENTED YOUNG PLAYERS IN THE WORLD. ROONEY HAS SHOWN AT EURO 2004 AND IN THE CHAMPIONS LEAGUE HE CAN PERFORM ON FOOTBALL'S MAJOR STAGES." JURGEN KLINSMANN

"ROONEY WILL BE ONE OF THE BIG PLAYERS IN THE WORLD CUP. I LOOK AT HIM AND THINK THAT MAYBE HE HAS ENOUGH ABILITY TO BE A BRAZILIAN... BUT NOT QUITE!" RONALDINHO

141 FA PREMIERSHIP
WEDNESDAY DECEMBER 14, 2005

MANCHESTER UNITED	4
WIGAN ATHLETIC	0

ATTENDANCE: 67,793

MAN UNITED SCORERS: Ferdinand 29, **Rooney 34 55**, Van Nistelrooy (pen) 70

Rooney was back to his superlative best as Manchester United stormed back to comprehensively outclass and thrash Wigan. He got on the scoresheet twice, netting United's second and third goals. He also hit the crossbar, albeit in the context of missing an open goal at very close range, and forced the visiting goalkeeper Mike Pollitt into some crucial saves. Ferdinand opened the scoring with his first goal for the club and van Nistelrooy also converted a penalty for the fourth goal, but the tally could have been much higher for both Rooney individually and United as a team.

WHAT THEY SAID ABOUT ROONEY: "Rooney will be one of the big players in the World Cup. I look at him and think that maybe he has enough ability to be a Brazilian... but not quite!" ***Ronaldinho***

⚽ **ROONEY GOAL** *(34 mins) Rooney, inside the Wigan penalty area, received a pass from Fletcher and despite being put under pressure by Matt Jackson, he overcame the Wigan man's attempted tackle before beating Leighton Baines and slotting the ball inside goalkeeper Pollitt's near post.*

⚽ **ROONEY GOAL** *(55 mins) Van Nistelrooy's left-foot pinpoint pass picked out Rooney, who raced clean through, inducing Pollitt to commit himself, before knocking the ball over the grounded goalkeeper and into the back of the net.*

142 FA PREMIERSHIP
SATURDAY DECEMBER 17, 2005

ASTON VILLA	0
MANCHESTER UNITED	2

ATTENDANCE: 37,128

MAN UNITED SCORERS: van Nistelrooy 10, **Rooney 51**

Villa tried to contain United but the plan failed and they were fortunate not to be routed. Van Nistelrooy and Rooney found the net for United but it could have been a lot more. Scholes, Giggs, Park, van Nistelrooy and Rooney all forced saves from Sorensen or were not far off the target. Park hit the woodwork and Rooney, with a spectacular overhead volley, forced a superb save from the Danish goalkeeper. United were more imaginative and simply outclassed Villa, with Rooney once again having an excellent, influential game.

WHAT THEY SAID ABOUT ROONEY: "The second goal was important to us. I think there will be a lot more goals from Ruud and Wayne – they are becoming a combination now." ***Sir Alex Ferguson***

⚽ **ROONEY GOAL** *(51 mins): Rooney fired home with a low drive past goalkeeper Sorensen after good work from van Nistelrooy and Park.*

143 CARLING CUP
QUARTER-FINAL
TUESDAY DECEMBER 20, 2005

BIRMINGHAM CITY	1
MANCHESTER UNITED	3

ATTENDANCE: 20,454

MAN UNITED SCORERS: Saha 46 63, Park 50
BIRMINGHAM SCORER: Jarosik 75

Rooney started on the bench as Ferguson made six changes to the side that won at Villa Park three days before. Rooney watched as Rossi, Ronaldo and Saha all went close in the first-half as United dominated. Rooney replaced Rossi at half-time and within 40 seconds United had taken the lead through Saha. Park made it 2-0 four minutes later and the match was wrapped up for United by Saha's second in the 63rd minute. Rooney's presence helped United turn their advantage into goals but it was Saha and Park who were the real stars of the night.

WHAT THEY SAID ABOUT ROONEY: "I thought we maybe should have had a couple of goals in the first-half but in the second-half we had a great start. I felt probably bringing Wayne on, the presence of him helped." *Sir Alex Ferguson*

144 FA PREMIERSHIP
MONDAY DECEMBER 26, 2005

MANCHESTER UNITED	3
WEST BROMWICH ALBION	0

ATTENDANCE: 67,792

MAN UNITED SCORERS: Scholes 35, Ferdinand 45, van Nistelrooy 63

Rooney found himself being man-marked by West Brom defender Paul Robinson. It seemed an effective ploy as United were restricted to half-chances for the first 30 minutes of the match. Then a sickening collision of heads between Robinson and team-mate Thomas Gaardsoe resulted in the left-back being stretchered off. Rooney, now free of his designated marker, was allowed to roam and influence play, bringing panic to the Albion defence. United imposed themselves more in the final third as a result and the goals came. Scholes opened the scoring in the 35th minute and Ferdinand headed home a Giggs corner in the sixth minute of first-half injury time. Van Nistelrooy added a third to end the game as a spectacle.

145 FA PREMIERSHIP
WEDNESDAY DECEMBER 28, 2005

BIRMINGHAM CITY	2
MANCHESTER UNITED	2

ATTENDANCE: 28,459

MAN UNITED SCORERS: van Nistelrooy 4, **Rooney 54**. **BIRMINGHAM SCORERS:** Clapham 18, Pandiani 78

A quiet start for Rooney but as the game wore on he became a persistent threat, particularly in the second-half. His influence contributed to a dominant spell after the break that could have reaped more than the single goal that he scored. Birmingham's Jamie Clapham had cancelled out van Nistelrooy's opener and Rooney went close with a shot to reiterate his dangerous reputation before he finally restored United's lead in the 54th minute. It looked as if Rooney's strike would prove to be the winner but Birmingham, who had battled throughout to match the visitors, levelled through Walter Pandiani with 12 minutes remaining. Moments before the equaliser, Rooney had delivered an excellent chip that just grazed the crossbar, which would have put the game out of Birmingham's reach. It was a disappointing outcome for United against the Premiership strugglers.

⚽ **ROONEY GOAL** *(54 mins) Van Nistelrooy let Smith's low centre continue into the path of Rooney who fired his shot out of the reach of Blues goalkeeper Maik Taylor and into the net to make the score 2-1.*

146 FA PREMIERSHIP
SATURDAY DECEMBER 31, 2005

MANCHESTER UNITED	4
BOLTON WANDERERS	1

ATTENDANCE: 67,858

MAN UNITED SCORERS: N'Gotty (og) 8, Saha 44, Ronaldo 67 90 **BOLTON SCORER:** Speed 33

Ferguson got a great 64th birthday present from his team with a stunning performance and victory over Bolton. Rooney was once again the unstoppable, influential force. He and Saha were a superb combination in attack, while Ronaldo grabbed the headlines with two goals and saw two more efforts hit the post. Rooney saw one shot narrowly go over the crossbar and then another narrowly wide of the post before unleashing a 20-yard strike that was saved by Jussi Jaaskelainen in the 29th minute. Rooney also set up Ronaldo's first goal before receiving a standing ovation for his performance when he was substituted by Park after 79 minutes.

WHAT THEY SAID ABOUT ROONEY: "He terrified us. I think I've just seen one of the most outstanding young players I've ever seen. He not only frightened us with his skill but also his work-rate and his physical attributes. He was brushing off our players and some of his touches were just magnificent. You can plan all you want but when a player of his ability is in that sort of mood what can you do?" *Sam Allardyce*

147 FA PREMIERSHIP
TUESDAY JANUARY 3, 2006

ARSENAL	0
MANCHESTER UNITED	0

ATTENDANCE: 38,313

A more restrained affair than previous encounters, with Arsenal dominating the first-half but not creating anything substantial. Rooney and van Nistelrooy were quiet until the Dutchman forced a superb save from Lehmann just before the break. United came more into the game in the second-half with Rooney going close with a looping header early on. He was one of five players booked but it was a game never in danger of boiling over like previous encounters.

148 FA CUP THIRD ROUND
SUNDAY JANUARY 8, 2006

BURTON ALBION	0
MANCHESTER UNITED	0

ATTENDANCE: 6,191

Non-league Conference outfit Burton Albion, managed by Nigel Clough and some 104 places below Manchester United, held Ferguson's side to an embarrassing goalless draw that could have been even worse. Rooney watched from the bench as Bardsley twice cleared off the line for United and Brown repeatedly stopping Burton with timely interceptions, tackles and blocks. Rooney appeared

JAN. 3 > v ARSENAL

in the 58th minute replacing young Italian Rossi and tried to break the deadlock with an overhead kick. He also provoked goalkeeper Saul Deeney into two decent saves but it remained goalless.

149 CARLING CUP
SEMI-FINAL FIRST LEG
WEDNESDAY JANUARY 11, 2006

| BLACKBURN ROVERS | 1 |
| MANCHESTER UNITED | 1 |

ATTENDANCE: 24,348
MAN UNITED SCORER: Saha 30
BLACKBURN SCORER: Pedersen 35

This game was overshadowed by a confrontation that involved Rooney and Robbie Savage. After both playes were involved in a tasty challenge, Savage grabbed Rooney by the throat and the United man responded by shoving his hand into the Welshman's face. A melee ensued and both players were lucky to get away with just bookings, meaning Rooney was suspended for the FA Cup replay with Burton. The match started at a blistering pace and throbbed with action throughout the half. United took the lead through Saha but Pedersen soon equalised. After the break some of the pace went out of the game but it still gripped the Ewood Park crowd.

JAN. 11 v BLACKBURN ROVERS

150 FA PREMIERSHIP
SATURDAY JANUARY 14, 2006

| MANCHESTER CITY | 3 |
| MANCHESTER UNITED | 1 |

ATTENDANCE: 47,192
MAN UNITED SCORER: van Nistelrooy 76. **MAN CITY SCORERS:** Sinclair 32, Vassell 39, Fowler 90

Van der Sar, Giggs and Rooney were the only United players to come out this poor performance with any credit. Rooney had a chance to score after being sent clear by Ronaldo but he couldn't get the better of goalkeeper David James. City held a deserved 2-0 half-time lead after a woeful first-half display from the visitors. United improved in the second-half until Ronaldo was sent-off. Although van Nistelrooy gave United hope of salvaging something, Robbie Fowler rubbed salt in the wounds in the closing minutes with his final goal for the club before rejoining Liverpool.

151 FA PREMIERSHIP
SUNDAY JANUARY 22, 2006

| MANCHESTER UNITED | 1 |
| LIVERPOOL | 0 |

ATTENDANCE: 67,874
MAN UNITED SCORER: Ferdinand 90

Rooney was here, there and everywhere as he chased possession of the ball in defensive, midfield and attacking positions, while still finding the energy to go on 50-yard surging runs. Despite his spirited endeavours, it was Liverpool who created the better chances, requiring van der Sar to save and then Ferdinand to clear off the line. United's first goalscoring opportunity did not arrive until the 43rd minute and then van Nistelrooy's shot didn't fully test goalkeeper Reina. Rooney moved out onto the right after the break and still pursued the ball. A dramatic finish to the game saw Ferdinand powerfully head home a Giggs free-kick in stoppage time.

JAN. 29 ▶ v WOLVERHAMPTON WANDERERS

152 CARLING CUP
SEMI-FINAL SECOND LEG
WEDNESDAY JANUARY 25, 2006

| MANCHESTER UNITED | 2 |
| BLACKBURN ROVERS | 1 |

Manchester United win 3-2 on aggregate

ATTENDANCE: 61,637

MAN UNITED SCORERS: van Nistelrooy 8, Saha 51 **BLACKBURN SCORER:** Reid 32

Rooney was required to play in a deeper role but it didn't stop him exerting his influence and he was involved in both of United's goals. After Fletcher had pounced on Michael Gray's error he gave possession to Rooney, who sped 30 yards goalward before flicking a pass towards van Nistelrooy. Gray tried to intercept but failed to control, and the ball ran for the Dutchman who fired the ball into the net. Steven Reid scored to level the tie, but the decisive goal went to United, with Rooney setting up Saha with a chipped pass, allowing the Frenchman to score with a curling shot. The game was one of long troughs and very high peaks of drama, which included the loss of Giggs after 12 minutes through injury, van Nistelrooy missing a penalty, and a dramatic half-time player dash to the tunnel as Savage and Ferdinand confronted one another. Significantly, however, the result meant a second successive domestic cup final appearance for Rooney.

153 FA CUP
FOURTH ROUND
SUNDAY JANUARY 29, 2006

| WOLVERHAMPTON WANDERERS | 0 |
| MANCHESTER UNITED | 3 |

ATTENDANCE: 28,333

MAN UNITED SCORERS: Richardson 4 52, Saha 45

The enforced absence of five key players led Ferguson to reluctantly partner Rooney and Ferdinand in central midfield. It did not prove to be such a big gamble after all as United strolled to victory over their Championship opposition with consummate ease. Rooney was his usual influential self but it was Kieran Richardson who grabbed the headlines with two goals, while Saha once again netted in a cup competition.

154 FA PREMIERSHIP
WEDNESDAY FEBRUARY 1, 2006

| BLACKBURN ROVERS | 4 |
| MANCHESTER UNITED | 3 |

ATTENDANCE: 25,484

MAN UNITED SCORERS: Saha 37, van Nistelrooy 63 68. **BLACKBURN SCORERS:** Bentley 35 41 56, Neill (pen) 45

Manchester United were on the wrong end of a seven-goal thriller in which a David Bentley hat-trick helped Rovers into a shock 4-1 lead. United almost staged an incredible fightback with two goals from van Nistelrooy, while Rooney almost clinched a fourth

WAYNE ROONEY'S STRIKE RATE SEASON 05/06

PREMIERSHIP		36 GAMES/16 GOALS	44%
FA CUP	2 GAMES/0 GOALS		0%
LEAGUE CUP		2 GAMES/0 GOALS	50%
EUROPE	5 GAMES/1 GOAL		20%
OVERALL		19 GOALS IN 47 GAMES	40%

in the 80th minute with a reflex shot that was saved by Friedel in the Blackburn goal. Earlier Rooney had tested the keeper with a drive that produced a fine parried save, but Saha was on hand to equalise for United. The headlines – aside from Bentley's deserved hat-trick – were for Ferdinand's dismissal two minutes from time for a tackle on Savage who was subsequently stretchered off.

155 FA PREMIERSHIP
SATURDAY FEBRUARY 4, 2006

| MANCHESTER UNITED | 4 |
| FULHAM | 2 |

ATTENDANCE: 67,844

MAN UNITED SCORERS: Park 6, Ronaldo 14 86, Saha 23 **FULHAM SCORERS:** McBride 22, Helguson 37

Rooney was on the bench and witnessed an unrelenting thrill-a-minute five-goal first-half. Park, who Rooney was to replace in the 69th minute, opened the scoring with his first Premiership goal and Ronaldo increased the lead from a free-kick eight minutes later. Fulham managed to halve the deficit but only for less than a minute because Saha found the net again. At half-time it was 3-2 and aside from the goals, both goalkeepers had made significant saves. Although the teams still continued to attack, there were no further goals until the 86th minute when Ronaldo got United's fourth.

156 FA PREMIERSHIP
SATURDAY FEBRUARY 11, 2006

| PORTSMOUTH | 1 |
| MANCHESTER UNITED | 3 |

ATTENDANCE: 20,206

MAN UNITED SCORERS: van Nistelrooy 18, Ronaldo 38 45
PORTSMOUTH SCORER: Taylor 87

By half-time this match was sewn up by Manchester United, thanks van Nistelrooy's header, a 25-yard shot from Ronaldo, and then another deflected shot from the Portuguese player after being set up by Rooney. After the break United eased off without ever being put in any serious danger. Before the goals and late on in the game, Portsmouth did give United something to think about, but they could not alter the outcome of the match.

157 FA CUP FIFTH ROUND
SATURDAY FEBRUARY 18, 2006

| LIVERPOOL | 1 |
| MANCHESTER UNITED | 0 |

ATTENDANCE: 44,039

LIVERPOOL SCORER: Crouch 19

Manchester United were knocked out of the FA Cup by a Peter Crouch headed goal after 19 minutes. It was not to be their day as they had lost Ferdinand before departing Manchester and then their arrival (and the kick-off) was delayed because of a road accident. Neville, on his birthday, and Rooney – reiterating his loyalty to United by kissing his shirt – received the ritual abuse from Liverpool fans and Smith suffered a badly broken ankle. Rooney's best chance came at a free kick when Giggs rolled him the ball, but the driving shot went narrowly wide.

WHAT ROONEY SAID: "I know when people will target you and wind you up, and I can cope with that much better… But I keep learning all the time and I think I am getting better and I think you can see that in my game. I love playing football but I think I'm like everyone else, I hate losing and love winning."

158 CARLING CUP
FINAL
SUNDAY FEBRUARY 26, 2006

| MANCHESTER UNITED | 4 |
| WIGAN ATHLETIC | 0 |

ATTENDANCE: 66,866

MAN UNITED SCORERS: **Rooney 33 61**, Saha 55, Ronaldo 59

Rooney won his first major trophy with a Man of the Match performance that inspired Manchester United to the biggest League Cup Final victory in the 35-year history of the competition. Rooney, playing alongside Saha in attack, gave a fantastic performance, scoring twice and creating many other chances as United were unstoppable. Wigan suffered a blow early on with the loss of first choice goalkeeper Pollitt with a hamstring injury. Pollitt, who had seen Rooney hit the crossbar with a header from a Neville cross, was replaced by John Filan. In the 33rd minute Rooney, via route one, got the goal United's pressure and possession deserved. He had the opportunity to increase the lead before the break after Giggs carved out an opening, but Rooney's volley lacked the power to beat Filan on that occasion. Three goals in six second-half minutes destroyed any hope Wigan had of a recovery. Neville, overlapping Ronaldo on the right wing, advanced and sent over a low cross that Saha met but Filan saved. The ball rebounded from the Wigan substitute goalkeeper and fortuitously hit the Frenchman's knee and rebounded into the net for his sixth Carling Cup goal of the season. Four minutes later Stephane Henchoz's hashed clearance gifted the ball to Saha, who sent Ronaldo clear to net United's third. Another two minutes on and a deserving Rooney

scored his second goal of the match. There could have been more goals with Rooney creating one chance for South Korean international Park, who was just inches wide of the target. The full-time whistle was blown by referee Alan Wiley and captain Neville lifted the trophy for the victorious United team, to ensure they ended the season with a trophy. Man of the Match Rooney collected his first major winners' medal.

WHAT THEY SAID ABOUT ROONEY: "We were playing against one of the best players in the world – if not the best player in the world – in Wayne Rooney." *Paul Jewell (Wigan manager)*

WHAT ROONEY SAID: "It's amazing. I'm delighted with the two goals. I haven't been scoring but the other players have and we've been winning. I was hungry because I had not scored for a while. It was not as bad as it could have been because at least the team were scoring, but I was disappointed with the situation and I wanted to put it right. I guess there is no better time to do it than a cup final. I am absolutely delighted. To win any trophy gives you a big buzz and this is the best feeling I have ever had."

 ROONEY GOAL (33 mins) United goalkeeper van der Sar punched clear up field, Saha flicked the ball forward and Rooney gave chase sprinting clear of Wigan defenders Pascal Chimbonda and Arjan De Zeeuw. He then unleashed a precision drive past Wigan substitute goalkeeper Filan.

ROONEY GOAL (61 mins) From a Giggs free-kick, Saha's flick-on bounced off the chest of Chimbonda. Ferdinand headed the loose ball into the path of Rooney, who guided the ball into the back of the net to make it 4-0, which ensured the Man of the Match award.

APR. 17 | v TOTTENHAM HOTSPUR

159 FA PREMIERSHIP
MONDAY MARCH 6, 2006

WIGAN ATHLETIC	1
MANCHESTER UNITED	2

ATTENDANCE: 23,574

MAN UNITED SCORERS: Ronaldo, Saha 90
WIGAN SCORERS: Scharner 59

Manchester United fielded an unchanged side from their Carling Cup victory but this time Wigan were determined not to be thrashed again. The home side dominated the first-half although they failed with the final touch. Shortly after the break Rooney, nowhere near as dominant as he was in the final, went close with a diving header that flew past the near post. However, Wigan did take the lead in the 59th minute through Paul Scharner. Helped by substitute van Nistelrooy, Ronaldo equalised, and then cruelly for Wigan in stoppage time Chimbonda put through his own net while attempting to clear.

160 FA PREMIERSHIP
SUNDAY MARCH 12, 2006

MANCHESTER UNITED	2
NEWCASTLE UNITED	0

ATTENDANCE: 67,858

MAN UNITED SCORERS: Rooney 8 12

Rooney was the star of a totally one-sided match. Straight from the kick-off it was clear this was going to be his day and by the 12th minute he had scored the two goals that won the game. The fact he didn't score his hat-trick, and that the Red Devils weren't at least five up at the break, was because chances were squandered. Rooney missed a couple of opportunities and, in the second-half, also hit the post with a chipped shot. Chances went begging for Saha, Park, O'Shea and, later, van Nistelrooy, but three points kept United in the title race.

🖤 **ROONEY GOAL** (8 mins) Newcastle defender Ramage found himself under pressure on the touchline from Silvestre and attempted a backpass to his goalkeeper Given. Rooney, showing great anticipation, intercepted the ball and lobbed it over the stranded goalkeeper and into the net for his first Premiership goal since the end of December.

🖤 **ROONEY GOAL** (12 mins) Saha and O'Shea combined to supply Rooney. Despite the attentions of Ramage, Rooney shook off his marker and rammed the ball powerfully past Given to leave the goalkeeper shellshocked.

161 FA PREMIERSHIP
SATURDAY MARCH 18, 2006

WEST BROMWICH ALBION	1
MANCHESTER UNITED	2

ATTENDANCE: 27,623

MAN UNITED SCORER: Saha 16 64
WEST BROM SCORERS: Ellington 78

It was Rooney's strike partner Saha who grabbed the headlines at The Hawthorns. Aside from keeping van Nistelrooy out of the side, Saha scored twice to give United victory, while Rooney, doing a competent job but not at his grandiose best, took the back seat.

162 FA PREMIERSHIP
SUNDAY MARCH 26, 2006

MANCHESTER UNITED	3
BIRMINGHAM CITY	0

ATTENDANCE: 69,070

MAN UNITED SCORERS: Taylor (og) 3, Giggs 15, **Rooney 83**

Old Trafford witnessed another easy victory for Manchester United and another fine performance from Rooney. Before scoring United's long overdue third goal he had grazed both posts after being set up respectively by a Giggs back-heel and a Ronaldo chipped pass. United's firm grip was established early on when Birmingham goalkeeper Taylor pushed a Giggs free-kick onto a post and into his own net, then Giggs was rightfully credited with United's second goal on 15 minutes. There should have been more goals but United relaxed and appeared not to have the will to go on a goalscoring rampage.

🖤 **ROONEY GOAL** (83 mins): Rooney latched onto a pass, slipping past defender Martin Larka before firing home from inside the box beating goalkeeper Taylor.

163 FA PREMIERSHIP
WEDNESDAY MARCH 29, 2006

MANCHESTER UNITED	1
WEST HAM UNITED	0

ATTENDANCE: 69,522

MAN UNITED SCORER: van Nistelrooy 45

A rather dismal game decided by a van Nistelrooy goal on the stroke of half-time. United started in rather reserved fashion, but as the game wore on they had periods of sustained pressure. However,

there were glimpses of brilliance from Rooney, including an amazing through ball that sent Fletcher in on goal but the ball ended up in the side-netting, much to the Scotsman's displeasure. Rooney also went close with an acrobatic volley that thundered off the crossbar and although the scoreline suggests a close encounter, the game was never in danger of falling out of United's grasp.

164 FA PREMIERSHIP
SATURDAY APRIL 1, 2006

BOLTON WANDERERS	1
MANCHESTER UNITED	2

ATTENDANCE: 27,718

MAN UNITED SCORERS: Saha 33, van Nistelrooy 79. BOLTON SCORER: Davies 26

One of those rare days for Rooney where his decisive touch let him down. Unmarked inside the penalty area he was perfectly placed for Ronaldo's cross but, unbelievably, his first touch was poor and the chance was gone. Later, after a Giggs shot had been saved by goalkeeper Jaaskelainen, the rebound came to Rooney but the finish wasn't good enough. Fortunately Saha and substitute van Nistelrooy were on target for United to come from behind and win the match. It was a result which kept the pressure on Chelsea at the top of the table, who had drawn that day at relegation-threatened Birmingham.

165 FA PREMIERSHIP
SUNDAY APRIL 9, 2006

MANCHESTER UNITED	2
ARSENAL	0

ATTENDANCE: 70,908

MAN UNITED SCORER: **Rooney 54**, Park 78

The Old Trafford crowd were rewarded with an exciting top-class match full of end-to-end action. Once again Rooney shone and was centre of attention. He scored the first goal for United and set up Park for the second after receiving Neville's pass and then beating Philippe Senderos before crossing for the South Korean. Rooney helped create other chances and tested Lehmann with a couple of efforts of his own, including a rasping shot. In one particular moment, Rooney saw himself denied either a goal or a penalty when referee Graham Poll failed to see Kolo Toure 'save' the striker's goalbound effort with his hands after tumbling over his own goalkeeper.

🖤 **ROONEY GOAL** (54 mins): Rooney expertly brought down Silvestre's left-wing cross before blasting the ball past Lehmann on the half-volley.

166 FA PREMIERSHIP
FRIDAY APRIL 14, 2006

MANCHESTER UNITED	0
SUNDERLAND	0

ATTENDANCE: 72,519

After nine successive wins Manchester United were held to a goalless draw by relegation-doomed Sunderland. United should have won the game comfortably but in goalkeeper Davis, Sunderland had an invincible force. Rooney, who forced a fingertip save from the goalkeeper, van Nistelrooy, Ronaldo and Solskjaer were all denied and the result all but ended any hope United had in catching Chelsea at the top of the table.

167 FA PREMIERSHIP
MONDAY APRIL 17, 2006

TOTTENHAM HOSTPUR	1
MANCHESTER UNITED	2

ATTENDANCE: 36,141

MAN UNITED SCORER: **Rooney 8 36**
TOTTENHAM SCORER: Jenas 53

The deciding factor in this match was Rooney. Tottenham, who were closing in on fourth place and a Champions League spot for next season, were the better team on the day, dominating for long periods, but they squandered a host of chances. In contrast, when opportunities fell his way Rooney was lethal. He scored twice to take his season's tally to 19 goals

🖤 **ROONEY GOAL** (8 mins) Van Nistelrooy supplied Ronaldo who, in turn, delivered a pinpoint cross for Rooney to score one of his easiest goals with a tap in past Tottenham goalkeeper Robinson.

🖤 **ROONEY GOAL** (36 mins) Park dispossessed his South Korea compatriot Lee Young-Pyo and set up Rooney, who picked his spot before firing the ball past Robinson to put United into a 2-0 first-half lead.

168 FA PREMIERSHIP
SATURDAY APRIL 29, 2006

CHELSEA	3
MANCHESTER UNITED	0

ATTENDANCE: 42,219

CHELSEA SCORERS: Gallas 5, J Cole 61, Carvalho 73

A sight no England fan wanted to see: Rooney being stretchered off the field in agony – with his World Cup hopes hanging in the balance. He picked up the injury in the 78th minute, landing awkwardly on his right foot following a tackle by Blues right-back Paulo Ferreira. The pain etched on the striker's face indicated the injury was serious and it was later diagnosed that he had broken the fourth metarsal in his foot. The minimum six-week recovery period would take Rooney up to the start of England's World Cup campaign. For the record, Chelsea lifted the Premiership trophy after this comfortable win.

1 INTERNATIONAL FRIENDLY
WEDNESDAY FEBRUARY 12, 2003

ENGLAND	1
AUSTRALIA	3

ATTENDANCE: 34,590 (Upton Park, London)
ENGLAND SCORER: Jeffers 70. **AUSTRALIA SCORERS:** Popovic 17, Kewell 42, Emerton 84

Rooney became England's youngest international at 17 years and 111 days when he came on as a half-time substitute against Australia. Rooney, who replaced fellow striker Michael Owen, was one of 11 substitutes used by England coach Sven Goran-Eriksson in a wholesale change of line-up from the first-half. England did not perform too well in the opening 45 minutes, trailing 2-0, but Rooney, along with fellow debutants Francis Jeffers and Jermaine Jenas, impressed after the break in a youthful-looking side. Almost immediately Rooney made an impact, carving out a chance for Darius Vassell who squandered the opportunity. Rooney wanted to seize his chance on such a farcical evening and showed glimpses of his outstanding ability. He was rewarded by being involved in the move that led to England's goal in the 70th minute: he passed out to Jenas on the right and the Newcastle man struck a superb cross for Jeffers to score at the near post with a glancing header. Australia finished the brighter, however, as Brett Emerton found the net to confirm Australia's first-ever win over England.

2 EURO 2004 QUALIFIER
SATURDAY MARCH 29, 2003

LIECHTENSTEIN	0
ENGLAND	2

ATTENDANCE: 3,548 (Rheinparkstadion, Vaduz)
ENGLAND SCORERS: Owen 28, Beckham 53

England gave a comfortable, if not impressive, performance in claiming the expected victory over the minnows of Liechtenstein. Goals by Owen and David Beckham gave England the 2-0 lead before Rooney was called off the substitutes' bench to replace Emile Heskey in the 80th minute. Not much time to make much of a mark but a goalscoring opportunity did come Rooney's way from a Kieron Dyer cross, but his header was mistimed.

3 EURO 2004 QUALIFIER
WEDNESDAY APRIL 2, 2003

ENGLAND	2
TURKEY	0

ATTENDANCE: 47,667 (Stadium of Light, Sunderland)
ENGLAND SCORERS: Vassell 76, Beckham (pen) 90

Eriksson gave Rooney just four hours' notice before kick-off that he would be making first international start. The teenager rewarded him with an excellent, infectious performance. Rooney partnered Owen up front at the expense of Heskey. From the kick-off he showed himself to be fearless in the edgy opening period of play. Both England and Turkey did not flinch but Rooney's vision and understanding looked to have given the hosts the upper hand. In the 11th minute, he seized on a dropped ball by Turkey goalkeeper Rustu Recber but the shot was blocked and Beckham followed up with an off-target effort in front of an open goal. Just before half-time Rooney put Owen clean through after a fantastic run and superb pass but, unfortunately, Rustu, dived at his feet and won the ball. Rooney was equally impressive in the second-half but England also had to thank

FEB. 12 v AUSTRALIA

goalkeeper David James in dealing with the real Turkish threat. Vassell, who had replaced the injured Owen, broke the deadlock for England in the 76th minute and the points were only assured after skipper Beckham converted an injury time penalty after Dyer had been fouled by Ergun Penbe. The Newcastle midfielder had just come on as an 89th minute substitute for Rooney, who received a standing ovation from the crowd.

WHAT THEY SAID ABOUT ROONEY: "He's a great talent, we knew that before. But now we know he's ready for the big matches. I can't see any reason why I should leave him out if he plays like that."
Sven-Göran Eriksson (England coach)

"I have never seen a full debut before as good as that. He was so full of confidence." *Steven Gerrard (Liverpool & England)*

"If our expectations are high that's probably good for the boy and will help keep him up there."
Bill Kenwright (Everton chairman)

4 INTERNATIONAL FRIENDLY
TUESDAY JUNE 3, 2003

ENGLAND	2
SERBIA & MONTENEGRO	1

ATTENDANCE: 30,900 (Walkers Stadium, Leicester)
ENGLAND SCORERS: Gerrard 35, J Cole 82
SERBIA SCORER: Jestrovic 45

After a first-half in which Gerrard, England's best player on the night, gave the home side the lead and then saw it cancelled out by Nenad Jestrovic's strike, Rooney was one of five half-time England substitutes replacing Owen. In total, the sides made 20 substitutions between them from the break onwards, which contributed to a rather broken up second period. Eriksson justified his numerous changes, arguing that he wanted to protect key players at the end of a tough season. Chelsea midfielder Joe Cole scored the winner from a 20-yard free-kick eight minutes from time, while Rooney almost extended the lead in injury time with an effort that was brilliantly saved by Serbia goalkeeper Dragan Zilic.

WHAT THEY SAID ABOUT ROONEY: "The first time I picked him, I was asked why. I said that when he gets the ball, he makes things happen. Not every time but many times when he gets the ball, he can beat people, sees the pass or makes the shot."
Sven-Göran Eriksson

"Wayne Rooney is the most exciting young talent we've seen in years and his emergence is hugely exciting to both youngsters and people like myself who have been right through the game."
Geoff Hurst (England World Cup winner)

5 EURO 2004 QUALIFIER
WEDNESDAY JUNE 11, 2003

ENGLAND	2
SLOVAKIA	1

ATTENDANCE: 35,000 (Riverside Stadium, Middlesbrough)
ENGLAND SCORERS: Owen (pen) 62 73.
SLOVAKIA SCORER: Janocko 31

England had to come from behind to take all three points and it was stand-in captain Owen, making his 50th appearance for his country, who won a penalty and then dispatched the resulting kick. He doubled his account by netting what proved to be the winning goal with his head. England took another three points on their way to Euro 2004 but Rooney, at the end of his first full season in professional football, was a little subdued. He was responsible for a tackle on Vladimir Labant that led to the Slovakian leaving the game after 39 minutes and then, some 19 minutes later and with England still trailing, he too left the field having been substituted by Vassell.

WHAT THEY SAID ABOUT ROONEY: "I'm happy with Rooney. The fans and the critics expect Rooney to be the best on the pitch every time he plays. But we have not to forget that he is only 17. He has to learn. He is one of the biggest talents I've ever had."
Sven-Göran Eriksson

6 EURO 2004 QUALIFIER
SATURDAY SEPTEMBER 6, 2003

MACEDONIA	1
ENGLAND	2

ATTENDANCE: 20,500 (City Stadium, Skopje)
ENGLAND SCORERS: Rooney 53, Beckham (pen) 61. **MACEDONIA SCORER:** Hristov 26

Rooney, aged 17 years and 317 days, became England's youngest ever goalscorer with a second-half equaliser. The record had previously been held by his striking partner Owen. England started poorly with a woeful first-half display that saw Macedonia take the lead through Georgi Hristov. At half-time Eriksson took off midfielder Lampard and replaced him with Heskey to create a three-pronged attack alongside Rooney and Owen. Within eight minutes the tactical change had paid off with Rooney scoring his first England goal. Just past the hour and England scored their crucial second after John Terry was fouled by Aginaldo

Braga, earning a penalty from which Beckham scored. It was England's seventh successive win, equalling their best post-war winning sequence.

WHAT THEY SAID ABOUT ROONEY: "The talent is there, the quality is there with Wayne. Of course he has a lot to learn, but if things go to plan, he can go very, very far. Wayne can score goals, he is a very strong player, so congratulations to him for becoming the youngest ever England goalscorer."
Sven Goran-Eriksson

"Everyone knows what a great player Wayne is. He's a great lad with a great family and a great club behind him but we have always known the type of performance he is capable of producing."
David Beckham

⚽ **ROONEY GOAL** (53 mins) England skipper Beckham found Heskey on the edge of the area with a superb flighted pass. Instead of shooting, the Liverpool striker then headed the ball down into the path of Rooney who fired the ball home for his first England goal.

7 EURO 2004 QUALIFIER
WEDNESDAY SEPTEMBER 10, 2003

ENGLAND	2
LIECHTENSTEIN	0

ATTENDANCE: 64,931 (Old Trafford, Manchester)
ENGLAND SCORERS: Owen 46, **Rooney** 52

It was hard going but England did beat minnows Liechtenstein as expected, thanks to a significant contribution from Rooney. He was cast in a deep-lying role behind Owen and James Beattie, who was to hit the woodwork with his best effort. Rooney's position also allowed him to create several chances as Liechtenstein's goalkeeper Peter Jehle found himself, as always, constantly busy. Rooney scorched a first-time shot high and saw Jehle tip his looping header over the bar. An unstoppable run down the left led to a cross that set up Beckham for a sweeping shot that grazed the Liechtenstein crossbar. Rooney then tried to score with an overhead kick but the effort was too high. Liechtenstein survived to the break but in the first minute of the restart England were finally ahead. Rooney found Gerrard with a pass and the Liverpool skipper sent in a cross that Owen flicked with his head into the net past the wrong-footed Jehle. Six minutes later and Rooney was on target for his second successive game to put England within a single point of qualification. In the 70th

minute, with his job done, Rooney was replaced by Cole and received another standing ovation.

WHAT THEY SAID ABOUT ROONEY: "For a 17-year-old boy he has started international football in an excellent way. We'll see him score for England in the future… He's a very good football player and he can get better with age." *Sven-Göran Eriksson*

⚽ **ROONEY GOAL** (52 mins) Beckham's right-wing cross to the far post was pulled back by Gerrard for Rooney to sweep the ball into the net.

8 EURO 2004 QUALIFIER
SATURDAY OCTOBER 11, 2003

TURKEY	0
ENGLAND	0

ATTENDANCE: 42,000 (Sukru Saracoglu Stadium, Istanbul)

Rooney, in the place of the injured Owen, partnered Heskey in attack in the intimidating atmosphere of the Sukru Sracoglu Stadium. England needed – and got – a point to qualify for Euro 2004 in Portugal. England gave a very disciplined performance and were presented with few chances to score. Scholes headed over the bar and Rooney, set up by Beckham, tried to lob the goalkeeper and his effort landed on the roof of the net. England's best chance

JUN. 5 >> v ICELAND

> "WAYNE ROONEY IS THE MOST EXCITING YOUNG TALENT WE'VE SEEN IN YEARS AND HIS EMERGENCE IS HUGELY EXCITING TO BOTH YOUNGSTERS AND PEOPLE LIKE MYSELF WHO HAVE BEEN RIGHT THROUGH THE GAME."
> GEOFF HURST

was a Beckham penalty, awarded after Gerrard had been fouled by Tugay. Beckham slipped and mishit the spot-kick way over the bar. At half-time there was an incident in the tunnel when Beckham confronted Alpay, who had taunted him after the penalty miss. England, however, owed their success to a resilient and disciplined defence that kept Turkey at bay. Rooney and Heskey found no way through and were replaced by Dyer and Vassell, in the 69th minute and the 73rd minute respectively.

9 INTERNATIONAL FRIENDLY
SATURDAY NOVEMBER 16, 2003

ENGLAND	2
DENMARK	3

ATTENDANCE: 64,159 (Old Trafford, Manchester)
ENGLAND SCORERS: Rooney 5, Cole 8
DENMARK SCORERS: Jorgensen 8 (pen) 30, Tomasson 82

There was a thrilling start to this friendly international with Rooney giving England an early lead with his third international goal. Martin Jorgensen, free from Gary Neville, equalised. The Danish celebrations were still going on when Rooney set up Joe Cole to drill home with his left foot. That was the nature of an open game that saw England defeated because of their own defensive frailties. Matthew Upson conceded a penalty with a foul on Jorgensen, who equalised again from the spot after 30 minutes. The winning goal came from Jon Dahl Tomasson

after goalkeeper Robinson had saved successive efforts from Peter Lovenkrands and Jorgensen in the 82nd minute. By then Rooney, who had hit the post with a great volley shortly after half-time, was off the pitch as one of eight substitutions made by England coach Eriksson (the Danes made seven). This time it was Scott Parker in the 65th minute who was Rooney's replacement. Overall, Denmark deserved to win the game.

⚽ **ROONEY GOAL** *(5 mins) Rooney started the move and finished it off by pouncing on a deflection with a rising, powerful shot past Sorensen to make the score 1-0.*

10 INTERNATIONAL FRIENDLY
WEDNESDAY FEBRUARY 18, 2004

PORTUGAL	1
ENGLAND	1

ATTENDANCE: 27,000 (Estadio Algarve, Faro)
ENGLAND SCORER: King 47
PORTUGAL SCORER: Pauleta 70

This was a game of very few chances and, inevitably, plenty of substitutions. Rooney started and lasted until the 71st minute, when Smith took over his role. Rooney was one of several players who were subjected to some uncompromising tackles from the Portuguese, although it did not prevent him from eluding one or two on a run that created a chance for Beckham. Spurs defender Ledley King put England ahead just after the break but Pauleta, from a free-

kick, levelled the scores just before Rooney's departure. Rooney, unfortunately, had the miss of the night when, in the 28th minute, Fernando Couto slipped and presented Rooney with a close range tap in. However, he failed to control the ball and the chance of a shot on goal was lost.

11 INTERNATIONAL FRIENDLY
WEDNESDAY MARCH 31, 2004

SWEDEN	1
ENGLAND	0

ATTENDANCE: 40,464 (Gamla Ullevi Stadium, Gothenburg)
SWEDEN SCORER: Ibrahimovic 53

This was England's last international before Eriksson was to name his provisional 23-man squad for the Euro 2004 finals. Without Owen, Rooney led the attack, initially partnered by Vassell, who lasted just 11 minutes before an injury forced him off. Rooney then found himself in a new attack pairing with Tottenham's Jermain Defoe, making his international debut. Rooney and, in particular, Defoe were lively and within two minutes they combined to create a solid chance: Defoe tried a long-range effort from a Rooney pass, but he hit the post and the ball rebounded across the face of the goal. Rooney also went close just before the break but his shot was blocked, and by the time he was inevitably substituted by Smith, England had fallen behind to a Zlatan Ibrahimovic goal. Although England had created the best chances – Bayern Munich midfielder Owen Hargreaves also hit the upright – Sweden

had the lion's share of possession and managed to hold on for a hard-fought victory. England had once again failed to beat the Swedes whom they last defeated back in 1968.

12 INTERNATIONAL FRIENDLY
TUESDAY JUNE 1, 2004

ENGLAND	1
JAPAN	1

ATTENDANCE: 38,581 (City of Manchester Stadium, Manchester)
ENGLAND SCORER: Owen 21
JAPAN SCORER: Ono 52

Eriksson fielded his first-choice XI in this Euro 2004 warm-up fixture with Rooney, who gave an inconsistent performance, partnering Owen. England created chances but Japan matched them and deservedly earned a draw. Owen put England ahead after 21 minutes, pouncing on a loose ball after goalkeeper Narazaki fumbled Gerrard's shot. Japan responded with chances of their own and got the equaliser they deserved when Shinji Ono netted. Rooney set-up Owen shortly afterwards in search of a winner but he was denied by Narazaki's legs. On 77 minutes, Rooney was replaced by Vassell – one of eight England substitutions in the last 20 minutes of an entertaining and closely-fought match.

13 INTERNATIONAL FRIENDLY
SATURDAY JUNE 5, 2004

ENGLAND	6
ICELAND	1

ATTENDANCE: 43,000 (City of Manchester Stadium, Manchester)
ENGLAND SCORERS: Lampard 24, **Rooney 26 38**, Vassell 56 77 Bridge 67
ICELAND SCORER: Helguson 41

Rooney was only restricted to the first 45 minutes of this final warm-up match but he gave a blistering performance in which he scored twice and could have had more as England routed Iceland. Rooney was almost let in early on by left-back Ashley Cole, and then Frank Lampard opened the scoring with a dipping strike. Two minutes later Rooney scored and before he netted a spectacular second, he had mesmerised the Iceland defence with his excellent close ball control. Iceland got a goal back through Watford striker Heider Helguson before the break. Rooney, one of nine half-time substitutions by England, took his bow and his replacement Vassell obliged by grabbing two goals of his own, with Wayne Bridge getting on the scoresheet with the first goal of his international career.

WHAT THEY SAID ABOUT ROONEY: "I'm pleased for Wayne. We all know what a great talent he is and today he proved it. Let's hope he can continue that form into the European Championship."
Sven-Göran Eriksson

"Wayne has received a bit of criticism over his temperament in the game against Japan and for an 18-year-old kid, a lot of the media have been talking about whether he should be in the team. But he showed what he can do in just 45 minutes – imagine if he would have been on for the full 90 minutes."
Jamie Carragher

⚽ **ROONEY GOAL** *(26 mins) Gary Neville, receiving the ball from a Beckham throw-in, slipped past a defender before setting up Rooney, who slotted the ball into the net from inside the penalty area to make the score 2-0.*

⚽ **ROONEY GOAL** *(38 mins) Rooney received the ball from Scholes and then unleashed a shot into the top right-hand corner from almost 30 yards out.*

WAYNE ROONEY'S ENGLAND STRIKE RATE

TOURNAMENT FINALS	8 GAMES/4 GOALS	50%
TOURNAMENT QUALIFIERS	13 GAMES/2 GOALS	15%
FRIENDLIES	12 GAMES/5 GOALS	42%
OVERALL	11 GOALS IN 33 GAMES	33%

JUN. 13 ▶ v FRANCE

> "A FEW OF US TOLD HIM TO TAKE OUT HIS FRUSTRATION BY SCORING GOALS, AND THAT'S WHAT HE DID. WHEN YOU GET BOOKED AS AN 18-YEAR-OLD YOU CAN GO OUT OF THE GAME OR FIGHT BACK – AND HE FOUGHT BACK." DAVID BECKHAM

 14 EURO 2004 FINALS
GROUP B
SUNDAY JUNE 13, 2004

FRANCE	2
ENGLAND	1

ATTENDANCE: 64,000 (Estadio Da Luz, Lisbon)
ENGLAND SCORER: Lampard 38
FRANCE SCORER: Zidane 90 (pen) 90(+3)

Rooney became the second youngest player ever to appear in a European Championship finals match and helped England to what seemed an ideal winning start. But Rooney had to watch in horror from the bench as his team-mates were suckered by two Zinédine Zidane goals in the last moments of the match. Rooney was crucial to England's disciplined approach as he time and again displayed excellent holding play. Both sides were intent on attacking from the outset and early on Scholes and Rooney combined to release Owen, only for William Gallas to bring the move to a halt. On 38 minutes France conceded a free-kick when Beckham was fouled by Bixente Lizarazu. Beckham fired in the resulting kick and Lampard headed home the cross past Fabian Barthez to give England the lead. It was the first goal France had conceded since June 2003, some 1,077 minutes before. Rooney's direct play bothered France and in the 73rd minute he was brought down by Silvestre, who was booked. Beckham, however, squandered the penalty, allowing Barthez to save. Shortly afterwards, Rooney was replaced by Heskey. England looked set for victory but then in the final minute Heskey conceded a free-kick on the edge of the area and Zidane curled it home past James. Then Gerrard sent a poor backpass to his goalkeeper as Thierry Henry lurked. James ended up bringing down the Frenchman and Zidane stepped forward to convert the penalty to give France an amazing smash-and-grab win.

15 EURO 2004 FINALS
GROUP B
THURSDAY JUNE 17, 2004

ENGLAND	3
SWITZERLAND	0

ATTENDANCE: 30,000 (Cidade de Coimbra, Coimbra)
ENGLAND SCORERS: Rooney 23 75, Gerrard 82

Rooney became the youngest ever goalscorer in the history of the European Championships as he inspired England to a comprehensive 3-0 win over Switzerland. However, it was not easy going in the 30 degree temperatures and England's best chance resulted in a booking for Rooney when he caught Swiss goalkeeper Joerg Stiel after a Lampard through ball eluded him. The Swiss were having the better of the play early on but then Rooney broke the deadlock against the run of play. The headed goal gave England the breathing space they needed and then, on the hour, Eriksson's side was further boosted when Switzerland were reduced to ten men after Bernt Haas was sent-off for two bookable offences committed within ten minutes of each other. England took advantage and Rooney scored his second goal (only the third Englishman to have scored twice in a European Championship finals game) and once Gerrard had netted Gary Neville's right-wing cross, Rooney was replaced by Dyer to be rested for the all-important third group game against Croatia four days later.

WHAT THEY SAID ABOUT ROONEY: "A few of us told him to take out his frustration by scoring goals, and that's what he did. When you get booked as an

18-year-old you can go out of the game or fight back – and he fought back." *David Beckham*

"He was fantastic, two beautiful goals. He worked very hard as well. To put in that performance at this level – it's incredible." *Sven-Göran Eriksson*

WHAT ROONEY SAID: "It's always great to break a record, but it's the team that matters. I just go out and play the game and I was lucky enough to score two goals. There's not much to say about them. Michael Owen put the ball on my head and I couldn't miss, really, and for the second I just hit it hard enough and luckily it went in. Like any young lad I get nervous before a game, but once you get in to it you get a bit more relaxed and you go out there and do your best… I like to play with a bit of temper, I think it makes me play better. I'm not going to stop because it's a major tournament like this."

⚽ **ROONEY GOAL** *(23 mins) Beckham hit a diagonal flighted pass to Owen. Rooney met his cross and headed past the goalkeeper to open the scoring.*

⚽ **ROONEY GOAL** *(75 mins) Rooney struck a powerful shot that hit the post and then ricocheted off the unlucky goalkeeper Joerg Stiel and into the net.*

16 EURO 2004 FINALS
GROUP B
MONDAY JUNE 21, 2004

CROATIA	2
ENGLAND	4

ATTENDANCE: 63,000 (Estadio da Luz, Lisbon)
ENGLAND SCORERS: Scholes 40, **Rooney 45 68**, Lampard 79
CROATIA SCORERS: Kovac 6, Tudor 74

In a thrilling match of 32 goal attempts, of which 22 were on target, and six goals, England qualified for the last eight of Euro 2004. Rooney was at his best, scoring twice to become the tournament's leading scorer. England fell behind to an early Nikos Kovac goal after six minutes. However, they responded by surging forward while Croatia were happy to play on the counter-attack whenever a move broke down. In the 40th minute England finally equalised when Gerrard and Lampard combined to send Owen sprinting clear. The livewire striker was confronted by goalkeeper Tomislav Butina who did well to block but the ball rose up to Rooney who headed back across goal for Scholes to score with a stooping header. On the stroke of half-time Rooney gave England the lead with a powerful shot, and he extended the lead further in the 68th minute with his fourth goal of the tournament. Shortly afterwards, with the job seemingly done and England fans chanting his name, Rooney was replaced by Vassell in the 72nd minute. But Croatia weren't finished and reduced the deficit through Igor Tudor two minutes later. It needed Lampard's surging run and deft shot past Butina in the 79th minute to assure victory but it was Rooney who attracted all the headlines. He had proved his worth as a truly world class striker and was already being billed as the player of the tournament.

WHAT THEY SAID ABOUT ROONEY: "I don't remember anyone making such an impact on a tournament since Pelé in the 1958 World Cup in Sweden." *Sven-Göran Eriksson*

⚽ **ROONEY GOAL** *(45 mins) Rooney, set up by Scholes, fired home an unstoppable shot from 22 yards out that flew past Croatia goalkeeper Butina.*

⚽ **ROONEY GOAL** *(68 mins) Owen put Rooney through and he calmly placed the ball past Butina and into the back of the net.*

17 EURO 2004 FINALS
QUARTER-FINAL
THURSDAY JUNE 24, 2004

PORTUGAL	2
ENGLAND	2

After extra-time; Portugal win 6-5 on penalties

ATTENDANCE: 65,000 (Estadio da Luz, Lisbon)
ENGLAND SCORERS: Owen 3, Lampard 115
PORTUGAL SCORERS: Postiga 83, Rui Costa 110

With England leading 1-0, thanks to Owen's goal after three minutes, Rooney's tournament came to a premature end. Having had his foot clipped by Jorge Andrade, he hobbled off the field with what was a broken fifth metatarsal in his right foot. He was not to play again until September 28 – 14 weeks later. Before Rooney learned that dreadful news his team-mates were suffering agonies of their own. England came within seven minutes of beating the European Championship hosts when Helder Postiga equalised. Sol Campbell had a late 'goal' disallowed and extra-time followed. England fell behind to a Rui Costa goal but Lampard levelled the scores with five minutes remaining and forced the dreaded penalty shoot-out. Three of England's natural penalty takers – Rooney,

Scholes and Gerrard – had all been substituted during the match. The respective captains Beckham and Rui Costa both missed their kicks leaving the score at 4-4 as the contest went into sudden death. Both Ashley Cole and Postiga were successful but then Vassell, who had come on as a substitute for the injured Rooney, saw his penalty kick saved by goalkeeper Ricardo. The Portuguese number one then stepped up and converted the match-winning kick past James to knock England out of the European Championship.

WHAT ROONEY SAID: "What happened in Euro 2004, to go out of the tournament and get injured on the same night, was probably was one of the hardest and worst feelings I've felt in football."

18 WORLD CUP QUALIFIER
SATURDAY OCTOBER 9, 2004

ENGLAND	2
WALES	0

ATTENDANCE: 65,224 (Old Trafford, Manchester)
ENGLAND SCORERS: Lampard 3, Beckham 76

Rooney, fit again after injury, was recalled to the England starting line-up and selected to play in a deep-lying striker role behind Owen and Defoe as Eriksson played an overt 4-3-3 formation. It was a strategy that worked well, allowing Rooney to dominate the game as soon as it started. Every time he got the ball the Welsh felt they were in trouble. Early on he beat Mark Pembridge and headed goalward to fire a low drive that provoked goalkeeper Paul Jones into a save by pushing the shot against the post and out of play. Defoe and Rooney combined to set up Owen but his shot was repelled

by the legs of Jones. In the second-half, Rooney fought off Mark Delaney to burst into the area and fire a tight-angled shot that brought another superb saved from Jones. Late in the game, before being substituted by King, Rooney was on hand after Beckham had a point-blank shot remarkably stopped by Jones. But as he followed up, the effort was blocked by defender Danny Gabbidon. Rooney had time to beat three defenders but another excellent tackle by Gabbidon denied him a goalscoring chance. Lampard had given England a third minute lead and Beckham secured the points with a superb goal in the 76th minute.

WHAT ROONEY SAID: "It was good to have three of us up front and I think it worked well. We have a lot of pace between us and I had loads of space to try and play other players in. I didn't score but we got the result we wanted and that's what matters. I think I played pretty good in there. I like playing that role and I had a lot of space. But all I want to do is play for my country and it's a great feeling to be in the team whatever the formation."

WHAT THEY SAID ABOUT ROONEY: "I think it worked very well. All three played well and we had good balance in the team, and gave a good professional performance. We kept cool heads and that was important in such a game."
Sven-Göran Eriksson

19 WORLD CUP QUALIFIER
WEDNESDAY OCTOBER 13, 2004

AZERBIAJAN	0
ENGLAND	1

ATTENDANCE: 15,000 (Tofik Bakhramov Stadium, Baku)

ENGLAND SCORER: Owen 22

England got the three points after enduring cold, wet and blustery conditions. The only goal of a poor game by captain Owen after 22 minutes proved enough in the end. Rooney played the deeper role in a three-man attack behind Owen and Defoe but the trio were often isolated from the rest of the team. However, that did not prevent Rooney getting involved when he could. He had an opportunity from a close range free-kick inside the area but saw his shot strike the defensive wall. Two other goalbound efforts by Rooney were parried and punched away respectively by Azeri goalkeeper Jahangir Hasanadze. In the 85th minute Rooney, who was booked for a foul on Anatoly Ponomaryov earlier, was replaced by Joe Cole.

20 INTERNATIONAL FRIENDLY
WEDNESDAY NOVEMBER 17, 2004

SPAIN	1
ENGLAND	0

ATTENDANCE: 48,000 (Estadio Santiago Bernabéu, Madrid)

SPAIN SCORER: Del Horno 10

Rooney's darkest hour on the international stage. It was an ill-tempered friendly not helped by appalling racist chants from the Spanish crowd towards England's black players. Asier del Horno put Spain ahead after ten minutes and nearly extended their lead from a dubiously awarded 24th minute penalty which England goalkeeper Robinson saved to deny Raul. Rooney's frustration and aggression got the better of him and he was making some rash, unsavoury challenges. Joaquin was the subject of one untamed tackle and Rooney was fortunate not to be cautioned. Then a dangerous, forceful push on goalkeeper Iker Casillas saw the Spanish goalkeeper end up in the crowd. Greek referee George Kasnaferis had no hesitation in booking Rooney – and it could have so easily have been a red card. Another wild challenge on Michel Salgado had Eriksson substitute the unhappy Rooney in the 41st minute, replacing him with Smith. Overall England were outplayed and put in a very disappointing display on an unpleasant night in Madrid.

WHAT THEY SAID ABOUT ROONEY: "Wayne Rooney has got a problem regarding discipline, but he is young and is learning. However, he has got to learn pretty fast otherwise not only will he be punished but the teams he plays for will be punished too… He was lucky not to be sent-off rather than just

MAR. 26   v NORTHERN IRELAND

"I DON'T REMEMBER ANYONE MAKING SUCH AN IMPACT ON A TOURNAMENT SINCE PELÉ IN THE 1958 WORLD CUP IN SWEDEN." *SVEN-GÖRAN ERIKSSON*

taken off. By doing that, I think England coach Sven Goran-Eriksson helped him."
Alan Shearer (BBC pundit)

"I gave Wayne Rooney a yellow card before he was taken off and at the time I thought that was the right decision bearing in mind it was a friendly match. But had it been a competitive match either in a tournament or a qualifier then maybe I would have seen things differently." *Referee Kasnaferis*

21 INTERNATIONAL FRIENDLY
WEDNESDAY FEBRUARY 9, 2005

ENGLAND	0
HOLLAND	0

ATTENDANCE: 40,705 (Villa Park, Birmingham)

A goalless draw where the defences had the best of the night and more than 40,000 fans went home ultimately disappointed. Holland had long periods of possession and England had occasional moments of creativity. Rooney, along with Shaun Wright-Phillips, supported main striker Owen. Rooney did carve out a chance for Gerrard early on but the Liverpool man shot over the bar. Rooney made way for Middlesbrough winger Stewart Downing, making his first appearance for England, in the 61st minute.

WHAT THEY SAID ABOUT ROONEY: "Rooney can play centre-forward, second striker, the right, the left and he can play offensively in the midfield diamond. I don't think where he played was a waste of his talent. If that was the case he would have been

wasting his time for 90 per cent of the games at Manchester United." *Sven-Göran Eriksson*

"Rooney is an outstanding talent, already a great forward in the world. I have not seen many to compare with him in many years."
Marco Van Basten (Holland coach)

22 WORLD CUP QUALIFIER
SATURDAY MARCH 26, 2005

ENGLAND	4
NORTHERN IRELAND	0

ATTENDANCE: 65,239 (Old Trafford, Manchester)

ENGLAND SCORERS: J Cole 47, Owen 51, Baird (og) 54, Lampard 62

In Eriksson's 50th match in charge, England sailed to a comprehensive 4-0 victory in which Rooney did everything but score. After a goalless first-half in which he had headed a Gary Neville cross against the post, forced a diving save from Irish goalkeeper Maik Taylor with a 25-yard drive, sent a shot just narrowly wide of the Irish goal, and created chances for his team-mates, all of which were kept out by Taylor, England overcame Northern Ireland. Rooney had a shot charged down in the opening minute of the second-half but then within a minute Joe Cole had broken the deadlock thanks to a Rooney cross and a thunderous shot by Cole into the far corner of the net. Six minutes on, Lampard, who had an excellent match, combined with Rooney to set up Owen to shoot home. Three minutes later, Rooney got round

Colin Murdock at the byline and crossed into a crowded penalty area and the unlucky Chris Baird turned the ball into his own net. Rooney then set up Lampard eight minutes later and the midfielder's deflected shot off Murdock's head made it 4-0. Rooney had run the Irish defence into disarray and still found time to create an opportunity for Lampard that hit the crossbar. He also fired wide himself from a Beckham pass before making way for Defoe in the 80th minute.

WHAT THEY SAID ABOUT ROONEY: "He tried to shoot from the halfway line when he knew he was coming off. He's a striker, he wants to score goals."
Rio Ferdinand

23 WORLD CUP QUALIFIER
WEDNESDAY MARCH 30, 2005

ENGLAND	2
AZERBAIJAN	0

ATTENDANCE: 49,046 (St James' park, Newcastle)

ENGLAND SCORERS: Gerrard 51, Beckham 62

Rooney started in blistering form, having one shot blocked, another go over the bar and a header directed at goalkeeper Kramarenko in the first 15 minutes of the game. Azerbaijan, as expected, played with a packed defence and midfield, making it hard for England to break them down. So, despite Rooney's positive start, England needed to play with patience and await the breakthrough. It came six minutes into the second-half after Rooney beat two defenders and pulled the ball back from the byline for Gerrard to thump into the net off the crossbar. Beckham assured victory 11 minutes later and Rooney tried to increase the margin of victory with a 69th minute volley that produced a great save from Kramarenko and then he headed a Beckham cross against the post. Lampard had also hit a post and Rooney was substituted late on by Dyer.

> "I THINK WE'VE GOT SOME SUPER PLAYERS AND AN EXTRA SPECIAL PLAYER IN ROONEY. IF YOU LOOK BACK IN THE HISTORY OF THE WORLD CUP, GREAT SIDES HAVE ALWAYS HAD SPECIAL PLAYERS THAT JUST LIFT THE TEAM QUITE A BIT MORE. PLATINI HAS DONE IT FOR FRANCE, MARADONA FOR ARGENTINA AND I THINK ROONEY CAN DO THAT FOR ENGLAND." GLENN HODDLE

24 INTERNATIONAL FRIENDLY
WEDNESDAY AUGUST 17, 2005

DENMARK	4
ENGLAND	1

ATTENDANCE: 41,438 (Parken Stadium, Copenhagen)
DENMARK SCORERS: Rommedahl 60, Tomasson 63, Gravgaard 67, Larsen 90
ENGLAND SCORER: Rooney 87

England suffered their worst defeat since 1980 on a night where only Rooney, the scorer of England's 87th minute consolation goal, came away with any credit for the visitors. He was the only man likely to create something for England; he had the ball in the net in the first-half, only for it to be ruled out for a foul on Pal Nielsen, and he also had claim for a penalty turned down after Christian Poulsen seemed to hold him back on another occasion. After a goalless first half, Denmark tore England apart with three goals in seven minutes from Dennis Rommedahl, Jon Dahl Tomasson and Michael Gravgaard. Soren Larsen scored Denmark's fourth in stoppage time after Rooney found the net for the first time for England since Euro 2004.

⚽ **ROONEY GOAL** *(87 mins) Beckham hit a through ball down the right for Rooney to latch onto. Rooney then fired home a right foot shot past Sorensen.*

25 WORLD CUP QUALIFIER
SATURDAY SEPTEMBER 3, 2005

WALES	0
ENGLAND	1

ATTENDANCE: 70,715 (Millennium Stadium, Cardiff)
ENGLAND SCORER: J Cole 53

Rooney was cast as the lone striker, primarily supported by Wright-Phillips and Joe Cole, in a 4-5-1 formation. England dominated the game although there was a scare in the first-half when goalkeeper Paul Robinson needed to produce an outstanding save to deny John Hartson. Both Rooney and Cole squandered early chances, while Wales goalkeeper Danny Coyne denied Rooney, after he had combined with Gerrard. Later in the game, an excellent chipped shot from Rooney was tipped over the bar by Coyne. Cole got the only goal of the game, via deflection off centre-half Gabbidon.

OCT. 12 v POLAND

26 WORLD CUP QUALIFIER
WEDNESDAY SEPTEMBER 7 2005

NORTHERN IRELAND	1
ENGLAND	0

ATTENDANCE: 14,000 (Windsor Park, Belfast)
NORTHERN IRELAND SCORER: Healy 73

A frustrating and embarrassing night for England and Rooney as Northern Ireland caused an upset with their first win over the English since 1972. Rooney played wide on the left, Beckham in a midfield holding role and Owen returned in place of Joe Cole. Eriksson's tactical plan did not work and England were thwarted by the Irish throughout the first-half. Rooney, who was booked for a foul on Keith Gillespie that meant he was suspended for the next qualifier against Austria, left the field at half-time visibly frustrated and brushed aside attempts by Beckham and Ferdinand to calm him down. Rooney and England were unable to make headway after the break and went behind to a 73rd minute David Healy goal. Owen came closest to an equaliser but he was denied by goalkeeper Taylor.

WHAT THEY SAID ABOUT ROONEY: "Wayne was frustrated tonight and he showed that. That's what happens in games like this. If things are not going well the frustration shows and Wayne's a young player. But Wayne will handle that in his own way. He's at a great club, he's got a manager that can control that." *David Beckham*

"At half-time, it was discussed but it's always a pity to take off such an important player. You know that he can win the game for you. So it's always a difficult decision to take. His discipline was good in the second half." *Sven-Göran Eriksson*

"Wayne Rooney is wasted switching between the right and left hand side. He's got to play through the middle, playing to his strengths." *Terry Butcher (England legend)*

27 WORLD CUP QUALIFIER
WEDNESDAY OCTOBER 12, 2005

ENGLAND	2
POLAND	1

ATTENDANCE: 65,467 (Old Trafford, Manchester)
ENGLAND SCORERS: Owen 43, Lampard 81
POLAND SCORER: Frankowski 45

By the time this match kicked off, England knew they had already qualified for the World Cup, but this victory over Poland meant they finished top of the group. Rooney, back after suspension, was in good form and fired a second-minute free-kick around the wall but just shy of the near post. Later in the first half he fired a 25-yard shot just over the bar. Rooney carved out several chances for his side but the execution in the final third was not as it should be. Owen put England ahead just before the break but saw it cancelled out by Tomasz Frankowski before the half-time whistle. A draw looked on the cards until Lampard, Rooney and Joe Cole combined to supply Owen. He clipped the ball over a defender for Lampard to finish the move with a superlative volley into the net in the 81st minute.

WHAT ROONEY SAID: "I haven't scored a competitive goal since Euro 2004. I hope I am storing them up for next summer. It is a massive tournament and I want to go there and try and do the best I can and score some goals… I was happy getting out there and I was made up with the result.

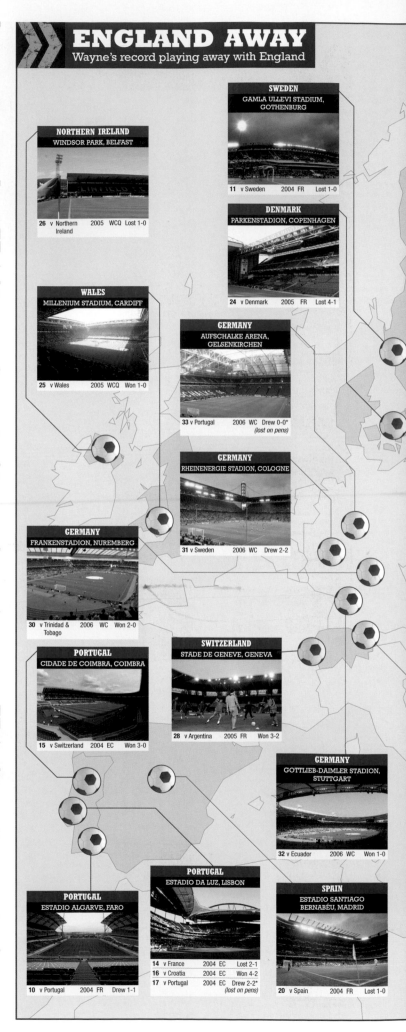

ENGLAND AWAY
Wayne's record playing away with England

SWEDEN
GAMLA ULLEVI STADIUM, GOTHENBURG
11 v Sweden 2004 FR Lost 1-0

NORTHERN IRELAND
WINDSOR PARK, BELFAST
26 v Northern Ireland 2005 WCQ Lost 1-0

DENMARK
PARKENSTADION, COPENHAGEN
24 v Denmark 2005 FR Lost 4-1

WALES
MILLENIUM STADIUM, CARDIFF
25 v Wales 2005 WCQ Won 1-0

GERMANY
AUFSCHALKE ARENA, GELSENKIRCHEN
33 v Portugal 2006 WC Drew 0-0* *(lost on pens)*

GERMANY
RHEINENERGIE STADION, COLOGNE
31 v Sweden 2006 WC Drew 2-2

GERMANY
FRANKENSTADION, NUREMBERG
30 v Trinidad & Tobago 2006 WC Won 2-0

PORTUGAL
CIDADE DE COIMBRA, COIMBRA
15 v Switzerland 2004 EC Won 3-0

SWITZERLAND
STADE DE GENEVE, GENEVA
28 v Argentina 2005 FR Won 3-2

GERMANY
GOTTLIEB-DAIMLER STADION, STUTTGART
32 v Ecuador 2006 WC Won 1-0

PORTUGAL
ESTADIO ALGARVE, FARO
10 v Portugal 2004 FR Drew 1-1

PORTUGAL
ESTADIO DA LUZ, LISBON
14 v France 2004 EC Lost 2-1
16 v Croatia 2004 EC Won 4-2
17 v Portugal 2004 EC Drew 2-2* *(lost on pens)*

SPAIN
ESTADIO SANTIAGO BERNABÉU, MADRID
20 v Spain 2004 FR Lost 1-0

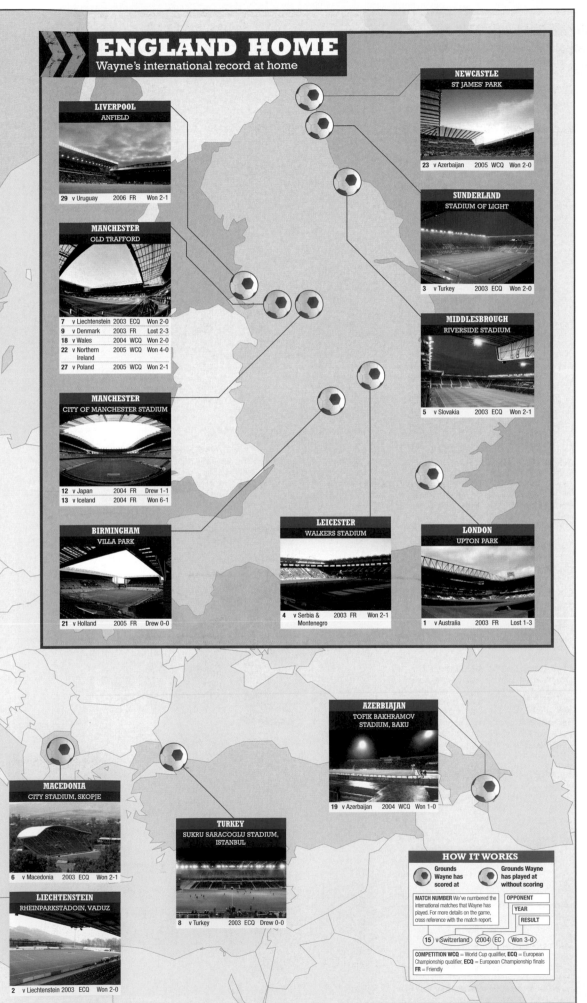

ENGLAND HOME
Wayne's international record at home

NEWCASTLE
ST JAMES' PARK

23 v Azerbaijan 2005 WCQ Won 2-0

LIVERPOOL
ANFIELD

29 v Uruguay 2006 FR Won 2-1

SUNDERLAND
STADIUM OF LIGHT

3 v Turkey 2003 ECQ Won 2-0

MANCHESTER
OLD TRAFFORD

7 v Liechtenstein 2003 ECQ Won 2-0
9 v Denmark 2003 FR Lost 2-3
18 v Wales 2004 WCQ Won 2-0
22 v Northern 2005 WCQ Won 4-0
   Ireland
27 v Poland 2005 WCQ Won 2-1

MIDDLESBROUGH
RIVERSIDE STADIUM

5 v Slovakia 2003 ECQ Won 2-1

MANCHESTER
CITY OF MANCHESTER STADIUM

12 v Japan 2004 FR Drew 1-1
13 v Iceland 2004 FR Won 6-1

BIRMINGHAM
VILLA PARK

21 v Holland 2005 FR Drew 0-0

LEICESTER
WALKERS STADIUM

4 v Serbia & 2003 FR Won 2-1
   Montenegro

LONDON
UPTON PARK

1 v Australia 2003 FR Lost 1-3

AZERBIAJAN
TOFIK BAKHRAMOV
STADIUM, BAKU

19 v Azerbaijan 2004 WCQ Won 1-0

MACEDONIA
CITY STADIUM, SKOPJE

6 v Macedonia 2003 ECQ Won 2-1

TURKEY
SUKRU SARACOGLU STADIUM,
ISTANBUL

8 v Turkey 2003 ECQ Drew 0-0

LIECHTENSTEIN
RHEINPARKSTADOIN, VADUZ

2 v Liechtenstein 2003 ECQ Won 2-0

HOW IT WORKS

⚽ Grounds Wayne has scored at   ⚽ Grounds Wayne has played at without scoring

MATCH NUMBER We've numbered the international matches that Wayne has played. For more details on the game, cross reference with the match report.

OPPONENT
YEAR
RESULT

15 v Switzerland 2004 EC Won 3-0

COMPETITION WCQ = World Cup qualifier, **ECQ** = European Championship qualifier, **ECQ** = European Championship finals
FR = Friendly

We won and that was our main priority, to top the group and put in a good performance. The attitude we showed was brilliant. We were already through to the World Cup but we wanted to top the group and we did it. I think the desire and work-rate has always been there but we played a lot better than in previous games. It shows what we can do."

28 INTERNATIONAL FRIENDLY
SATURDAY NOVEMBER 12, 2005

ARGENTINA 2
ENGLAND 3

ATTENDANCE: 29,000 (Stade de Geneve, Geneva)
ENGLAND SCORERS: Rooney 39, Owen 87 90
ARGENTINA SCORERS: Crespo 34, Samuel 53

A thrilling friendly fixture in which England twice came from behind and sensationally clinched victory with an injury-time winner. It was a skilful, open game and early on Robinson was needed to make crucial saves to deny Juan Riquelme, Carlos Tevez and Javier Zanetti. Both teams had goals disallowed, with Owen (offside) and Hernan Crespo (foul) the scorers who found their efforts overruled. Rooney went closest to opening the scoring after being put through by Gerrard. Crespo gave Argentina the lead shortly afterwards but Rooney cancelled out the lead in the 39th minute. Walter Samuel put Argentina back in front in the 53rd minute, moments after Rooney, on a quick counter attack, had set up Gerrard who shot wide. Time was running out but Rooney never gave up, driving his team to attack. In the closing five minutes he fired a volley a little too high and soon after chipped over Roberto Abbondanziei who managed to scramble back to his goal and push the ball round the post. Then a Gerrard cross found Owen who headed home an equaliser to set up a grandstand finish. A further opportunity was instigated by Rooney with a left wing cross, but Beckham's subsequent header was saved. A draw looked certain but then, in stoppage time, Joe Cole's floated centre was headed home by Owen again for a stunning England victory.

WHAT THEY SAID ABOUT ROONEY: "He is the complete footballer and he's still only 20. That's not bad. Rooney made a huge impact. He's considered one of the best players in the world and I hope that he will show the same form next summer. He can do everything, he was even winning headers against their centre-backs, which was incredible."
Sven-Göran Eriksson

"I think we've got some super players and an extra special player in Rooney. If you look back in the history of the World Cup, great sides have always had special players that just lift the team quite a bit more. Platini has done it for France, Maradona for Argentina and I think Rooney can do that for England." *Glenn Hoddle*

"Wayne Rooney is a key player. He is very dangerous and aggressive." *Jose Pekerman* (Argentina coach)

⚽ **ROONEY GOAL** (39 mins): Ayala concedes possession to Beckham who instantly flicks the ball on for Rooney to fire the ball past goalkeeper Abbondanziei.

29 INTERNATIONAL FRIENDLY
WEDNESDAY MARCH 1, 2006

ENGLAND 2
URUGUAY 1

ATTENDANCE: 40,013 (Anfield, Liverpool)
ENGLAND SCORERS: Crouch 75, J Cole 90
URUGUAY SCORER: Pousa 25

Another dramatic stoppage time goal – this time from Joe Cole – gave England victory. The visitors had gone ahead through Omar Pousa's stunning first-half effort that wasn't cancelled out until the 75th minute by Peter Crouch, who had replaced Rooney in the 65th minute. Rooney had caused all sorts of panic to the Uruguayan defence and was given plenty of time on the ball. He combined with Michael Carrick to set up Cole, who shot wide after 20 minutes. A long-range effort from Rooney on the half-hour was saved by Fabian Carini and just after the break, he had his best chance with a shot that had sub goalkeeper Sebastian Viera scrambling to push the ball wide.

"WE ARE A BETTER TEAM WITH ROONEY, THERE'S NO DOUBT ABOUT THAT." SVEN GORAN ERIKSSON

30 WORLD CUP FINALS
GROUP B
JUNE 15, 2006

ENGLAND	2
TRINIDAD & TOBAGO	0

ATTENDANCE: 41,000 (Frankenstadion, Nuremberg)

SCORERS: Crouch 83, Gerrard 90

Just 47 days after suffering a broken fourth metatarsal bone in his right foot and just 13 days after kicking a ball for the first time since the injury, Rooney made his World Cup debut. Despite the severe injury England boss Eriksson still included him in the World Cup squad, allocating him the number nine shirt. Displaying robust powers of recovery, Rooney earned his recall to the side nine days earlier than the most optimistic medical opinion predicted he could be available for selection. Rooney was a 58th minute substitute replacement for Owen (who had played barely six hours of football in 2006 himself) with the match goalless. Rooney showed some good initial link play with good passes and running but he found it difficult to get involved in the play. His best opportunity – a half-chance really – came in the 82nd minute when Lampard tried to slip the ball through into the area to Rooney. Trinidad & Tobago's Chris Birchall intercepted but Rooney recovered the loose ball and lined up to fire a shot. Unfortunately, Birchall had continued to chase the ball and produced a well-timed tackle. A minute later Rooney's strike partner Peter Crouch broke the deadlock, heading home a Beckham cross and in the first minute of stoppage time Gerrard unleashed a fantastic shot from the edge of the area and into the top left-hand corner. England were assured of the victory and a guaranteed place in the second round although it was an uninspiring performance.

WHAT ROONEY SAID: "I stayed positive and always believed I'd play in the World Cup. The thought never entered my mind that I wouldn't be here."

WHAT THEY SAID ABOUT ROONEY: "We are a better team with Rooney, there's no doubt about that." *Sven Goran Eriksson*

31 WORLD CUP FINALS
GROUP B
JUNE 20, 2006

ENGLAND	2
SWEDEN	2

ATTENDANCE: 45,000 (RheinEnergie Stadion, Cologne)

SCORERS: J Cole 33, Gerrard 85; Allback 50, Mellberg 90

Rooney was starting a match for the first time since April 29 and was partnering Owen. It was a strike force that was last used by England very effectively against Argentina. But after 51 seconds disaster struck when Owen twisted awkwardly and was later diagnosed with lateral cartilage damage and a ruptured anterior cruciate ligament. Owen crawled off in agony ruling him out of the World Cup (and the game for some time) and the Owen-Rooney partnership was snuffed out before it began. Peter Crouch was Owen's replacement and Rooney was immediately asked to play out of his normal position. As expected Rooney worked as hard as ever but he was frustrated by the Swedish central defensive partnership of Teddy Lucic and Olof Mellberg who would block or divert his efforts at close range. Joe Cole gave England the lead with a stunning long range volley but Marcus Allback equalised shortly after the break with the World Cup's 2,000th goal. Sweden were appearing to get the upper hand and the England bench suspected Rooney was tiring and he was replaced by Gerrard after 69 minutes. All Rooney wanted to do was play football and he expressed his frustration at having his game curtailed by thumping the dugout and then throwing-off his boots! He watched from the sidelines as his

JUN. 20 v SWEDEN

replacement gave England the lead with five minutes remaining but then some appalling defending allowed Mellberg to touch home an equaliser. The draw meant both teams were through with England progressing as group winners.

32 WORLD CUP FINALS
SECOND ROUND
JUNE 25, 2006

ENGLAND	1
ECUADOR	0

ATTENDANCE: 52,000 (Gottlieb-Daimler Stadion, Stuttgart)

SCORER: Beckham 60

Following the injury to Owen, there was more pressure than ever on the shoulders of Rooney and when coach Eriksson opted for a 4-1-4-1 formation, Rooney had to carry the weight of England's attack as a lone striker. For much of the game Rooney found it tough, often finding himself isolated, through no fault of his own, from the rest of the team. England pummelled too many long balls for Rooney to chase, particularly in the first-half and he was often left chasing lost causes. However, as the game wore on, with Lampard and Gerrard giving him much closer support and Rooney defying concerns about his ability to last a full 90 minutes, the situation improved. Rooney had the legs of Hurtado and managed crosses from the byline but the chances were squandered, notably one golden opportunity by Lampard. In the end the listless match was decided by a Beckham free-kick on the hour that just squeezed inside Cristian Mora's right-hand post.

WHAT THEY SAID ABOUT ROONEY: "Wazza said to me before the game that my free kicks had been poor, and that's why we were laughing after I scored." *David Beckham*

"I spoke to Frank and Michael [Carrick] and we were pleased with how the system got better as the game went on. We got more support to Wayne in the second-half... Wayne got better as the game went on and that was down to the support he got. It will be crucial for the team if he keeps getting fitter." *Steven Gerrard*

"England banked too heavily on Wayne Rooney, who did not have the support going forward. Because of this, very few opportunities were created." *Alvin Cornell (FIFA Technical Study Group)*

WHAT ROONEY SAID: "It was difficult on my own up front, but I got a lot of support from midfield and it worked for us in the end. I feel myself getting fitter all the time. In the last 30 minutes I did better than in the first 60. That's a positive sign for me."

33 WORLD CUP FINALS
QUARTER-FINAL
JULY 1, 2006

ENGLAND	0
PORTUGAL	0

After extra-time; Portugal win 3-1 on penalties

ATTENDANCE: 52,000 (AufSchalke Arena, Gelsenkirchen)

Rooney was controversially sent off for violent conduct after 62 minutes. The incident saw him battling for the ball with three Portuguese players, among them Ricardo Carvalho. The Chelsea defender slid in from behind and Rooney, unbalanced, accidently stood on the unfortunate opponent's groin. Referee Horacio Elizondo signalled for a Portugal free kick – although arguably Rooney may have won a free kick himself – as Portuguese players surrounded the official, among them Rooney's Manchester United team-mate Cristiano Ronaldo. Ronaldo's intervention – which included displaying a card gesture – upset Rooney and he pushed Ronaldo. Referee Elizondo only then showed the red card to a disbelieving Rooney, although he later said the card was for the incident with Carvalho. The seriousness of the charge – violent conduct – could have led to a lengthy international suspension for Rooney but FIFA finally decided on a two-match ban and a £2,400 fine. Ten-man England, who minutes earlier had also lost their captain Beckham through injury, battled bravely. Rooney and Beckham, however, could only watch as the game ebbed towards extra-time and then penalties. Just like two years before, against Portugal in the European Championship quarter-finals, England were knocked out 3-1 on spot kicks. Only Owen Hargreaves converted for England while Lampard, Gerrard and Carragher all missed.

WHAT THEY SAID ABOUT ROONEY: "I saw Ronaldo going over giving the card gesture and I think he's bang out of order... He had four or five Portuguese men all over him and I walked away thinking we were going to get a free kick... Wayne won't get any blame from me because I love him and he's done so much for this team. And he's going to do so much more in the future." *Steven Gerrard*

"I'm sure Wayne Rooney does more good things than bad things. He has a temperament, you have to live with that. I have spoken to him about it in the past but I always said you can't take the temperament away from Wayne Rooney because then he wouldn't be that kind of player. Don't kill him. You need him. I might not need him next year but you do. Take care of him. I am absolutely two hundred per cent sure that Rooney will come back from this. But make it easier for him to come back than you did with David Beckham. You need him and he's a fantastic football player." *Sven-Göran Eriksson*

"For me it was a clear red card, so I didn't react to the Portuguese players. There was shoving on both sides, but no reason to caution anyone." *Horacio Elizondo (referee)*

"Wayne should have had the free-kick 15 or 20 seconds before. Any other team, any other player, they go down and the ref gives a foul but we are honest. Wayne tried to stay on his feet and tried to win the ball. He'd got two people fighting against him. That's the kind of honesty that we show." *John Terry*

WHAT ROONEY SAID: "I remember the incident clearly and have seen it several times since on TV. I am of the same opinion now as I was at the time that what happened didn't warrant a red card. If anything, I feel we should have had a free kick for the fouls committed on me during the same incident. I want to say absolutely categorically I did not intentionally put my foot down on Ricardo Carvalho. He slid in from behind me and unfortunately ended up in a position where my foot was inevitably going to end up as I kept my balance. That's all there was to it."

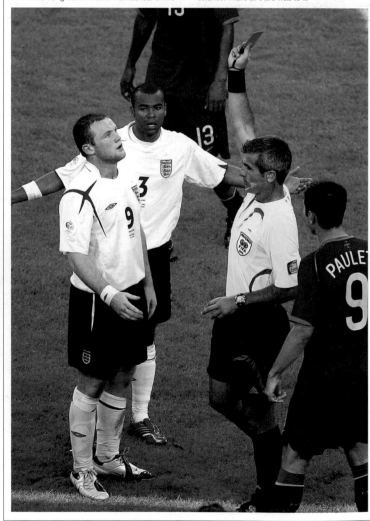